Women in Pre-Islamic Arabia: *Nabataea*

Hatoon Ajwad al-Fassi

BAR International Series 1659
2007

This title published by

Archaeopress
Publishers of British Archaeological Reports
Gordon House
276 Banbury Road
Oxford OX2 7ED
England
bar@archaeopress.com
www.archaeopress.com

Archaeopress
10 years

BAR S1659

Women in Pre-Islamic Arabia: Nabataea

ISBN 978 1 4073 0095 5

Printed in England by CMP (UK) Ltd

Cover illustration: Two Nabataean female musicians with a man in the middle, in their local dress and veil (Amman museum, Zayadine 1991: 55). By courtesy of the Department of Antiquities, Jordan

All BAR titles are available from:

Hadrian Books Ltd
122 Banbury Road
Oxford
OX2 7BP
England
bar@hadrianbooks.co.uk

The current BAR catalogue with details of all titles in print, prices and means of payment is available free from Hadrian Books or may be downloaded from www.archaeopress.com

To My Friend and Life Partner
Abdel Aziz

To my Angel Son
Ajwaad

To my Hope Daughter
Zein al-Sharaf

بسم الله الرحمن الرحيم

Contents

List of Plates

Dr al-Fassi with a Sinai Bedouin

Acknowledgements

There is no doubt that this book could not have been completed without the support and help of an endless list of people to whom I became gratefully indebted. The support I received in dealing with the 'methodological' problem is where I will start.

I would like to convey my gratitude to many organisations that supported my academic research and welfare through scholarships and grants, including the 'Chevening Scholarship' and 'Seven Pillars of Wisdom Trust' as well as the 'Hardship Fund' and the 'Travel Grant' of Manchester University.

For my fieldwork trip, which was carried out in December 1989-January 1999, I am indebted to the departments of antiquity in Saudi Arabia, Jordan and Syria, The French Institute of Archaeology in the Near East (IFAPO) and the tribe of 'Ulayqāt in Sinai.

For the updating of this book, I would like to thank 'La Maison de l'Orient et de la mediterranée' for inviting me there during the summer of 2005 and making its library totally available. Special thanks are due to Dr Saba Farès from 'La Maison' and Dr Jean-Claude Decourt, the director of the department of 'Histoire et sources des mondes antiques HISOMA' at the 'Maison'. My thanks also go to Archaeopress publishing house, especially Dr David Davison, who showed interest in publishing the book without much hesitation, and waited patiently until I came back with my updated version, respecting the timeout I took to enjoy the new experience of motherhood. Thanks also go to my friend Ms Maureen Franks who proof-read the text with complete amitié.

On an individual level, I would like to thank, in Saudi Arabia, Prof. Abdul Raḥmān al-Anṣārī, the father of archaeology in Saudi Arabia and former member of Majlis al-Šūrā, Prof. Saad al-Rashid, former deputy-minister of the Ministry of Education for Antiquities and Museums, Mr Ḥussein Abu al-Ḥassan, from the High Comission for Tourism, Mr Aḥmad Abdul Karīm, former mayor of al-ʿUlā, Mr Muṭlaq al-Muṭlaq, from the Museum of al-ʿUlā, Mr Abu Ḫalaf al-ʿInizī, the guard at Madā'in Ṣāliḥ, Mr Farḥān al-Zāmil from the Museum of Taymā, Mr Haššāl al-Ḫuraiṣy, an old colleague in Tabuk, Mr Yaʿrub al-ʿAlī from the Antiquities of Tabūk and Mr Muʿawwaḍ al-ʿAṭawī the driver. From Dūmat al-Jandal, I would like to thank Mr Ḥussein al-Ḫalīfah, head of the museum, Mr Aḥmad al-Quʿayd from the Antiquities of Dūmat al-Jandal, Mr Ṣāliḥ al-Šarʿān from the antiquities of al-Qurayyāt, Sheikh Muḥammad al Mu'ḏin, Sheikh of Iṯrā. From King Saud University, I would like to thank Dr Mušallaḥ al-Murayḫī and Dr Saud Ḏiyāb, the Saudi cultural attaché in Paris.

In Jordan, I would like to thank Dr Ġāzī Bīšah, the former general director of Antiquities and Museums, Dr Fawaz el-Khraysheh the actual general director of Antiquities and Museums for giving me permission to use the photo of the three musicians on the book's cover, Dr Fawzī Zayadine, the deputy director of the department of Antiquities, Dr Khayriyyah ʿAmr, from the department of Antiquities, Mr Abdul Qādir al-Ḥuṣān from the antiquities of al-Mafraq, Mr Muwaffaq al-Musāʿīd, the guard of Umm al-Jimāl. From Petra, I would like to thank Mr Muḥammad al-Šōbakī, the director of the museum, Mr Aḥmad al-Nawāflah and Muḥammad al-Salāmīn, the tourist guides, Mr Abu Ḫālid al-Budūlī and Mr ʿImād Ḍarūs from al-Ṭafīlah's antiquities. From Irbid, I would like to thank Dr Zaydūn Muḥeisin, director of the Institute of Archaeology and Anthropology of Yarmūk University, Dr Maḥmūd al-Rōsān from the institute and Mr Zayd al-Ḥamad.

From Syria, I would like to thank Dr Sulṭān Muḥeisin, the general director of Antiquities and Museums, Mr Khalid al-Asʿad, the director of Palmyra Antiquities, Ms Wurūd Ibrāhīm and Ms Munā Mu'azzin from the Antiquities department, Mr Muḥammad al-Murawweḥ, the guide, Mr Ḥussein, the guard of Bel temple in Palmyra, and Mr Abū Rāmiz the driver. I would like also to thank Dr Jean-Marie Dentzer, the former general director of IFAPO in Jordan, Syria and Lebanon.

In Sinai, I would like to thank Mr Muḥammad Raḍwān and his family, from the tribe of ʿUlayqāt. I would like also to thank Mr Muḥammad Mabrūk from the geographic studies centre in Cairo, an expert in Sinai.

In Manchester, I would like to thank all members of Ashburne Hall, students, staff, tutors and Dr Elisabeth Healey, the former warden. In addition, I would like to thank the Middle Eastern Studies department's staff, especially Dr Philip Sadgrove, Head of Department and fellow colleagues, namely Dr Murteza Bedir. The John Rylands Library needs a special acknowledgement for the great support and accommodation they provided me with, especially the staff of the blue area in the fourth floor and porters. My thanks go as well to Mr Peter Parr and Prof. G. Rex Smith who read the text and provided me with their advice. My thanks go also to Prof. David F. Graf for reading the whole manuscript and enlightening me with suggestions, to Dr Bobby Sayyid for his constant intellectual challenge with every chapter given.

I am also most grateful and indebted to my former supervisor and present colleague and friend Prof. John F. Healey, for being a true scholar.

My friends in Manchester and elsewhere were and will always be an important factor of my intellectual and social development. Naming them cannot express the complex reciprocal relationship that has grown throughout the years. I shall however try my best. I would like to thank my Jordanian school friend with whom I explored Jordan's sites and Wādis, Asmā al-Šōbakī, the Libyan articulate activist pharmacist, Dr Sālmah al-Jāyer with whom we explored Scotland's lakes and valleys, Dr Haseena Lockhat with whom I explored the Syrian and Lebanese plains, with memories of deserts and borders, Dr Ghada Zoubianne, with whom I explored the Lebanese mountains and its marvelous south, not to miss our Mancunian struggles – big and small, Dr Ḥanan Baṭarfī, the mathematician with style, and Dr Habib al-Attar, the dramatist who turned life in Manchester into scenes from a light-hearted sitcom.

Each friend has left an imprint on my personality. With each one I share dreams and hopes. With Dr Fowziyyah Abū Khālid, the Arabian Poetess and socio-political critic, I share a love for the Land. With Dr Nasreen Ali, the articulate social scientist, I share the hope for a better brighter future, and with the "Sumerian" Dr Bobby Sayyid, I share the dream of the only Name. But are these words enough to express how deeply grateful I am as well as thankful and happy with this lifetime friendship? I don't think they are.

I would not have been able to achieve anything without the support of my family: mother and father, Hawazen and Nizār, my niece and nephew, Hind & Ziyad. My appreciation goes to my little brother, Muḥammad, who accompanied me without complaining on the tiring field trip of a month and a half which corresponded with Ramaḍān and winter. Their constant encouragement and help were always pushing me to achieve the best. Not to forget the support of my aunt Jawāhir al-ʿAnbar and cousin Abdallah Shams-addin al-Fassi.

My new status of being a wife and a mother added another dimension to my gratitude during the long period of up-dating the manuscript. The encouragement and inspiration provided and faith in my abilities that my husband Dr Abdelaziz Abu Hamid Aluwaisheg granted me was an invaluable constant reminder of his total support. However, Ajwaad's efforts to shut down my computer every time I was busy working and not playing with him turned out, luckily, to be no danger. Becoming a mother for the second time gave me a nice break from the usual worries and added another hand that tries to reach my computer keyboard's buttons. That was Zein al-Sharaf's. She was born at the end of November 2006. I'm grateful for their patience and love that was completely unconditional.

And finally, alḥamdu li-Allah, before and after. Thankfulness and grace to Allah the Mighty, the Beneficent.

Transliteration Correspondence

ʾ : ء	ḥ : ح
ʿ : ع	Ḫ : خ
Ā : آ	ḫ : خ
ā : آ	Š : ش
Ī : إي	š : ش
ī : إي	Ṣ : ص
Ō : و	ṣ : ص
ō : و	Ġ : غ
Ū : أوُ	ġ : غ
ū : أوُ	Ṭ : ط
Ḍ : ض	ṭ : ط
ḍ : ض	Ṯ : ث
Ḏ : ذ	ṯ : ث
ḏ : ذ	Ẓ : ظ
Ḥ : ح	ẓ : ظ

Abbreviations

AAE	Arabian archaeology and epigraphy
ADAJ	Annual of the Department of Antiquities of Jordan
AJA	American Journal of Archaeology
Ant.	The Jewish Antiquities, Josephus
AS	Anatolian Studies
BA	Biblical Archaeologist
BASOR	Bulletin of the American Schools of Oriental Research
BIA	Bulletin of the Institute of Archaeology
BiOr	Bibliotheca Orientalis
BMGS	Byzantine and Modern Greek Studies
BO	Bibbia e Oriente
BSOAS	Bulletin of the School of Oriental & African Studies
CH	Culture & History
CIG	Corpus Inscriptiorum Graecarum
CIS	Corpus Inscriptionum Semiticarum
CRAIBL	Comptes Rendus de l'Académie des Inscriptions et Belles-Lettres
EI	Encyclopaedia of Islam
EJ	Encyclopaedia Judaica
ERE	Encyclopaedia of Religion & Ethics
G	Greek inscriptions
ICS	Illinois Classical Studies
IEJ	Israel Exploration Journal
IGN	Institut Géographique Nationale
JAOS	Journal of the American Oriental Society
JEOL	Jaarbericht Ex Orient Lux
JNES	Journal of Near Eastern Studies
JRA	Journal of Roman Archaeology
JRAS	Journal of Royal Asiatic Society
JRS	Journal of Roman Studies
JS	Jaussen & Savignac in Mission Archéologique en Arabie I, II
JSS	Journal of Semitic Studies
JW	The Jewish Wars, Josephus
LCL	Loeb Classical Library
LIMC	Lexicon Iconongraphicum Mythologiae Classicae
Lisān	Lisān al-ʿArab, Ibn Manẓūr
Lit	Littmann in Nabataean Inscriptions
MA	Mediterranean Archaeology
Macc	Maccabées, 1st & 2nd book
N	Nabataean (inscription)
NAS	New Arabian Studies
NC	The Numismatic Chronicle
PAT	Palmyrene Aramaic Texts, Hillers & Cuissini.
PEQ	Palestine Exploration Quarterly
PSAS	Proceedings of the Seminar for Arabian Studies
RA	Révue Archéologique
RB	Révue Biblique
RES	Répértoire d'Épigraphie Sémitique
SCI	Scripta Classica Israelica
SHA I	Studies in the History of Arabia, Sources for the History of Arabia
SHAJ	Studies in the History and Archaeology of Jordan
SIJ	Safaitic Inscriptions from Jordan, Winnett

SNG	Sylloge Nummorum Graecorum
SS	Semitic Studies
SSR	Social Science Research
ZDMG	Zeitschrift der Deutschen Morgenländischen Gesellschaft
ZDPV	Zeitschrift des Deutschen Palästina-Vereins

Introduction

The *Manchester Guardian*, Wed, May 1st 1907, 12, under the heading 'A mysterious City':

> 'For twelve long centuries the very site of these stupendous remains was unknown to *civilised man* [my italics], until that August day in 1812 when Burckhardt toiled through the Sik with a water-skin, while his Arab guide carried a kid which was duly sacrificed at the tomb of Aaron'.

I. Introduction

The first words are always the most difficult, especially when they are written at the end, when all articulation possible has been executed and all expression has been exhausted. This is an extraordinary feeling – to be at the beginning whilst knowing the end of the plot. As difficult as it is I will nonetheless find new expression to introduce this work, after all it is customary that any new work be introduced with an adequate sequence of words and sentences. At least, I shall try to follow the steps of the Caliph al-Ma'mūn (813-833 CE) during his search for the secret of the pyramids when he succeeded in opening the hidden door that led to the largest pyramid's inner caves (al-Maqrīzī 1: 179-197). If this research can open even a small window through which a once glorious epoch can be viewed I will feel that some contribution to a distant past has been achieved.

At this point, it would be appropriate to explain why I chose to look at ancient Arabia's Nabataeans, and why women in particular. By choosing Nabataea as the political frame for this experiment, I had three inter-related motives, all connected to who I am. These were specifically my identity as a Muslim, an Arab and a woman.

My interest in the history of pre-Islamic Arabia is related to my identity as a Muslim woman living in an era in which Islamic attitudes towards women have been heavily criticised and put under the spotlight. Much of the unjustified criticism that has been directed at Islam and intensified after the catastrophy of September 11th has had to do with the status of women in Islam. In fact, most of the practices related to women's status are based on some local traditional practices that are not necessarily Islamic. Nor are they essentially Arabian, as this book will demonstrate.

In addition, there has been an association between nomadism, Islam and the subordination of women (see for example Mann 1986 I: 345). This was posited by emphasising the relationship between nomadism and patriarchy (Ahmed 1993), on the one hand, and Muslims being originally nomads, on the other (see McGraw Donner 1981: 26-28). Nabataea was a state particularly known for its relations to the nomads and one that included nomads in its identity. The process of this inclusion has weakened the idea that Arabians were merely or essentially nomads, by having an Arabian urbanised state. In other words, Nabataeans broke the stereotype that sees Arabians with only one form of social structure.

Nabataea and Nabataean history become central to the debates regarding the relationship between ancient Arabs and Islam. It became one of the central and distinguished states in pre-Islamic Arabia due to its distinctive perspective towards its neighbouring cultures. In this and in many other aspects it tried to remain outstanding, especially in its relation to the Parthians and Romans. Research suggests that it attempted to articulate a distinctive identity that is not Hellenistic, Roman, Jewish, Babylonian, or Egyptian; it had, rather, maintained its own language, script, art, political system and deities.

As for the relationship between Nabataeans and Arabs, this is an area of huge debate that has been partially settled. The general understanding is that Nabataeans had a close relationship with Arabia and Arabian culture, a contentious issue that will be explored further in the second chapter.

Recently, there has been worldwide interest in origins. History and heritage are seen as signs of national identity, a tendency that has been encouraged and sometimes exploited by some who claim ancient nations and cultures, rightly or wrongly, to be the ancestor of these modern entities. Such an approach was popularised in the post-Ottoman Muslim world at the beginning of the twentieth century with the establishment of nation states and the regionalisation of identities, where, for example, the Lebanese claim a Phoenician ancestry, the Egyptians a Pharaonic, the Tunisians a Carthaginian, the Iraqis a Babylonian and Assyrian ancestry. This identification was incorporated later in the pan-Arabism ideology in the fifties and sixties in particular. For pan-Arabists, finding a historical origin of some kind that accepts regionalisation was difficult, although Yemen was popularly believed to be the cradle of the Arabs. But where did that leave Nabataea? It was not a known state until the archaeological excavations carried out in Jordan from the beginning of the twentieth century, but that was still not common knowledge to the average Arab as the information was confined to those interested in archaeology or those reading archaeology journals, i.e. it was not a history available or accessible to the average pan-Arabist.

In this respect, research has found that Nabataea ideally represents one of the major Arabian states that were known before Islam, which Arabs can legitimately claim. It is possible to present the link between this early Arabian state and earlier ones such as Liḥyān, or those contemporaneous such as Ma'īn, Saba', or Ḥaḍramawt, or later states such as the Laḫmīds or the Ġassānids, as will be further discussed in chapter three.

Interestingly, I found that Arabian history has been marginalised in many mainstream studies about the ancient world in the West. This maybe explained as a reflection of attaching less value to other cultures including Arabia. Even researchers who are aware of the problem of excluding non-Western cultures, such as Amélie Kuhrt, did not escape excluding Arabia from her major study on The Ancient Near East. Whether it is a matter of belittling the importance of Arabia, or overvaluing other cultures, there is no doubt that, in general, it is related to the marginalisation of Arabia's ancient history, an attitude that this research attempts to rectify.

It is generally agreed that women's history has also been ignored within the larger project of writing histories, thus contributing to the marginalisation of women in real life. This is of course related to the fact that history has usually been written by men and refracted through the lens of men's observations (Lerner 1979-81:160), and hence presented from a male perspective. Revealing the importance of women's history will not happen by writing the history of high achievers only, i.e. by documenting the history of the exceptional, not just the history and experience of the mass (Lerner 1979-81: 145-46). Nor is it sufficient for women to argue for a redress of balance simply on the grounds of being of the same gender. It is important to understand how history has differentially affected men and women so that women's histories are not subsumed by the histories of men. This can be achieved by understanding the efforts and inter-dependence of the histories of the two genders in any society. What is vital in redressing the balance is to emphasise that any representative history cannot ignore one half of humankind. A female perspective is essential for writing women's histories and experiences. This has two purposes. First, it has the effect of restoring women to history by making them the subject of the enquiry and the focus of the narrative and secondly, it returns history to women. This issue will be discussed from a theoretical perspective in the first chapter, and later addressed throughout the whole book by applying the methodology presented in the first chapter.

In addition to feminist studies, this work uses epigraphy, archaeology and classical sources, as well as recent developments in historiography, to understand Nabataean society and Nabataean women in particular. There are two overall enquiries. The first is to investigate (in the fourth chapter) whether Nabataean women enjoyed a high status that was particular to their society and history. The second related enquiry is to investigate (in the fifth chapter) what made it possible for Nabataean women in the first century BCE-CE to become visible in inscriptions and numismatics (i.e. prominent in that period, place and time)? In other words what are the factors that allowed women such status? And were they factors particular to Nabataean women, their society or history? One of objectives of this book is to question the assumption of subordination of women in pre-Islamic Arabia.

It was the search for a female perspective and the restoration of history to women that led me to take up the issue of women in Pre-Islamic Arabia to find out how far patriarchy was inherent to their social structure, or to nomadism in this regard. Research discovered that patriarchy was not unique to 'Arabness', or to 'Arabians' or nomads. Rather, it was a system that prevailed in most of the ancient world.

Although this research is principally about ancient history and women in particular, it is important to begin by addressing some theoretical and methodological issues related to the writing of ancient history. Some of these issues will be considered at length in the first chapter but it is necessary to subsequent discussion on the history of pre-Islamic Arabian women and their relationship to power to set the scene from the outset and discuss some of these concepts below. The next section therefore begins with the concept of 'Hellenism' as a historical category applied to the region under discussion. We shall see that it has been utilised in an inappropriate fashion and that it needs questioning.

II. Frames of Reference

A. Hellenistic or post-Achaemenid

The problem with the term 'Hellenistic' is that it represents the form in which Western Hellenocentric modern scholarship and its non-Western followers have constructed and presented the ancient history of the 'Near Orient' from the fourth century BCE: they present the time from the conquests of Alexander the Macedonian as a period dominated by Hellenic culture. The term Hellenistic was first introduced by Johan Droysen in 1836 (Yaḥia 1978: 16) to distinguish it from the Hellenic classical Greek culture of the fifth-fourth century BCE that preceded it. Others understood it as a *melange* between the Hellenic culture and the west Asian cultures and civilizations, although some find that the Hellens have become more Orientalised than the west Asians have become Hellenized (ibid. 18).

While Eurocentrecism is a modern term, it is not a modern phenomenon, for it has been operating in different guises, one of which can be attributed to Hellenocentrism, both in ancient sources and modern histories of the ancient world. It is a vision of history that views the Greek world as the centre of the civilised universe, and views Alexander's conquests as a war of liberation, and an 'act to confer the attributes of their (the Greek's) implicitly greater culture upon passive foreigners' (Invernizzi 1993: 233; Kuhrt & Sherwin-White 1994: 311). In fact, Alexander was concerned all the time with justifying his wars. Such concern was shown in the accounts of early classical historians who would give different reasons for his invasions. For example the *casus belli* given for his war against the Arabs was their 'failure to offer the appropriate homage'; for Strabo and Arrian, the classical writers, the Arabs were the only people in that part of the world not to have made overtures, although the real reasons for the attack were his personal vanity and commercial exploitation (Bosworth 1996: 153). This trend continued after Alexander's death and was taken up by his successive generals. Antigonus' attack on the Nabataeans was famous for its lack of justification. He was embarrassed by the eloquency of the Nabataean elders who sent a messenger saying that they had not provoked such an aggression. However, Antigonus, acting in bad faith, showed that this was undertaken without his orders, and continued to find a proper *casus belli* for a second aggression (Bosworth 1996: 147-148).

Alexander, indeed, conquered the Achaemenid Empire, a well-established empire with a long heritage dating back to the Neo-Babylonian and Assyrian times; and with complex political administration and governmental organisation and social institutions. Although the Hellenic influence was described as 'advanced', politically, culturally and economically, it was exaggerated at the expense of the indigenous civilisations and culture and their impact on their own history. Theirs was a history that, for millennia before the Hellenic conquest, experienced advanced and well- established forms of economic and social life, be it represented in terms of cities, markets, coinage etc. (see Sherwin-White & Kuhrt 1993: 1-2). The main problem was that, in treating the history of the newly conquered areas separately from their predecessors and their successors, scholars neglected the broader historical setting, which in the end served to encourage their narrow Hellenocentric interpretations (see Alcock 1993: 172). This attitude has endorsed the history and the civilisation of the period from the fourth century BCE up to the Islamic conquests in the 7th century CE for the sake of the Greco-Roman culture, transforming it into an appendix to European historiography. The Achaemenid Empire, on the other hand, was a major actor in ancient history during the sixth, fifth and fourth centuries BCE. Their Empire had the distinction of being called the Great Empire, greater in extent and the largest stable political structure in history until the formation of the Islamic Empire. It was the first Empire ever to control two million square miles, a size that was surpassed by half a dozen contemporary states, such as Canada, China, USA, Brazil or Australia (see Taagepera 1978: 109). This Empire managed, for two hundred years, to include, under one sovereignty, the whole area called the ancient 'Near East', spreading over the Greek city-states of Asia Minor, and northwards up to Thrace, northern Greece. No other power was able to rule over this area in peace and autonomy again until the Islamic conquests (see Taagepera 1978: table 2). Or, as Garth Fowden stresses, the unification of this area has only twice been achieved, by Cyrus and by Muḥammad, who both created empires without peer (1993: 18-19). Alexander, after conquering the Persians, saw himself as the last Achaemenid Great King, and as Cyrus' heir. He behaved as one, dressed in Cyrus' attire, and re-established the Achaemenid satrap system. It has even been wondered why Alexander was called 'the Great' if it were not for the Hellenocentric dream that he made come true (Mann 1986: I: 246-7; Fowden 1993: 21-22). After Alexander's death, his successors did nothing less than adopt and adapt the Achaemenid culture, trying to become Persians themselves, especially the Seleucid States, which were called 'loose Persian-style states' (Mann 1986 I: 247; Sherwin-White & Kuhrt 1993: 1).

It has been noted that introducing new usages, rather than using conventional terminology, is a difficult step, which might make the work unintelligible to the scholar as well as to the lay-person. It is, however, a worthy attempt if the 'common terminology' or 'practice' implies an incomplete representation or imprecise categories in one's proposition (Hodgson [1958] 1974 I: 45-57). Therefore, I find it more appropriate for the period conventionally called 'Hellenistic' in Western Asia and northern Africa to be called instead the 'Post-Achaemenid' period, a term that is used by Fowden (1993: 18). This includes the period from the fragmentation of the Achaemenid Empire under the Diadachoi until the Islamic Conquests. It follows that, the Seleucids, Ptolemaics, and Roman governors of western Asia and Egypt should be regarded as post-Achaemenid kings, even if they did not follow the Achaemenid system. It is true that the Achaemenids did not conquer Arabia proper, but the relationships with Arabia existed for a long time (see Graf 1990a). And it is true that the Hellens did not conquer Arabia, but the tendency amongst many scholars, was to refer to the Hellenistic periodisation even if the subject discussed is Oman or Thaj in south eastern or eastern Arabia (see for example Boucharlat 1989 and Potts 1992). It is true that the term 'post-Achaemenid' is problematic as well, such as the difficulty in finding out how much the natives had adopted the Achaemenid way of life or culture. However, it is sufficient for the present study to raise the problem and question the common terms. Therefore, I shall use the term suggested, keeping 'hellenistic' between inverted commas.

For example, the Nabataean kings would be considered as contemporary to the last Achaemenids and as post-Achaemenids, since they had been on the scene since the Achaemenid period and later, similarly with the Ptolemaics Seleucid kings and their period.

B. The geographical frame: Middle East-Nile to Oxus

Finding a collective name to describe the wide area from Egypt in the west to Persia in the East, Asia Minor in the north to Southern Arabia in the south, which has been included in the term 'Near East' coined by Greek and Roman literature and by Biblical scholarship (Larsen 1987: 96, for Assyriology and the Hebrew Bible, 102-110), is not an easy task (Kuhrt 1995 I: 1-4). Nor is it easy to find a term that is essential to the area and the culture, but that has not been based on the political situation of any period, or is removed from any 'Other' ethnocentrism, and conveys more enduring criteria relevant to the social history intended here. This area was traditionally labelled by terms such as 'the Orient', 'the Near East' and, later on, 'the Middle East,' as opposed to 'the Occident', 'the West', be it Europe or North America or both of them, without any critical awareness of what such labels declare. For they emphasise Eurocentrecism towards the 'Other's' cultures and civilisations. They try to equate the Eurasian peninsula with the rest of the Asian continent, as expressed by Marshal Hodgson ([1958] 1974 I: 49).

The Greeks were not particular about giving the rest of the world its real name, as its nations were all categorised by them as 'Barbarians', divided into those known Barbarians of the vicinity, and the mysterious Barbarians who live far away (Inglebert 1997: 187), though they had some difficulty in justifying this term for dominant civilisations, such as the Persians or Phoenicians (Mann 1986 I: 213-216). Sometimes, however, they came up with a generic terminology to identify the other nations in relation to themselves; thus, they called their area the 'Orient' from where the sun rises according to their position, or 'the Near East', especially when they, the Greeks, came as conquerors after Alexander's victories. This was the period when classical writers were interested in the conquered or recently settled areas of the ancient world by the Hellenes. From that time, the contrast between the centre and the periphery was created, with all the assumptions that this concept carries about the Greeks being the makers of civilisation, the active, the inventive, and the creative ones. It was exploited more and continued throughout Western literature, observed by many modern scholars (see Hodgson [1958] 1974, Said [1987] 1995 and Asad 1993).

The second term, 'Middle East', was created in the beginning of twentieth century by the American naval officer and geopolitical theorist, Alfred Thayer Mahan (1840-1914), who published an article in the National Review that bore the title 'The Persian Gulf and International Relations' (see Adelson 1995: 22). Mahan, as an American from the West Atlantic, recognised the inadequacy of using the term 'Near East' in the new structure of the western world which, by the twentieth century, extended further to the west and therefore, needed modified terminologies to describe the world in relation to the modern equation of power relations, hence the 'Middle East' term. This vague term was also rejected by Marshal Hodgson ([1958] 1974 I: 60ff).

In this situation, there is a need to generate a different position that can express the criteria of this geographical entity in its own terms. Geographical terms such as 'West Asia' or 'North Africa', might sound clumsy and loose, as well as confirming the common error of dividing the Afro-Eurasian land mass into the continents of Europe, Asia and Africa (see Hodgson [1958] 1974 I: 49). At the same time, following a geographical choice, we cannot choose 'Western Eurasia' for this will mean what is conventionally known as 'Western Europe'. Hodgson argued against the term 'West Asia' as it excludes Egypt ([1958] 1974 I: 61). For the purposes of this research I will adopt Hodgson's adaptation of 'Nile to Oxus' ([1958] 1974 I: 61-62).

This term is advantageous in the sense that it includes a large area of land which was known as the vague 'Near East', as well as being a mere geographical term, not charged by political assumptions. The difficulty of finding a definite inclusive term is apparent here. Despite the disadvantages and problems such as the fact that the Achaemenids ruled Cyrene (west of the Nile) and India (east of the Oxus) which makes the term 'Post-Achaemenid' imprecise, I find that Hodgson's term could still be used for the time being, bearing in mind that the geographical term does not need to be identical with the historical term used. Saying 'Near East' does not mean that the geographical area should belong to the Assyrian period or the Achaemenid period. Thus, at present, the term 'Near East' would be expressed by the geographical reference 'Nile to Oxus' that includes the Land of the two Rivers, adding to that Asia Minor and the Arabian Peninsula ([1958] 1974 I: 61, 117 fn.9). In this regard, reference to the people of the Semitic culture as Semites is not used. I am well aware of the problems with the term 'Semitic'. It has however been accepted conventionally as a term, without reference to its Biblical origin.

Similarly, in a regional context, one is faced with the problem of naming the different geographical regions and cities, etc. Most of the names have reached us through Orientalist works, based on Biblical or Hellenic tradition, which tend, in general, to avoid the native names of those places. For example, the name of 'Mesopotamia', which first appeared in Greek works starting with Arrian's *Anabasis of Alexander*, corresponding to its usage at the time of Alexander, has continued to be used in western literature. The term was later used for a Roman province, though it meant different things in different times. Locally, however, it took many forms and names that can be generalised to the three main regions of Sumer, Babylonia and Assyria (see Postgate 1992: 3). Where the name Mesopotamia means literally the land between the two rivers, the Arabs by the seventh century CE onwards used, among other names Bilād al-Rāfidayn, i.e. the Land of the Two Rivers, which can stretch to the east of the Tigris and west of the Euphrates. As a collective name, they called it al-ʿIrāq, i.e. 'border of the rivulet, said to be so named because it situated upon the side or shore of the Tigris and Euphrates, or because it was in the approximity of sea shores' (Lisan, Lane: ʿrq; Yaqut: ʿIrāq). Realising the problems of using any of these names, I shall choose either Babylonia, or more loosely the Land of the Two Rivers, though long and clumsy, to denote Sumer-Akkad/Babylon and Assyria.

Not much further away, there is problematic area from the eastern Mediterranean to the Syrian Desert that stretches to the Arabian Desert of Nufūd. For this region the convention (e.g., by Hodgson) to call it 'Syria' in the old sense will be accepted, i.e. all the area which comprised what is known today as Lebanon, Palestine, Jordan and Syria (see Hodgson's discussion in [1958] 1974 I: 47-48).

Some problems emerged also in city names such as 'Petra', a Greek name, meaning 'rock', by which the city is very well identified today. Its original Nabataean name was, however, rqmw as it appeared in the Nabataean inscriptions. In Arabic, it means 'figured, decorated, and especially striped. It can also mean a tablet where one inscribes' (Lisan; Lane: rqm) (Mailser 1949: 316; Starcky 1965, b: no. 2). In this regard, I find it essential to give the people whose history is represented, the chance to have a voice, at least through using their own terms and names. And if they were to be modified, that should be done to the nearest language with which they can identify, i.e. Aramaic or Arabic. In other words, I would prefer to call the city rqmw using the Arabic form of al-raqīm, but for easier comprehension in the present study, I shall call it Raqamū-Petra.

These are only examples, but the reader needs to adjust to the new terms. In other cases, where new terms are needed, they will be discussed at the time.

C. The Dating Frame: AD-CE

Finding a useful dating system expressive of the period with which I am dealing was another problem that I encountered. Although dating systems can be conventional and used by different nations, such as the 'Seleucid system' was used by Babylonians, Syrians, Aramaeans and Arabs, for example, it cannot be separated from historical creation. That system was based on the beginning of Seleucid rule over the Babylonians. Similarly, the dating system of 'Boṣra', which commemorated the annexation of Nabataea and the establishment of the Roman Provincia Arabia, was used by the Romans as well as by some of the Arab monarchies. Each group of people, however, followed their own system, depending on the major events that formulated their community experiences. It marks a notion of independence, as in the case of dating after the ruling years of a king, as was common among the Nabataeans for example, as well as other realms.

For today's dating system, the convention is that of the Christian era, which starts, theoretically, from the birth of Jesus, and is common in the West and most of its former colonies in the world. A few exceptions are found, for example in China, Ethiopia, Japan, Iran and Saudi Arabia. This conventionality had and still has a close relationship with the position that the West is giving itself, where history goes only in one direction. To break from this hegemony, a new dating system came into fashion based on the 'Common Era'. Although this system set out to avoid a religious inclination, it could not break from the Christocentric ways of referring to time periods (Frymer-Kensky 1992: 10*), for if one asks whose 'Common Era' is being talked about, one will find again the expression of a Western perspective that has a calendar starting from where the Christian Era started.

This research did not, unfortunately, manage to break from this loop, nor find an alternative yet, for I am aware that to reach a dating system that will not be expressive of one group of people only, or at least of my own, will need a larger project than this one.[1] For the purposes of this research therefore I shall adhere to the Common Era dating, realising that it is not sufficient to meet the position taken in this work or to answer its intellectual concern.

The above sections have set the frames of elementary definitions required for the course of history writing, which includes giving alternative terminologies for common descriptive language. I will take up the critique of ancient-history writing further in the following chapter.

[1] In a recent paper (April 2007) presented to the 8th Annual Scientific Meeting of the GCC History and Archaeology Society, I gave an alternative dating system that will be published soon.

Chapter One

Rules of Engagement: The Politics of Writing Ancient History

I. Prologue

A Tale of Two Cities, First Part: ḤEGRA[2]

Wādī al-Qurā: 'An outpouring of green amid the harsh, obdurate desert, as if it had burst from within the earth or fallen from the sky. It was nothing like its surroundings, or rather had no connection with them, dazzling you with curiosity and wonder: how had water and greenery burst out in a place like this? But the wonder vanished gradually, giving way to a mysterious respect and contemplation. It was one of those rare cases of nature pressing its genius and wilfulness, in defiance of any explanation'.[3]

If it were left to Kamkam, the priestess, daughter of Wā'ilah, to speak about Wādī al-Qurā she would have said unbelievable things about the place. She would have spoken about the beauty of Dedan, the gentle breeze of Ḥegra and the sweetness of the springs. She would not have forgotten the magnificent red sandstone mountains. There is magic in these mountains and a curiosity that keeps the beholder captivated. Their secret is that they take the spectator on a mesmerising journey changing their form. At first glance they can show one thing and at the second glance they change their form thus holding the imagination forever. From one side they can look like a lion, and from another like an ostrich. She would have seen them as resembling the shape of a woman carrying a baby or perhaps a woman wailing for a daughter. This is an exceptional magic, a rare beauty, present only here where every mountain and rock tells its own story. A story narrated by those who have dreamt about reaching its summits, of those who succeeded and of the others who didn't.

Kamkam would have recounted stories, some of which go back to the time of 'Ād,[4] *but most of the stories would have been mainly about Ṯamūd, their prophet Ṣāliḥ and his she-camel, whose ḥawār's*[5] *massive rocks, still to this day (called al-Ḥawārah and Ḥuwairah) can be found outlining the northern horizon of the city where the rock was believed to have burst out with this giant young camel, who drank the daily share of all the other camels. Kamkam would have spoken about the wrath that fell on Ḥegra when it disobeyed Ṣāliḥ's God and conspired against the sign God sent to its people, the giant she-camel, so that in a time immemorial, ancient Ḥegra disappeared from the surface of earth.*

She would have also related the story of the Sheikh and his lovely daughter Buṯeynah, who loved the artisan (al-Ṣāne'), Badrī. He would meet her secretly. Every night he would tie up his horse at the rock that still holds the name of Marbaṭ al-Ḥuṣān,[6] *and climb up the mountain to the place where Buṯeynah's father had confined her fearing that one day her beauty would captivate someone. These confines did not prevent passion from burning and her lover would climb to her using her snake-like long thick braids. She had maintained these all her life, by applying henna and sesame oil, brushing and braiding them, and now they where the bridge between her and her lover. She would have repeated Buṯeynah's verses of longing which unravel her secret and made the days of the two lovers shorter than a dream:*

Wāweil al-Ḥadrī law yadrī
Buṯeinah 'ašrat Badrī
yā Ḥadrī law innak tadrī
ḍarabt rāsak bil-jadrī[7]

For soon, fate did not spare them the anger of the Sheikh. He took revenge upon them both and turned their myth of love into a tragedy, to which the bloody remains on the rock of Qaṣr al-Ṣāne' still bear witness.[8] *Knowing the fate of the doomed lovers, all lovers, newly wed and caravans that pass by Ḥegra would pay tribute to the lovers and offer sacrifices for them. They would also chant the hymn of their own sacrifice to the gods of love.*

Once the caravans, whether coming from the north and crossing the passage of Mabrak al-Nāqah,[9] *or from the south through the old town of Dedan,*[10] *reached the stone walls of Ḥegra, they would enter an enchanting world. This is a world of constant movement, smells of all kinds, noise from all directions, of builders, carpenters, artisans, peasants, water-carriers, beggars and whores, madmen and crippled women, horsemen and camel-riders, men and women, elderly and young leading a donkey or a camel,*

[2] Madā'in Ṣāliḥ, see map plates IV & VII.

[3] (Munif [1984] tr. 1994: 1).

[4] Ancient extinct Arabian people.

[5] A young camel when just born or until weaned.

[6] 'Where the horse is tied up'.

[7] JS 1909 I: 115.

[8] 'The artisan's castle'.

[9] Resting place of the she-camel.

[10] al-'Ulā.

children running about or behind chickens or sheep, poets and singers displaying their eloquence or chanting a lyric, slaves and foreigners from north and south in colourful strange attire, sellers and buyers bargaining and quarrelling, merchants proclaiming their merchandise, be it slaves, animals, or goods in all tongues. Goods were brought from the Indus or beyond, from Ḥabašah and Aksūm,[11] *from Saba' and Ḥaḍramawt, from Alexandria, Raqamū, Boṣra, Damascus, Tadmur,*[12] *Ḥaṭra, Seleucia,*[13] *Misān, Qaryat Ḏū Kahl,*[14] *al-'Uyūn*[15] *or Hajar.*[16]

Kamkam was a woman of simple words and perhaps she would have spoken more easily about her own domain or the important events of that year than telling stories of these beautiful and enchanting places. Her home was the house of Manāt. These are her words:

'from within the white city, you can appreciate the vast space that leads to the isolated blocks of mountains in the distance in all directions. To the south you can see when you pass the walls, especially when you follow the grazing sheep, al-Ḥureibah rocks and abū Loḥah's rock,[17] *al-Ṣunaymāt or the Ḥreimāt series of rocks in the west which is reserved as part of the rock cemetery of Ḥegra, like the northern Qaṣr Fahd and al-Maḥjar. This is a chain of hills, which is not far north of the other beautiful block of the mountain named after Buṯeinah as Qaṣr al-Bint in the direction of the sacred mountains of Aṯālib to the north-east. That leaves the space to the east. In that direction as you are leaving the great congregation hall of Iṯlib, making the detour heading towards the south-east, you'll reach the elegant house of Manāt which is carved by the pious people of Ḥegra, such as 'Abd Ḥāriṯah, s. of 'Īd, 'Arfūn and others. It is almost in the shape of a giant kam'ah*[18] *from the outside, and almost square from the inside, about 5-6 feet, opening into the Iṯlib direction, where the goddess can be blessed with Dushara's spiritual ambience. Although it is a smaller house than that in Dedan, it benefits from a better breeze and location, and I was able to manage it with less temple slaves. My daughter Kulaybah was a good help in maintaining the house; she took care, with two more slaves, of the maintenance, of cleaning and tidying, refilling the oil that feeds the lamps, supervising the quantity and kinds of incense burnt, and checking that the doors are safely fastened before the sun sets'. 'In turn', subsequently, Kamkam says, 'I take care of the gifts and money given to the house, of the fines that the intruders into the sanctity of the after-life houses (or the breaches of its rules) had to pay to the house of Manāt, as well as the usual tithes. This money was stored in a small room adjacent to the main hall of the sanctuary that is locked in by a wooden door, where no one enters but the priestess of the goddess. In addition to this, I would keep the money of the pious worshippers who trust their goddess with their fortune. It was left to me to decide how to spend all that comes into the house as an offering to the goddess, or whether to accept worshippers or travellers with no place to stay. Usually they would have been given a place in the house, but since there is no room for such a stay, most of them would use the big sanctuary in the Iṯlib. Last but not least, there are the banquets of the mourners and the feasts of the gods and goddesses. In that chamber, I also store my special herbs, which I use for those asking to be healed from bad spirits. Like my mother Wā'ilah, I have become known for my knowledge of herbs and healing. This is a secret teaching that she passed down only to me and I shall pass it to my daughter Kulaybah, by collecting the herbs and letting her help me prepare the ingredients of each cure'.*

Proudly, Kamkam says: 'The Ḥegran people, the Arabs from all towns as well as the travellers, know me by now and have experienced my wonders with herbs, some of which I order specially from the caravans going to Yemen, Ḥaḍramawt, India and Axūm. Some I plant myself in the garden behind the house, and others I collect from the farther side of the Wādī, especially those which grow by the banks at the special time of rain fall'.

'I will also decide whose offering to accept for carving a niche, for one cannot accept all the requests to have one's niche in the house. Instead, I would urge these pious men and women to make more offerings of gifts and prayers to the goddess. I also set the time for receiving the members of all clans, to answer their needs and find out what the divination will say. I would have all sorts of people coming to pay tribute, and all sorts of complaints as well, such as those of wives against husbands, buyers against sellers, mothers against sons, orphans against uncles, etc'.

'Summer comes in with its stagnant air and heat, with the date harvest that attracts flies and diseases, which come also from food that rots too quickly, though many women used to either dry or pickle their food without a large chance of success. The elderly and children are prone to death in summer, especially the newly born. Animals get even more affected by the summer's heat and diseases. The winter brings with its cold air other problems that afflect all parts of the body. The best remedy in addition to my herbs is goat wool: it prevents any unwanted cold air from being abosrbed'.

'Hot summer's flies are among the most annoying creatures on earth, especially at the time of the date harvest. Flies by then would stick on everybody's nose and eyes mercilessly. The best remedy, for us women, is to draw down our veils, and for men to mask themselves with their turban ends, so that we can escape the annoyance, which many get used to after living long in the Wādī. People also get used to the

[11] Ethiopia.

[12] Palmyra.

[13] Seleucia-upon-Tigris.

[14] al-Fau.

[15] al-Aflāj (central Arabia).

[16] Bahrain.

[17] Known also as al-Farīd rock.

[18] Wild mushroom.

Wādī's smells, which are a mixture of spices and perfumes, cardamom and cinnamon confused with the known and unknown incense burning on altars or in front of niches in the corners of the streets. All of that, together with the familiar and unfamiliar smells of cooking and grilling coming in as trails from the houses and caravanserais, or merely from the market, make up the special smell of Ḥegra'.

'Worst of all is the time of drought', Kamkam says wisely. 'Then, everybody will think that crying to Manāt will bring the blessing back, forgetting how often many, in their turn, in the days of abundance, will forget the goddess, especially since there has been more intermixing with the Syrians, Babylonians, Persians and Egyptians, and there is more fascination with their deities. This is a corrupted and ungrateful new generation. I have even seen the new trend of erecting statues and acquiring images of the Egyptian gods and goddesses, who are in the shape of half-humans, half- animals and birds, which they call Sikhmat, Tefnut, Wadget and others. It is true that the God of our Lord, Dushara, can be seen in the image of an eagle, erected on many houses and houses of after-life, but it just symbolises his strength and knowledge and not the idea that he is an eagle. In the days of blessings, however, more sacrifices were usually offered. Banquets are held all over the houses of the gods, all of which are centred on the Aṯālib and Manāt's house'.

'When it rains, at the right time in winter, in the right amounts, that becomes the time for feasting, for the new adults to celebrate their unions and for the peasants to celebrate their crops. But when rain is excessive, which could happen at any time when people become ungrateful to the gods, the wheat and corn harvest might either be ruined or drenched by floods that will turn the city into a muddy field. This used to happen some time ago. Luckily, the Nabataeans' together with the Liḥyānites' experience with water drainage made it possible for Ḥegra to enjoy huge water reservoirs and well carvings with minimal hygienic disturbance. The qanāt system, though not as elaborate or concentrated as it was in Dedan, is very well distributed around the city; the dams, the cisterns and water caches are plentiful everywhere. Visitors to Ḥegra envied and imitated our system'.

'We grew up hearing about the caravans that travel in all directions', Kamkam remembers. 'Some go to the great city of Raqamū, and carry on to the towns beyond, reaching the sea at Ġazzah. Other caravans head west where the sun sets, towards the sea of Liḥyān at Kurkumah,[19] *'Aynūnah or Maqnā after passing by many small towns such as Dīsa, on the way to Rawwāfah, from where one reaches the big city of Qurayyah. For those heading west to the sea they must see the famous city of Midian that imitates Ḥegra, however old it is. From there they connect with the desert of Sīn, from which they reach the Nile valley. Certain caravans travel east, where the sun rises, towards Taymā, the town of Ṣalam.*[20] *Through Taymā the route leads to Dumat Mārid,*[21] *the town of Wadd, our old moon god, and from there through Wādī al-Sirḥān they head north through the castles and villages of the Salt and ḥarrah, Iṯrā and Kāf,*[22] *reaching the springs of al-Azraq, crossing from there Ḥawrān's black sand via Umm al-Jimāl, Deir al-Kahf, Amtān, Ṣalḫad, until they alight in Boṣra, the city of wheat and vines. I don't know where the caravans continue after that, or where their routes end' she continues, 'but, there are many more territories beyond, about which our men tell us stories and adventures. Nowadays, men travel all the time in both seasons, summer and winter; the caravans of camels strut along with their load of incense and perfumes, frankincense and myrrh, spices and balsam, silk, linen, and cotton material, cups and vases, of glass, bronze and fine pottery, silver hair pins, beads and necklaces, bronze mirrors inlaid with silver and ivory and much more. With every caravan, gifts and donations for the house of the gods are expected, new clothing, a cassock or kiswah for the temple priestesses. These will be offered at the throne of the deities whose betyls are carved with watching eyes and whose closed mouths signify the wisdom of silence.*

Kamkam points out that, 'This year is different from the other years, even from that when we first moved to Ḥegra. I still remember that day. I was in my early spring years. My mother, Wā'ilah daughter of Ḥarām, the great priestess of Manāt, together with all the rest of our household and many Dedanites, left Dedan, the city abundant with springs, qanāts, fields and orchards, houses of the gods and forts. For our Lord 'Obadah succeeded in stretching the influence of Nabaṭū to Dedan, benefiting from the fall of the kings of Alexandria into the hands of the Romans by conquering our last King Mas'udu. Since Ḏū-Ġābah, our once great god, failed in protecting us, the populace deserted him as well, and instead, sought to please the emerging Dushara. Fortunately, Manāt, our great old goddess, helped us to survive this chaos and in no time life prospered in the new city, which used to be secondary to Dedan. Now it is an important city, with the huge investment the Nabaṭū had brought into it to make it attractive for its inhabitants, who are mainly from the state administration, rich merchants and even soldiers, as well as visitors from all over the place'.

'The population began to increase, with newcomers coming from the surrounding towns, or from those passers-by who chose to settle. We, the Dedanites', Kamkam proceeds, 'were the majority. Most of us were from Liḥyān and Salamians, while a few came from Taymā, Yaṯrib, Raqamū and from the nearby tribes, such as Muzaynah and Bajja. No wonder that Ḥegra during the last twenty years of 'Obadah's reign was able to reach such a glorious

[19] Ancient Egra, see Ġabban 1993: 21, plate XIX.

[20] See plates VII, XV, XVI, XVII, XVIII & XXI.

[21] Dūmah (Dumat al-Jandal) see plate XX.

[22] See plate XXI.

status. Soon, the plains of Ḥegra became prosperous and the stone and mud-brick houses suddenly flourished and competed in beauty and elegance. All the houses imitated the architecture of the Emir Ḥāriṯah's graceful palace and castle, which any traveller entering from the north could see, once they passed the gates of the city. Kamkam says that Ḥāriṯah attracted architects, masons, artisans, and merchants to the new city and established in it altars and houses for the great gods and goddesses'. She adds: 'he built altars for Manāt, the Shepherd of our fortune and life, and for her companion Qays, as well as for Hubal and Allāt, our mother and the mother of all the gods, but above all remains first of all Dushara, the pastor of the Nabaṭū kings. The governor also established the administration with a court and the house of records where taxes and fines are collected and recorded'.

'This year', Kamkam carries on, 'is different from any other year, for our Lord the King 'Obadah has died and the people of Ḥegra are in turmoil, talking all the day and night, wondering what the governor will say or do. Later on the news, disputed and contradictory, arrived with the caravan. Some said that the Aḫū, or as it is known officially Aḫū, brother of our Lord, Sullay, or as he is known locally, Ṣāliḥ, has seized the throne. Some said that Ṣāliḥ was killed, and a third group said that he is in Rome, which will help establish him on the throne. It is true that Ṣāliḥ, in the last few years acquired a vast fortune, power and influence. It started when he succeeded in leading the Roman troops astray in the desert. Their troops were said to have pitched their tents near Ḥegra for days and months, burying hundreds of their men around there, until they were able again to move along to the country of Saba', also called 'the Happy Land'.[23] *Since that year, the fourth of Lord 'Obadah's reign, which witnessed the humiliating defeat of the Romans and their departure, hopefully never to return, the name of Ṣāliḥ, the Aḫu malka', appeared on every lip. Gradually and consequently, he became the one who orders and forbids. Nothing happens in the state without his consent. This has pushed 'Obadah more and more into the shadow. Stories about him became the entertaining talk of the gossiping men and women, as they gathered around the burning ġaḍā wood in winter, especially the story of his doomed love for Salome, the Jewess. These stories were turned into tales that were transported from one town to the other by the caravaners, the way they used to pass around the stories of Cleopatra and her lovers'.*

'The final word came with the last caravan, which carried a number of Ḥegran men, whose days of travel had been long and painful to their mothers, children, wives and lovers. Truly, their long absence was rewarded with a luxurious life style that even Dedan did not enjoy, but this continuous travel, save for a few months or so before they are again on the back of camels heading in one of the earth's many directions, was tiresome for their women's hearts and hands. The women of Ḥegra are known for their strong will and wise management: They wake up at dawn before anyone in the town to milk the goats, light fires with the collected wood and manure, mix flour and knead the dough which has been left to rise from the night before, bake the bread from either wheat, corn or wheat and barley, depending on the season, and feed the little ones and the old. They count on the elder children to take the goats and sheep to the lands outside of the city-walls to pasture wherever they will find grass. In the house women check on the chickens and pigeons, water the small vegetable patches and pick up what they need for cooking that day. They are also known for making high quality carpets and rugs from a fabric that they spin and weave, especially from sheep's wool. Making house furniture of straw mats is women's entertainment on special occasions, such as when preparing offerings to a bride. So is producing mats and baskets made of palm straw of all sizes for dates and fruits'.

'Nowadays, with more men working on the caravan trails, you find more and more women depending on themselves to fulfil their needs, especially since the governor has been tough on all acts of delinquency and has made Ḥegra safe to wander about in even after dusk. Women now sell and buy, harvest the crops or even sow the seeds or at least supervise slaves, hired men and boys, rear their children, manage the family affairs by themselves, often with the help of other women within the household or from the elderly. You see them come often to pay their tribute to Manāt, dedicate epitaphs with their beloved names on them, offering more to the gods in the hope that their men will come back soon safe. Indeed', Kamkam interjects, 'I was the right person to help them. The oracles of Manāt did wonders, and still do. On the other hand, you would also see more and more prostitutes, who instead of sacrificing themselves to help in the temples, give themselves to the few men left in the city, or to the foreigners passing through.

'With the last caravan from Raqamū, also arrived the last word on the situation in the palace. The name of the new king was Aeneas, who had become the malik and was crowned with the royal name of Ḥāriṯah. It is said that his mother is the daughter of the late King Mālik, and she is the one who backed his claim to the throne. Others said that it was his wife, who is the daughter of 'Obadah, and that it was she who helped him to succeed her father, thus discarding the ambitions of the Vizier. As for Ṣāliḥ, it is said that he stayed in Rome trying to defend himself against the accusations of poisoning the late 'Obadah, which is a scandalous assertion! Apparently, however, Ṣāliḥ did not succeed in convincing Augustus of his version of the story, or in obtaining the throne of the Nabataean kingdom. A group of caravaners later added that the rumour was strong that Ḥāriṯah had in his turn provoked the wrath of Rome, because he did not seek Augustus' permission before he proclaimed himself king'. Kamkam added with anger saying: 'this was the oddest of all the stories. After all, this is the way our King

[23] Arabia Felix.

and Lord should act. Roma must be dreaming. barīk 'al ḥayy ḥartat'.

'This year', the story goes on, 'the first year of Ḥāriṯah's reign, is a different year by all measures. Firstly, new coins that Ḥāriṯah has struck from the first month of his rule started to circulate. On them his mother appeared, to our astonishment, on the foreground of the face of the coin. It was clearer than the old ones. Here one can see how the queen looks. Her earrings, her veil and even her braids were clear. Everybody thinks that there must be a story behind this. But with the next caravan, only a few months later, more enigmatic rumours arrived with a new issue of the Ḥaritite coins. This time they carried on the face the picture of the king and next to him his wife Ḫuld malikat Nabaṭū. Yes, with her name on it. This topped the news for this season. How the queen was able to put her name on a coin was not explained. It was scandalous to some people. However, it should not be. For even Cleopatra used to strike her coins with her name and legend on the coins that the Egyptian merchants use, so why', Kamkam was asking, 'couldn't our Queen and mar'atanā do any less'? She went on with delight, 'the news was worthy of burning fresh frankincense on our Goddess's altar as well as the altars of Dushara and all the gods. Truly, some men and even elderly women condemned this novelty and found it improper. It is not entirely, however, a new thing. When 'Obadah struck the first coins with the picture of our queen only, the people of Dedan and Ḥegra even threatened not to touch or use these coins, but this did not last long. They soon accepted the new rules. On the other hand, how can they disapprove of such a thing, when they give the sacrifice daily in the name of Allāt and Manāt; how can they disapprove when they know how sacred is our Queen, the High Priestess, Protector of our Mother Goddess? They simply had no other choice but to comply'.

'And, with time passing and their frequent travel to other cities and other villages, our men started to come back with new habits, in their way of speaking, behaving, even dressing. They also got used to finding their wives taking care of their household and taking good care of their fields and property. Something else was new; they were not able any longer to force their wives to accept other wives and their children, nor were they able to stop them from getting their own houses, and even after-life houses for their daughters and their close family, exclusively for them. One started to find women, even if they were divorced, having their own tombs, for which they would put up an order for specific inscriptions and decorations in order to house their corpses, and the remains of their daughters. This tradition became a custom among women, especially those of the wealthy merchant families, and even among women from other places such as Taymā.

My state, however, is different', Kamkam explains, 'for we, the priestesses, don't marry mortals, and we do not need to do that. We offer ourselves to our great goddess Manāt. Our grandmothers offer each daughter, generation after the other, as a sacrifice to the service of the Goddess. Therefore, we also build or buy our own after-life houses. I, myself, was keen to do so, since as I approached my late twenties, I did not have much longer to live. With the offerings and gifts I received, I was able to ask the Raqami creative architect Wahab'Ilāhī, son of 'Abd'Obadah, to design and engrave my kafra, which I shall share with my daughter Kulaybah, as a burial place, for us and for our offspring when they die, supported by the curses of all the gods and goddesses if anybody dares to remove any limb or corpse from the tomb, as well as fines on them for our grand 'afkal, as well as the king and his administration. These statements are very useful in protecting the tombs in this growing city full of foreigners. I chose my after-life house on Jabal Buṯeineh,[24] this mountain which is situated between the sacred mountains of Aṯālib and the city of Ḥegra, overlooking Manāt's sanctuary, so that I can stay close to all of these beloved places'.

'In the beginning, and when I decided to have my own tomb in the same style that men have, I almost faced their loathing. But it was the tomb of the priestess, which cannot be treated but with respect, and even emulation. So shortly after I settled my order to Wahab'Ilāhī, many women followed my example, especially the wealthy women, who can afford the money, in addition to the divorcees, and those who were bored with living merely as secondary wives. Moreover, many have been encouraged, mainly by the news arriving from Raqamū about Queen Ḫuld and the activities she is carrying out, of the dedications she is offering to the gods, especially to the Mother Goddess, and how the women of Raqamū started to appear with her in the public courts and theatres in their full ornament and veiled attire. The news also arrived that Queen Ḫuld has even adopted the crown of the Goddess Isis, the Egyptian equivalent to our Goddess Allāt, Mother of the Gods. It was inevitable, consequently, that more and more women gained the enthusiasm and courage to follow the model of our Queen and even inform her of their wishes and grievances in life. Her act enabled them to articulate their own needs and aspirations'.

'That year', Kamkam concludes, 'as if it was today was full of surprises but, vivid with new hopes and dreams. May the Goddess and all the gods bless our malik and malikah'.

II Writing Ancient History?

Is the above history? It could be said that it is fiction, and fiction cannot be history. But can any ancient historian say, with confidence, that this description is not valid, and/or that the above story did not happen as described? Can any ancient historian claim to know the past as it actually was? (Munslow [1997] 1998: 16). If history is a kind of writing, what distinguishes it from other kinds of writing? At its most basic conventional definition, history is 'the study of the past'. Such a view is fairly common and seemingly

[24] al-bint.

unproblematic, but it is incomplete. Can history be defined by its method? Does history not mean reporting an objective empirical fact?[25] Is this not a historical method? Is not what distinguishes history from mere stories the rule of evidence and the need for facts?

Such an approach towards history has been the subject of criticism by post-positivists/anti-foundationalists (who are rather problematically lumped together under the label of postmodernism), who see history as 'a constituted narrative' (Munslow [1997] 1998: 14). Postmodernism introduced challenges to historiography, as the study of writing history (Carena 1989: 1-2) in its basic components, such as fact, objectivity and truth, by questioning their absolute validity. These components are the staples of conventional historiography. Such a view of history ignores its relationship to power and ideology or the objects of historical enquiry. History is made up of tentative hypotheses, determined, among other things, by the individual historian or reporter, the language and ideology, both as media of authority and power. We should also not dismiss the fact that we read ancient sources with modern minds (Southgate 1996: 7-9; Munslow [1997] 1998: 12-13; Hopkins 1999: 2). The application of this postmodern approach to history encourages empowerment, validates different standpoints and opens up new possibilities and interpretations. Within this framework, modern schools of thought, such as post-colonialism and feminism, found their way to introduce new perspectives and their own interpretations. It was achieved by challenging the power relations of the dominant paradigm, be it western culture or male gender.[26] Using a postmodern critique of conventional history raises the awareness of historiographical issues and as such it is a reminder that history is the story that historians imagine about the past, following certain rules of the genre (Southgate 1996: 106-07), or as Hopkins puts it: 'History is, or should be, a subtle combination of empathetic imagination and critical analysis' (1999: 2).

In the realm of ancient history, the problem is no different. Ancient history also needs to be placed within its social and cultural context in order to be open to understanding and interpretation which include answers to questions of purpose and aim. 'What is the purpose of history in general and ancient history in particular?' remains one of the main critiques that Keith Hopkins makes about certain writings of ancient history.[27] Hopkins is critical of the argument on the lines of: 'our first task is to get straight what can be learnt from the sources'. Taking Hopkins' argument further, I will review the main critiques he makes against ancient history in general and try to apply it to Nabataean history writing. His views can be organised into four themes: conceptual, intellectual, methodological, and the aesthetic (1978: 180, 182). His themes echo the work of other prominent researchers in various fields (including: Talal Asad, Martin Bernal, Omar Carena, Edward Said, S. Sayyid, and Keith Whitelam), who theorise for alternative possibilities in anthropology, ancient history, historiography, literature, archaeology, politics and Biblical studies. Their works demonstrate how certain institutional, political and cultural networks have contributed to constructing and preserving a particular paradigm in those disciplines. At this point we shall examine how the conventional ancient historians dealt with the Nabataeans.

Pétra et la Nabatène by Jean Starcky, published in 1966[28] is one of the main historical works that established our current knowledge of the Nabataeans. Starcky made great use of his encyclopaedic knowledge of epigraphical material, not only pertaining to the Nabataean but also Greek, Latin, Hebrew, Aramaic, Palmyrene, and other languages and scripts, as well as his expertise in biblical and classical studies. Thus, his work is a good example of what Keith Hopkins calls the 'empiricist approach' to ancient history writing (1978: 180, 182). Starcky, however, wrote this article for a dictionary specific to Biblical themes, and he wrote it late in his life. That does not, however, exempt his work from being critiqued for using a certain style of history writing that was produced by this distinguished pioneer. It is important to acknowledge such writers for what they have written but also be aware of the difficulties inherent in such writing.[29]

Jean Starcky's long article in the supplement for *Dictionnaire de la Bible* (Col 886-1017) is mainly about Raqamū-Petra. However, he dedicated the second part of it to Nabataean history in particular. He divided the article into two main sections. The first is about the rock of Edom in both the Bible and the post-biblical traditions. The second discusses Raqamū-Petra and the Nabataeans. In turn, this second section was divided into three main parts, the first on history, the second on civilisation and the third on religion. The history section was again divided into three units, the first, dealing with the origin of the Nabataeans, the second, dedicated to the Nabataean kings and the third, to the Roman province of Arabia, which included Romanisation, the implantation of Christianity and finally, the Islamic period. Upon reviewing his article, the following was noted:

In the entire article Starcky did not critique his sources, be it epigraphical or classical. He did not ask once whether

[25] For the critique of empiricism/positivism in ancient history see J. Haldon 1984/85: 95ff.

[26] They did not, however, escape being themselves deconstructed by the same tools and equally questioned in terms of power and intentions. Nevertheless, the barrier of authority has fallen and historiographical awareness is already raised.

[27] See also the criticism by Omar Carena on writing the history of Mesopotamia and the ancient 'Near East' and the lack of methodological reflection among modern historians (1989: 15-19).

[28] I chose Starcky because he is a yardstick in Nabataean studies. His works were considered 'the authority' and 'the reference' in the field. But, although the article discussed above is relatively old, it is still fresh and alive, and a classic by which scholars are still inspired.

[29] See also the criticism by Omar Carena on writing the history of Mesopotamia and the ancient 'Near East' and the lack of methodological reflection among modern historians (1989: 15-19).

or not inscriptions, classical sources, or archaeological interpretations give an accurate picture of the Nabataean society. He did not problematise the truth, evidence or the objectivity of his sources. He took his sources for granted as full authority on the subject, without taking into account any questioning of their biases or faults or the fact that they may report the abnormal rather than the normal. Nor did he take into account an awareness of the biases of modern historians who interpret a 'dead' culture with modern experiences. There is no discussion of historiography or epistemology in his work. This does not mean that Starcky's work is somehow "theory-free", rather his theoretical insights are hidden from view. After all, even empiricism is theoretically grounded: it is only this grounding that performs the alchemist's trick of turning base data into facts.

Starcky's history is a valuable chronological descriptive collection of all the historical and epigraphical available data. By neglecting any explanation of the descriptive interpretation, history, however, loses its sense and point. A collection of facts does not reveal the historical indication of them. It is ironic that ancient history has been dominated by empiricist historiography even though in many ways it is the least likely of all historical periods to have strong documentary and evidential sources. It would appear that absence of hard facts in ancient history is often compensated for by strong devotion to empiricism. It is possible, therefore, to criticise using many means (see Haldon 1984/85: 95ff.). Since classical, epigraphical or biblical sources are limited to the place and time in which they were produced, the aim should be not only to avoid sanctifying them but rather to go beyond.

As seen above, relying on the descriptive narrative and neglecting to ask questions highlights, in my opinion, what ancient history suffers from. Asking questions such as: to what extent were the acts, beliefs, values, intentions and justifications of Nabataean individuals, kings or queens investigated or analysed? Were the various features of the social structure studied in relation to the actors in Nabataean society? Was its structure related to the living behaviour of Nabataeans, either as kings and queens or as social and religious groups?[30] The art of history that Starcky recounted can be described as linear, sunk in excessive classical and epigraphical micro-details, without the attempt to merge all these interpretations or sources. His work's separation between archaeology, biblical studies, classical sources, and epigraphy has resulted in Nabataeans being seen in the abstract. Raqamū-Petra in particular is seen as either made of inscriptions or of tombs and archaeological artefacts rather than made of people, about whom historians are writing history. For example, by the end of the section on the king Ḥāriṯah I (904-905), one learns of all the sources referring to him, but Starcky does not go beyond to explore how this king felt himself, his ambitions, tactics, fears, and challenges in relation to the complex international politics surrounding him and his people at the time. Another example: when Antony gives the Nabataean's revenue to Cleopatra but Mālik I refused to pay (909-910). Antony, therefore, gave Herod the charge of collecting the money by force. The two armies, the Judaean and Nabataean (under the successive king, ʿObadah II), met at Ḥawrān first, then near Philadelphia-Amman (911-913). No questions were raised by Starcky such as, why Herod? How did the existing relationship between the two states reflect this conflict? Why Ḥawrān not Raqamū-Petra or the south rather than the north? Was that related to economic factors, tax collection or merely a strategic tactic? What were ʿObadah's plans in his refusal: did he count on a way out? Was he counting on his fortifications, men or other factors? None of this was questioned by Starcky.

Taking one of Starcky's works as an example of what is not very helpful for the study of ancient history, is an exercise to look at history from another point of view. For the purposes of this study, this question of received historic methods is most important.

From an epigraphic viewpoint, history can certainly be argued and represented by using epigraphical material, but is it possible to write an entire history this way? Can inscriptions, together with classical literature, be a sufficient representation of the history, culture and society of the Nabataeans? Most of those who are trained in epigraphy, for example, consider epigraphy or the text as such to be the ultimate evidence, instead of seeing it 'as source of knowledge of its author, and not (or previously being) source of knowledge of narrated events' (Liverani 1973: 193). This makes history, at the end, a series of inscriptions, which generalise over the whole. Such inscriptions, which were written for a specific purpose and audience, by specific individuals and in a specific period, are not necessarily representative. The type of study that follows Starcky's model mostly falls into writing history by describing the material and its philology, such as the shape of letters, comparison with other letters or languages. By focusing on the linguistic derivation, and concentrating on the origin of institutions, one misses the problem of consistency or subtle relationships of power and authority. It is probable that the main problem stems from the assumption that history can be treated by philology, or by merely knowing ancient languages, whereas historians should be prepared to be familiar with the methodology and historical literature, and be able not only to translate the ancient texts but also to evaluate them and read them critically from the viewpoint of a historian (Carena 1989: 19).

A. *Feminism*

Starcky's approach illustrates much strength and also the limits of empiricist methodology of ancient history. In addition, there are a number of major issues that his study fails to address. Prominent among those issues are

[30] See the questions in Hopkins 1978: 183.

questions of feminism and Orientalism – discourses that were not fashionable in his time. In what follows I shall discuss the impact of these issues on the study of Nabataean society in general and Nabataean women in particular.

In Starcky's work, women are rarely mentioned, apart from insignificant references to this or that queen in passing. Such marginalisation of women has been questioned by the development of a feminist perspective in interpreting and writing history. By the 1990s feminism became well established. Its questions, theories, problematisations of the dominant male culture have borne fruit in the explosion of literature concerning feminism and in the spread of women's studies departments, mainly in the West. What is of interest here, as mentioned above, is the new perspective and challenge that feminism offers to the study of history. It opens up hidden horizons after centuries of neglect which had dismissed the achievements of the woman as an active participant in making of history and society.[31] For Starcky, women were always just there in the background and out of focus, not essential actors in history.

Taking the criterion of 'visibility' as a sign of power, one could argue that Nabataean women were very visible. However, it could be true only if the royalty and elite were put into 'focus'. They are women who appear in official documents or are credited in the sources with independent action. They will be viewed as more powerful than those who are not. Though this is an arbitrary division, it is the only way to make sense of the evidence of women's lives, which is far from complete' (Hill 1999: 26). Thus, this Study could be seen as the story of the Nabataean woman, her role and part in the making of Nabataean society. Through mainly that of the queen and the elite: their beliefs, ambitions and motivations, analysing their share, or explaining why and how they became visible. Such a position will be taken by a woman historian's perspective. It considers how the social structure with all its features was reflected in women's status. How did an activity, such as the caravan trade, affect women in pre-Islamic Arabia? Also how trading influenced the social system in such a way as to give an opportunity for women to demonstrate a public presence. Research suggests that changing the angle from which one looks at Nabataean civilisation and history can help in understanding the rise in women's status that crystallised at the end of the first century BCE and flourished in the first century CE. Furthermore, no independent study has been made of Nabataean women.[32] This is one of the reasons why this introduction did not include a literature review, and that is what this study is hoping to make up for.

[31] See the classical work of Simone de Beauvoir, The Second Sex (1949); the writings of Gerda Lerner such as: The Majority Finds its Past, Placing Women in History (1979-1981), and Arab writers such as Huda Elsadda, Sumayya Ramadān and Umayma Abu Bakr in their edited book on Women's Time and the Alternative Memory (1998).

[32] One of the most important contributions to the role of Nabataean women came in the last chapter of D.J. Johnson's thesis on Nabataean Trade: Intensification and Culture Change (1987).

B. Post-Colonialism: Orientalism and Eurocentrism

The aim of post-colonialist writing (and the critique of Orientalism and Eurocentrism) is to question the way the West undertakes to speak for the rest of the world in its writings.[33] In what follows, the impact of post-colonialism on ancient history will be investigated in more detail.

> 'There is nothing mysterious or natural about authority. It is formed, irradiated, disseminated; it is instrumental, it is persuasive; it has status, it establishes canons of taste and value; it is virtually indistinguishable from certain ideas it dignifies as true, and from traditions, perceptions, and judgements it forms, transmits, reproduces... All these attributes of authority apply to Orientalism'
> Said ([1978] 1995: 19-20).

What Edward Said was referring to in this quotation is a form of the dominant paradigm in the relationship between the West and non-West. It is the authority of knowledge that the Western narrative constructed, and claimed to own, throughout a long period of time, and through which it exercised and voiced its power. Said's contribution, as elaborated in his book on Orientalism is about what he labelled the 'Orientalism discourse' and story, meaning that the West constructed the 'East' or 'Orient'. This was achieved through the mechanism of a particular network of power relations which made the Orient a Western theme park, perfectly moulded to meet its needs for power, ethnic, religious and political projections, which defined the Orient as inferior, uncivilised, primitive and subordinate. He shows how Orientalism as an institution has provided the West with identity and authority, on which it, consciously or unconsciously, projected its negative opposite in the domain of power relations. Subsequently, the Orient was turned into a passive subject of thought and action. He argues, furthermore, that the West, in order to serve the categories mentioned, managed, produced and maintained the Orient politically, sociologically, militarily, ideologically, scientifically and imaginatively. Thus, an Orient was institutionalised within Western scientific branches of knowledge such as racial studies, linguistics, archaeology, anthropology, etc., making the Orient 'suitable for study in the academy, for display in the museum, for reconstruction in the colonial office, for the theoretical illustration in anthropological, biological, linguistic, racial, and historical theses about mankind and the universe' ([1978] 1995: 1-3, 7-8). The argument goes on with Said's book on Culture and Imperialism where he demonstrates how the West took on its burden to 'represent' the cultures of the non-West as a way to control them. He puts stress on the difference between the representations of foreign cultures, which all cultures tend to make, as a way to control them, and between making representations of foreign cultures and between mastering

[33] See the criticism of writing world history in Taagepera 1978: 123-125. See also Stuart Hall on the 'West and the Rest' (1992).

or controlling them literally (1994: 120). Within that frame, he discussed the ideological vision implemented and sustained by direct domination and physical force (ibid. 131). Practices that were demonstrated through different forms of culture which comprise, among others, arts of description, communication and representation in aesthetic forms, mainly through the form of the novel. He considers the narrated novel as a principal method through which 'colonized people use to assert their own identity and the existence of their own history'. Said sees that 'the power to narrate and or to block other narratives from forming and emerging, is very important to culture and imperialism' (ibid. xii-xiii).

The problem which non-Western history and historians were facing, among other things, was how to rewrite, re-narrate and reclaim their own history and story. Asad rejects the Western conceptions underlying non-Western models of history. Such western concepts he maintains, discard any claims to authenticity on the part of other peoples, and their unitary culture and tradition (1993: 2-3). The awareness of an alternative conception and a different perspective in interpreting non-Western histories has been growing in the last few decades in different areas of history, such as, among others, Biblical studies, Assyriology, Persian studies, Roman Egypt and Islamic history (Keith Whitelam, Amélie Kuhrt, Susan Sherwin-White, R.S.Bagnall and Nina V. Pigulevskja), However, little work of this genre has been carried out in ancient Arabian history, chiefly by David F. Graf in many of his articles (see his methodology in 2003: 52ff.).[34]

In following this direction, this work will attempt to tell the story of one's own people as an ancient historian trained in both Arabia and the West.[35] It proposes to follow a new course. Previous writers will be acknowledged but a new type of authority will be sought. This will be achieved by the means of mastering the evidence, in addition to following the processes that transfer and transcend the authority of the ancient source, using selection, interpolation and criticism. This study will try to find ways that enable a breaking away from the fixed rigidity of the past by allowing and introducing an alternative paradigm that is inclusive of other interpretations of the history.

1. *Critique of Classical Writers*

As seen in Hopkins's four-point guideline, the sources which record the acts and feelings of actors needed also to be checked in terms of their biases and intentions. It is also important to take into consideration that what is historically accounted for is the abnormal (Hopkins 1978: 183), i.e. what the modern ancient historian needs to address is what ancient sources took for granted and what they were silent about.

Greek historiography has been indebted, since its early stages, to the Persians. Although no records of Persian historiography have survived, reference to it was common in the Greek's sources, especially since the Greeks' early concern was Persian history and affairs. In Arnold Momigliano's view, Greek historiography was, from its early stages concerned with that of Persia, and 'was practised by men whose acquaintance with Persian traditions is beyond dispute'. In other words, he suggests that Greek historians' activities can only be explained within a Persian context, or specifically, within Persian historiography (1990: 5-10). After establishing that Greek historiography was heavily influenced by its opposition to Persian, Michael Mann shows how their attitude towards reasoning has also influenced their historiography. Greek historians, in this respect, were interested in the characteristics of male humanity at large, and were keen, for example, to project their multi-state system in this process (1986 I: 216).

Accordingly, Greek historians expressed admiration for the Nabataeans, lovers of freedom whose king ruled democratically (Diodorus 19: 94: 1-6; Strabo 16: 4: 26).[36] They were in fact projecting their categories, i.e. their own 'rationality' and 'democratic' system. As in the case of a great deal of ancient history, much of what is taken as sources for Nabataean history, such as classical writings, archaeological artefacts and the epigraphical remains, presents a problem, mainly due to the Hellenocentric interpretation of ancient societies. That is demonstrated by the way they project their own values and experiences on a nation that was an enemy at first, then later recognised as a respected and independent nation. Describing it by nomadic attribution is by no means sufficient to give a clear picture, nor is it unproblematic. Nomadism was a convenient description for those societies that either resisted or were different from the Greek model. In the case of resisting, these nomads are described to be freedom-seeking nations, unwilling to be enslaved. On the other hand, they lead a life of brigandage and pillage, and both descriptions were ascribed to the Nabataeans (Diodorus ii: 48: 1; see al-Abduljabbar 1995: 103-106). In examining the Greek report of Herodotus on Scylas, the Scythian king, Susan Sherwin-Write and Amélie Kuhrt point to the principal characteristics of 'civilisation' and 'Hellenisation' in the eyes of Greeks, which can be grouped into; language, costume, architecture and housing, religious rites, and political practices. In Greek eyes, civilisation means dressed in the Greek fashion, speaking Greek, living in houses, preferably in a similar architecture to the Greek with marble statues and columns, believing in deities with

[34] More recently Fahad M. al-Otaibi completed his Ph.D thesis on Nabataean history using a post-Colonialism approach (2005).

[35] About the importance of the identity of the historian in interpreting history see Tikva Frymer-Kensky's self introduction (1992: ix).

[36] In this example of the Strabo story, he gave the Nabataean king the quality of being 'democratic'. Although this word's meaning in Greek is known, it is unknown how this can be applied to Nabataean society or its political system.

shape and statues, having temples and altars and possibly mysteries, in addition to the unique Greek political system of democracy for the free citizens. Following these lines the Greek observer will consider a nation to be civilised once it copies the Greek way. These were also the characteristics which attracted Herodotus's attention when approving of the Scythians (1993: 145-147).

Hellenistic writers in the following centuries, who wrote from within a Greco-Roman culture, were no different in their assumptions, or in what attracted them to other nations. After dividing the world into two camps, sedentary-civilised and nomadic-barbaric, it was possible to realise where Nabataeans were situated. In the case of the Nabataeans, two major sources report about them: Diodorus the Sicilian and Strabo, both of the first century BCE, in addition to the Jewish Roman historian Josephus, writing in the first century CE (see discussion on all three historians in al-Otaibi 2005: 92-116). Diodorus, however, counts on an earlier source. He tells the story of the Nabataean conflict with Antigonus' son and army in 312 BCE. His account, based on Hieronymus,[37] deals with the Nabataean social structure (men take care of their women, their economy, asphalt industry, seasonal market, monopoly of frankincense trade, organised system of defence by the rock, patrolling system, their knowledge of writing, their diplomacy, skills in hewing water caches, reservoirs, their socio-economic legal rules such as, not to build a house, plant, cultivate, or drink wine) (19: 94). Strabo's account is taken from a friend of his, the Hellenized Phoenician Athenodorus, who lived in Raqamū-Petra, probably, at the end of the first century BCE. He reported on the 'civilised' Nabataeans: their legal rules, their lack of law-suits among themselves, their incentives for building houses, political and social observations: e.g. that the king was democratic, and worshiped the sun (16: 4: 26).

Any critique should refer to the above examples of these two principal classical sources, which historicise the Nabataeans in the fourth and first centuries BCE. The important point here is that the qualities Hieronymus attributed to the Nabataeans are unlikely to have given the full picture of Nabataean society. Rather they seem to have been selected. This is not an oddity if one accepts that what attracts curiosity to other cultures is usually what is unusual or what is comparable with one's own society.[38] Nor it is possible to take this account on face value politically. This may extend from the smallest social difference to political statements. Nomadism as a social and economic style of living has more dimensions to it for Greeks than merely a type of society. It was used to project their own values of civilisation on the one hand, and, when these groups resist their rule and colonisation, they were called 'freedom seekers' who do not and have not been enslaved to any ruler, on the other. It has been noted that these attributions reflect, in fact, a justification for a defeat on the Greek part. In the case of the Nabataeans, this was a justification for Hieronymus' failure to conquer them in the Antigonian campaign of 311 BCE (see al-Abduljabbar's argument in 1995: 106-109).

Josephus in turn, although from a Jewish community that is adjacent to the Nabataeans and in more direct contact with them, adopted the Roman umbrella even against his own people, especially since he was given Roman citizenship with a salary and was expected to write a propagandist history for the Romans. That was clear in his work about Jewish Wars, where the image of Nabataeans was not better than is found in the Roman accounts. Nabataeans in his histories were reduced to the personality of their controversial Vezir, Syllaeus, and were depicted as murderers, wicked, opportunists and uncivilised (see more elaboration in al-Otaibi 2005: 104-109)

David Graf takes the point of 'freedom-loving' people's term much further in another direction when discussing the specific vocabulary chosen and used by some Greek historians. These people may be Nabataeans or Scythians. In choosing these terms the Greek historians were, he argues, using them as a subtle instrument to criticise actual political situations in Greece which was changing and losing its democratic values by the time of the 'Hellenistic' post-Achaemenid kingdoms (1990b: 52-53). Moreover, this example shows how certain terms used in the classical accounts, which have their own interpretation within Greek culture, are interpolated into Nabataean culture. It is found, furthermore, that terms such as democracy and freedom were not only inserted with Hellenic connotations mentioned above, but have been also taken up by today's historians and linguists, mostly western, whose interpretations have similarly been affected by their Western experience.[39]

It is true that trying to reconstruct ancient history or society is not only about evidence. It is about how one can be certain that evidence is evidence of fact. At the same time, neither the classical sources can be discarded, nor accepted

[37] Hieronymus of Cardia (364-260 BCE), Diodorus' chief source in books 18- 20, was a friend and fellow countryman of Antigonus from Eumenes, who then became the companion of Antigonus, Demetrius and Gonatas. Save for a few preserved fragments the work of Hieronymus is lost. Anitigonus placed Hieronymus in charge of the asphalt industry on the Dead Sea, and to this history owes the detailed account about that sea and of the Nabataean Arabs (Diodorus, introduction: ix: Russell M. Geer: p vii ff.).

[38] See for example Hieronymus' account of the Nabataeans drinking wine or later, with Athenodorus, not drinking wine. The status of wine drinking continued to be an important marker of the account for other societies. This is exemplified through the uptake of this point by Athenodorus who may have felt it interested his Roman audience. Although it is not possible to tell how much Strabo selected from Athenodorus' narration, it is interesting to note in this account what would be considered odd and abnormal in Greco-Roman society. This culminated in misunderstanding of some terms such as 'tomb' for a 'dump', which thereby constituted a false story about Nabataean funerary rites which lasted for a long time (see Wright 1969: 113ff.).

[39] For example, see Teixidor 1995: 112-13, who measures the Nabataean urbanism with the Greek-Hellenistic model, which includes having for example a gymnasium, agora, theatre and a certain type of architecture.

as an ultimate authority. It is important to question them, realising that the sources selected by Greek commentators are based on the observations coloured by qualities that cannot be divorced from their own experiences of living in Greek or Roman societies. The problem, which was elaborated lengthily by David Graf (1990b: 51-53), is that these accounts in both situations are very much tied, influenced and constructed by the narrator's background, culture and concepts, in ancient or modern times. I like the phrase that Treadgold uses, he says: 'To study them we need not share their views, but we should resist the temptation to reinterpret them in modern terms' (2001: 3).

2. *Critique of Modern Historians*

The last point in Hopkins' methodological guideline was about the audience, to whom the historian with her or his own biases must interpret a dead culture (1978: 183). This section will be dedicated to the historian's methods in interpreting the past, using for this purpose some examples relevant to Nabataean history. Assumptions about ancient history that were accepted by many modern historians of the ancient Nile to Oxus are not different from any other area of the Orientalist enterprise. Based on an epistemology that is essentialist and empiricist, Orientalism has been able only to suggest a static culture in continuous decline politically and socially, especially once it meets the West (see Turner 1978: 6-7).

A fixed idea has been established among the majority of modern scholars that the Nabataeans passed historically through two phases, an earlier nomadic and a later sedenterised phase that 'developed under Greek and Roman influences' (Hammond 1973; Groom 1981: 202), represented by the accounts of Diodorus and Strabo mentioned above. These ideas were based on the association made, among other things, between building houses and civilisation or between not drinking wine and nomadism as equal to uncivilised (for example, Starcky[40] 1966: 938-939; Groom 1981: 202; Macdonald 1991: 116). Such associations were constructed, as was described above, and cannot be removed from a certain context. It is a reflection of what the West, ancient[41] or modern, defines as 'civilisation' or 'nomadism'. Some scholars suggest that the Nabataeans were a bedouin tribe or part from some sort of a confederation which continued throughout their history (Negev 1976: 235; Knauf 1989: 60; Macdonald 1991: 116), which implicitly suggests a static state and society. Such an unproven assumption and labelling cannot be taken seriously any more. It is noted, however, that most of the modern western historians of ancient history are not yet aware of the connotation of using certain terminologies. Tribes and nomads for example have been exchanged with 'ethnicity' by modern anthropologists in an attempt to avoid charges of 'Eurocentric bias' that carries the implication of 'primitive cultures' and people inferior in contrast with western and eastern cultures (Graf 2003: 52). On the other hand, the term 'nomad' is confused with terms such as bedouin and tribal, which can be the same or different or lead to one another. This needs clarifying in any case. This is found also in Starcky's description of Nabataean law in the first century BCE, which he named coutume tribale (1966: Col. 939-40) without defining what he meant by that, missing the fact that tribal society does not necessarily imply a nomadic society: they will be tribal possibly in the sense of preserving tribal genealogy, and probably some cultural values.[42]

In recent years, some historians have revisited this position and challenged it. Among them is David Graf, who has pointed out the contradictions that such an assumption leads to, arguing that the notion of nomadism or pure pastoralism contradicts with the details reported in Diodorus' account, such as having knowledge of writing, hydrological skills, the involvement of Nabataeans in the asphalt industry and trade of the Dead Sea, and their service as Mediterranean middlemen in the south Arabian incense trade (1990b: 53). Abdullah al-Abduljabbar, on the other hand, argues that the account of Diodorus/Hieronymus, which represents only one aspect of the Nabataean society at the time, did not describe a nomadic society but actually, he gave an account of a settled, sedentary polity (1995: 109, 118-120). The problem of this argument is the fall into a defence position where he tries to prove that Nabataeans were not nomads, i.e. uncivilised. By doing that he accepts unconsciously the Greek categorisation of what a civilised society should look like.

III. Conclusion

Ancient history, especially ancient history of the 'Near East', is largely dominated by a historiography derived from the nineteenth century; its positivism and empiricism have produced accounts that in many ways do not do justice to the period or the region. There are many ancient historians who realise that these explanations can benefit greatly from using wider range of disciplines, whether they come from linguistics (e.g. Liverani) or subsistence economics (e.g. Hopkins). The study of Nabataean women presents an opportunity to write an ancient history of the Nile to Oxus that is not locked in its empiricist prison. If all history is history of the present, then this writing about ancient North Arabia cannot help but to be influenced by its ambient conditions, which include the critiques of positivism and recognition of what Cornell West has called the passing of the 'age of Europe' (1989: 87; Sayyid 1997: 152).

[40] Starcky listed the properties that support the nomadism and sedentarism of Nabataeans. In doing that he omitted, intentionally or unintentionally, from the nomadism period the fact that they knew how to write. The omission shows his unjustifiable discomfort with this piece of information, or that he realised that it does not fit in with a nomadic culture, so discarded it, keeping its discussion to the section on writing.

[41] Though Greeks were not considered 'West' in ancient times.

[42] Macdonald points out the possibility that some tribes mentioned in the 'Safaitic' inscriptions had members settling in towns and villages of the Ḥawrān (1993: 353).

It would therefore be relevant to suggest that assumptions should be revised in order to write history without prejudices and as closely as possible from the period or society under discussion. Assumptions should also be critiqued to eschew misinterpretations of ancient societies, which can be easily drawn too. It would be most enlightening to be able to know how Nabataean women felt, what they believed in, dreamed of, or thought about. Is history not about narrating, imagining and reconstructing, or fictionalising, on the basis of modern experiences, by accepting that what is dealt with is modern audience, medium, language, environment, and being aware that one cannot reconstruct the past perfectly? (Hopkins 1978: 180; Munslow 1997: 2). I am, however, aware of the limitations that such a project might face. It will not be easy to break from all the past literature or from Starcky's model, nor to solve all the methodological problems facing us. But at this stage, there is the advantage of being aware of the problems, of the models that need to be avoided, and the model one strives for and wants to follow to gain an overall view of Nabataean history within the history of Nile to Oxus.

Chapter Two

Imaging Nabataea

I. Ethnicity and *ethnie*

The difficulty of trying to account for the ethnicity of the Nabataeans demonstrates a general difficulty that ancient history encounters with ethnicity itself (see Renfrew 1987: 4-5, 76-77, 287-88; Heather [1996] 1997: 3ff.). Nineteenth century historians did not have this difficulty as they saw ethnicity as a product of 'genetically determined physical characteristics' (Renfrew 1987: 215; Heather [1996] 1997: 3).[43] The discrediting of ideas about 'race' as a biological category something akin to 'species' among human populations has helped to radicalise the question of ethnicity (Renfrew 1987: 5). It has been argued that ethnicity is not simply equivalent to race, to geographical origin, to language, or to culture (Bagnall 1997: 8). The view that 'peoples, races and tribes are socially created' and that 'they are the product of confined power interactions over a long period between persons who are caged within boundaries' (Mann 1986 I: 92), suggests that ethnicity is not given but fabricated. Therefore, analysis of any ethnic identity has to account for not only how that ethnicity comes about but how it is maintained.

Until recently, scholars have had difficulty in categorising the 'Nabataeans'. Should categorising be by language, religion, culture, geography or political entity? Or how was their identity determined? Was it in the same nineteenth century rhetorical tradition of pigeonholing identity in criteria of race, language and culture (Ali 1999: 7)? How, in fact, did the Nabataeans recognise and perceive themselves, or how were they perceived by others?[44] How was their claim to an identity recognised or accepted? In other words, what constitutes Nabataeans, and in what symbols and practices would we find Nabataeanness? Although the evidence available is not complete, it is still necessary to ask what layers make up the Nabataean identity and their relation to ethnicity.

According to Siân Jones, what ethnicity involves is 'the subjective and situational construction of identity in opposition to particular 'others' in the context of social interaction' (1997: 143).[45] She concludes that ethnic identities are 'produced in specific socio-historical contexts, characterised by relations of power' (ibid.). Along the same lines, R.S.Bagnall argues that ethnic terms are '*always* based in historical circumstances and forces, and people struggle to control them' (1997: 8). Reconstructing identities of the past cannot be done in a neutral context. We should be aware of this and work towards avoiding the unintentional fabrication of ethnic identities to meet modern, for example, social or political, interests. Anthony D. Smith introduces the French term *ethnie* for an ethnic group[46] or an ethnic community as a designator that 'unites emphasis upon cultural differences with the sense of an historical community'. He argues that an *ethnie* is essentially social and cultural, rather than a unity generated from the same clan or tribe (1987: 21-22). The features of an *ethnie* are an accumulation of shared history and are formed out of shared interpretations and expressions of experiences which are passed down to the next generation, thus building a history of ethnicity that distinguishes one group from another. There are certain signifiers, however, that mark an *ethnie* from any other human group, such as having a collective name, a common myth of descent, a shared history, a distinctive shared culture, an association with a specific territory, and a sense of solidarity (ibid. 22-31). He sums it up by saying that 'ethnicity has remained as a socio-cultural 'model' for human organisation and communication from the early third millennium BCE until today' (ibid. 32).

Did the Nabataeans constitute an *ethnie*? In the following section I will use Smith's six features (collective name, shared myths and memories, common ancestry, historic territory, distinct culture, and sense of solidarity) to determine to what extent Nabataeans constituted an *ethnie*. From the onset, one needs to be aware that a single signifier does not tell the whole story, nor does it denote who the Nabataean was. The complex structure of any

[43] See for example Theodore Nöldeke on 'Some Characteristics of the Semitic Race', where he concluded that 'the genius of the Semites is in many respects one-sided, and does not reach the level of some Indo-European nations, especially the Greeks' (1892: 1-20).

[44] For an elaboration on the concept of defined and perceived identities see Ali 1999: 12-13.

[45] Graf adopts a similar view by accepting that 'ethnicity is to be regarded as a product of contact and relations, not of isolation' (2003: 55).

[46] This means 'groups of people who recognise themselves as distinct, and who see this distinction as part of their birthright'; or according to a quotation from Dragadze, the Soviet ethnologist, he defines *ethnos* as 'a firm aggregate of people, historically established on a given territory, possessing in common relatively stable particularities of language and culture, and also recognising their unity and difference from other similar formations (self-awareness) and expressing this in a self-appointed name (ethnonym)' (Renfrew 1987: 216): a definition that accommodates the concept of *ethnie* introduced by Smith.

society proves that it is difficult to rely on a sole signifier as a level of identity, or to view signifiers as stable markers in the way they index identity.

A. *The Collective Name*

Was the name *nbṭw* the collective name for the Nabataeans? Healey and Graf made a clear distinction between what we mean by Nabataeans and what the Nabataeans meant by this name. Although all Nabataean contemporaries and ancient Greek sources and early Roman imperial era historians called them interchangeably Nabataeans or Arabs, Healey stresses our lack of knowledge about how the Nabataeans perceived themselves, to say nothing of whether they perceived themselves as Arabs (1989b: 38; 1996b: 3), and David Graf considers any 'search for a common ancestry and ethnically pure race is hopelessly futile' (2004: 145). To clarify this point it is important to find out whether the word used for Nabataeans is representative of them, taking into consideration that our knowledge of Nabataean culture and society was provided by the written and archaeological sources, whereas, the sources for Nabataean identity are merely epigraphic (Graf 2004: 145), mostly from post-Nabataean period or from non-Nabataean script. Below, the use of the Nabataean name by Nabataeans will be traced, as well as the way they were named after by their contemporaries.

1. The word *nbṭw* appears in Nabataean inscriptions in two ways. Firstly, it is used to identify the people or tribe whom the king was ruling, for he was known by his title 'king of the *nbṭw*'. The title is found on coins and inscriptions, showing that there was a population under his rule and this was the name ascribed to them. It seems there was a need of identification of the Nabataean king because he was probably ruling over different groups. It also appears to be the name by which the state is known among their contemporaries. Secondly, it appears with reference to the traditional law, which applies to the sanctity of Ḥegran tombs expressed in this form: *ḥrm kḥlyqt ḥrm nbṭw wšlmw*, 'inviolable according to the nature of inviolability among the Nabataeans and Salamians' (Macdonald 1991: 107; Healey 1996b: 4). The reference to the traditional law appears only three times, all in the Ḥegran tombs (JS 1, 8, 19), linking them to an ancient law that ruled either the Nabataeans or their associates, the Salamians (or Sulaymians),[47] or instead, to a law that was particular for Ḥegra itself. The Nabataean kings and their allies expanded until Ḥegra and Dedan and, probably, had to make some agreements with the local groups, i.e. the Salamians. It is probable also, that what is called 'the inviolability of the Nabataeans and Salamians' refers to an agreement to observe the laws of the two groups, especially by the new rulers, the Nabataeans, in the application of the funerary laws.

There is no definite explanation for the meaning of the term *nbṭw*, whether it was a family name, a clan, or a tribe. Etymologically, the root is found in Semitic languages as a noun, verb and proper name, meaning in Standard Babylonian and Assyrian (*nbṭū, nabāṭu*) 'horizon'. *Nabāṭu* means 'to shine brightly' in Assyrian (Brinkman *et al* 1980: 11/1: 31, 22-24) and in Sabaic it means to 'dig a well down to water' (Beeston *et al* 1982: 91). Also it is found in South Arabian proper names, such as *nbṭ'l, nbṭ'ly, nbṭ'm, nbṭkrb, nbṭm*, and *nbṭyf*, in Minaic, Qatabani and Sabaic (Harding 1971: 579). In Arabic, similar to Sabaic, the noun means 'what first appears of the water of a well', or 'the water that issues forth from the bottom of a well when it is dug'. The verb means 'he produced or fetched out, by his labour, digging the water of the well'. Accepting the Sabaic which corresponds with the Arabic definition, *nbṭw* would perhaps point to a people who had advanced irrigation techniques. As is well known, such techniques were associated with the settlements of Raqamū-Petra, Ḥegra and Boṣra; the main areas that we identify as being Nabataean.

To what extent did the notion of Nabataeanness penetrate Nabataean society? In a few cases individuals used the self ascription 'Nabataean' as an ethnicon, but none of them were in Nabataean texts, but in other scripts, one in Palmyrene,[48] three in 'Safaitic' inscriptions,[49] and a fifth in a bilingual Nabataean-Greek inscription from Cos (IGR III. 1257) in (Macdonald 1991: fn. 38; Healey 1996b: 4; Macdonald 1998: 185-6; Graf 2004: 148). Furthermore, the majority of the Nabataean graffiti and inscriptions were about individuals asking the gods for protection. They usually referred to themselves by a short name, and they rarely affiliated themselves with a tribe or clan, let alone to Nabaṭū, the affiliated name of the Nabataean kings. That could possibly be because they were secure in their identity. Or that they did not need this kind of discrimination in their own community.

2. Among their contemporaries of Greek and early Roman imperial texts, they were referred to as 'Nabataeans', 'Arabs' or 'Arabians', and their kings as 'PN King of the Arabs', interchangeably (Josephus Ant. xiii: 387, 88, 89-92, 414; xiv:

[47] I argued elsewhere that the *slmw* refers to the tribe Sulaym, known at the time up to early Islam to live in the area of Wādī al Qurā, i.e. Ḥegra and Dedan (al-Fassi 1993a:100-102)

[48] (CIS, II, 3973) '.. *'bd 'bydw br 'nmw [br] š'dlt nbṭy' rwḥy[']dy hw' frš [b]ḥyrt' wbmšryt' dy 'n' lšy' 'lqwm 'lh''*, ''Abd 'ubaidw s. of Ġanam, s. of Sa'd-Allāt the Nabataean, the Rawḥiyan (from the tribe of Rawḥw) who was a cavalier in the fort and camp of 'Anah, for the god Shya' alQawm..'.

[49] *lmn'm bn 'ršmnwt bn 'bgr bn ''tl hnbṭy', 'l'tq bn 'sd hnbṭy* (not far from Rijm Mushbik, south of Ḥawrān, Macdonald, al-Mu'azzin and Nehmé 1996: B1-B2). Another in CIS V: 1 'sd bn rb'l bn 'sd bn rb'l *[] snt [.] nbṭ wyslmy wbrh ḥlqt šty hdr wt'r hsmy* (2820 in rajm Qa'qul, in the vicinity of Zelaf of Wadi Šām), and one cited in V.A. Clark's unpublished Ph.D. thesis (1979) no. 661: *l drb bn qn h-nbṭy* (Macdonald 1991: fn. 39; Macdonald 1998: 186; Graf 2004: 148).

14, 20-21, 32, 120-122, 370-73) so we find: 'the Nabataean Arabians' (Strabo 16:4:18); 'countries of the Arabian tribes, I mean the Nabataeans and the Chaulotaeans and the Agraeans' (Strabo 16:4:2); 'Arabs, who bear the name of Nabataeans', 'The Arabs who are called Nabataeans' (Diodorus 2:48:1, 19:94; Pliny 5:65); 'Aretas ruler of the Arabs' (2Macc 5:8). The terms Arabs and Nabataeans were considered to be equivalent. This association was also made previously by the Assyrians between Arabs and Qedarites (Eph'al 1984: 8). This seems to suggest that one needs to be aware that the notion of 'Arabness' that we have, may not have been that well defined in the past. However, Graf argues that 'if the Nabataeans of North Arabia were known as 'Arabs' to their neighbours, and spoke 'Arabic' (see below), we should not hesitate any longer to call them 'Arabs' either' (2004: 151).

B. *The Common Myth of Descent*

Do we know if the Nabataeans claimed to have a common descent? Do we know if they claimed to belong to Arabian stock? In fact, we do not yet have decisive evidence for the origin of the Nabataeans, and this fact has been the centre of long discussions among scholars (al-Theeb 1997: 234-238). Hypotheses have been suggested that they were Arabian immigrants from South Arabia (Starcky 1955: 87; 1966: 900-903, Glueck 1965:3-4), western Arabia (Parr, Healey), eastern Arabia (Milik 1982: 264-65; Graf 1990a: 145), The Land of the Two Rivers (Langdon 1927: 530-533; Graf 1990b: 67-69), northern Najd (Winnett & Reed 1970: 100; al-Theeb 1997: 237-38), a continuation of the Edomites (Bartlett 1990: 34), descendants of Qedar (Knauf 1989: 60; Dijkstra 1995: 42-46). Or to have been related to the Nabayot of the Assyrian records and Hebrew Bible (Baldwin 1982),[50] or that they 'arose from the same cultural matrix' of the Hagarenes of Hasa (Graf 1990a: 145), and finally that they belonged to the confederation of Liḥyān (Farès-Drappeau 2005: 125). Most of the above views agree on the fact that Nabataeans originated from Arabia. But the dispute is unsettled about which part of Arabia they came from and from which stock they were descended.

Although the Nabataeans can 'confidently be ascribed to an Arabian milieu', for they spoke Arabic, had Arab personal names, worshipped Arabian gods, were called Arabs by Greek and Latin authors, 'sounded and looked like Arabs', and behaved like Arabs, i.e. 'were Arabians culturally', they were not Arabians in the modern sense of 'belonging to a particular racial-social-political grouping' (Healey 1989b: 42; 1996b: 3).

C. *Shared History*

Shared history concerns the way the glorious past of a group and the narrative of shared experiences are built up from shared memories. Unfortunately, there are few texts that can demonstrate this in relation to the Nabataeans. Most of the evidence comes in disjointed stories in the classical works. The few glimpses of historical events that the Nabataeans experienced suggest expansion and inclusion of territories and cities in different periods of the six centuries known of their history, such expansion or inclusion was not at all alien to the nature of ancient states. In fact, this suggests that there were different populations in different periods, but with a core traditional population that lived throughout. History will be shared among those who created the polity, and later with those added or enclosed within it.

D. *Distinctive Shared Culture*

This can be derived from a large number of aspects: language, religion, script, art, laws, customs etc., all of which can be attributed to a sense of a distinctive shared culture.

1. *Language and Script*

It is possible to say that script, either in graffito or monumental form, written in what is known as the Nabataean language, which is Aramaic with Arabic influence, is a signifier for an ethnic Nabataean writer or a Nabataean ethnie. But someone's identity is not determined by use of a script or language. For example, writing this thesis in English does not mean I am an Englishwoman. 'Scripts (and, indeed, languages) are not the exclusive property of any one group' (see discussion on Safaites in Macdonald 1993: 310; and on Nabataean in Macdonald 1998: 185-189), nor are they boundary markers of distinct lifestyles (Graf 2003: 55). Writing in one language or another has been common since ancient times and even today, according to differing political, geographical, economic and cultural situations, and was in no way a means to designate an ethnic group (Renfrew 1987: 288), or as Michael Macdonald calls it the *liaisons*

[50] Gary D. Baldwin, in a search for the Nabataean identity, examined the possibilities of identifying them as Aramaeans, Arabians and Hebrews(1982: 51-122). He came to the conclusion that the Nabataeans were Arabians (1982: 117), and also that the four terms Nebaioth, Nabaiati, Nabaṭū and Nabataeans are etymologically synonymous(1982: 115), regarding them as akin, if not identical to the Kedarites, Dedanites, Masaeans, also to the Sabaean, Minaean, Qatabani and Ḥimyarite kingdoms of South Arabia and were closely associated to the Midianites, Kenites, and Rechabites of the Bible(1982: 117-118). His conclusion, based on examining Assyrian, Biblical and Classical sources, does not answer the question of, who were the people or the peoples that composed the Nabataean state at the time of their first emergence in a classical source, in 4th century BCE. Whether we agree or disagree with his identification and with the continuation of the Nabataeans from a previous period into the fourth century, it is the period from the fourth century onwards of their history that we are concerned with here. I agree, however, on the need for dealing critically and prudently with the classical sources, for I consider Baldwin's conclusions to be much too hasty. Moreover the linguistic problem of the terms Nebaiti, Nebaioth, etc. has been explained on by Broome (1973) and was revisited by Abu Taleb (1984), also Eph'al provided a comprehensible study of the notion of ancient Arabs (1984: 6-11).

dangereuses between epigraphy and ethnicity (1998: 189).[51]

In the Nabataean case, one notices that inscriptions found within the Nabataean realm were written by different ethnic groups, judging by their names, not only in Nabataean script, and 'Safaitic', but also in Greek, Latin, Palmyrene and others. The best examples are, firstly, an inscription written in Palmyrene script (CIS, II, 3973; RES 285)[52] dated to later than the Nabataean realm 132 CE, by someone calling himself a Nabataean, though the Nabataean kingdom as a polity had already disappeared. Secondly, the inscription of Rawwāfah (Milik 1972: 55-6)[53] is written in Nabataean by the tribe of Thamud, also in a post-Nabataean period 166-169 CE and the famous bilingual Nabataean-Thamudic inscription from Ḥegra dates from 276 CE (JS 17; al-Ansari *et al* 1984: 32-33; Healey & Smith 1989; al-Murayḫī 1999). In fact Nabataean script survived until the rise of Islam in 7th Century CE through which Arabic script took over. Hence, the Nabataean script is not the single signifier, though indeed there was a script and a language that can be attributed to the Nabataean state as such, which was known within and outside its boundaries. In brief, language and/or script are not the only designator and not enough on their own to identify a Nabataean identity.

2. *Religion*[54]

Religion in pre-modern societies played an important role as 'a symbolic code of communication and focus for social organisation'. Also, within certain communities, it became a reinforcing factor igniting ethnic sentiments which combined to form distinctive 'religio-ethnic communities' (Smith 1987: 34-35).

Nabataeans incorporated in their religion many deities: local, regional and national gods and goddesses. There seems to be, however, little evidence that there was a common and exclusive pantheon for the settlements that constituted the Nabataean state (see Graf 2004: 148-150). The one possible exception may be the status of Dushara, who seemed to enjoy worship in a widely dispersed area, both geographically and epigraphically (see Healey 1996a: 37-45; 2001: 80-106, especially 82-83). For example, dedications are found in Raqamū-Petra, Ḥegra, Boṣra, 'Abda, etc. and inscriptions are found in Greek, Latin, 'Safaitic', 'Thamudic' and Nabataean. To what extent did this distribution of Dushara citations correspond to the boundaries of the Nabataean polity or its exclaves? The available evidence suggests that Dushara was exclusive to the Nabataeans, worshipped in a special fashion of a 'monotheizing tendency' that corresponds with what was known in pre-Islamic Makkah (Healey 2001: 83-85). There is, however, the question of Dushara's sanctuary in Puteoli (Pouzzoles) (CIS, II, 158, 157; Lacerenza 1988, 1994; Roche 1996: 86-89) and the votive inscriptions to Dushara in Delos (Roche 1996: 83), Miletus (RES 675, 1100; Roche 1996: 80-83), and Rome (Roche 1996: 89-95). Is this temple or these shrines testimony to Nabataean merchants or other carriers of Nabataean values (i.e. what I would call an exclave), or are they evidence of the spread of the worship of Dushara? Given that most of these inscriptions have been dedicated by Nabataean individuals it would appear that they were Nabataean merchants. Thus, we could argue that Dushara worship was a quality of Nabataeanness and therefore, Dushara worship can be seen as one of the main markers of Nabataean *ethnie*.

3. *Material Culture*

Does evidence derived from material culture point to a distinctive Nabataean identity? Can one find Nabataeanness in the remains of architecture, pottery painting, etc. of Raqamū-Petra, Boṣra, Ḥegra, 'Abda...? Siân Jones warns that 'a static one-to-one correlation between particular monuments or items of material culture and a particular ethnic group is untenable, because the significance of such material culture is continuously reproduced and transformed in changing social and historical contexts by different people occupying varying positions within society' (1997: 140). Bearing this warning in mind, it is still possible to conclude that there is sufficient consistency in material culture found in Nabataean settlements to sustain a common cultural style. The way in which the Nabataeans esteemed their culture is expressed eloquently in architecture, art, painted pottery (Mackenzie 1990; Parr 1996)[55] and their urge for independent politics, which index an entity trying to be emphatically distinct. All of this hints at cultural resistance among the Nabataeans, which would explain their unique history and culture in a region dominated by foreign influences from all directions.[56]

E. Specific Territory

Pre-modern political formations were not clearly demarcated by boundaries. Political control tended to be determined by control over settlements and people rather than territory as such (see Lattimore 1962: 469ff.). There is no clear and definitive map of the Nabataean polity as it fluctuated in different periods, shrinking and extending.[57] Having said this, it is possible to identify a Nabataean core

---

[51] Even though Macdonald falls into the same paradox when he assigns Safaitic script to nomads that were external to the sendentary communities of southern Syria (see the critique in Graf 2003: 29ff.).

[52] See the footnote above.

[53] See plate XVI.

[54] To what extent religion is a universal category applicable to phenomena outside the Christian (or Judaeo-Christian) tradition? I will return to this problem subsequently.

[55] Parr stresses on the fact that Nabataean fine painted pottery was not a copy but rather a local, original invention (1996: 215).

[56] In this respect Morris elaborates on this point saying that 'the more pressure there is on a group, the more emphatically they mark themselves off symbolically from their neighbours and rivals, in what we call "style wars" ' (1992: 28).

[57] See the map for Nabataean utmost expansion in the middle of the first century BCE, plate II.

around Raqamū-Petra, extending to Ḥawrān in the north, southern Wādī al-Sirḥān in the south-east, southern Ḥegra in the south, the Naqab in the west. It probably reached Ġazzah, and Sinai,[58] partly belonging to the Arabian Peninsula and partly to Syria. No definite lines, however, can be drawn. This area, which is bordered by towns and garrisons and other Nabataean markers, can be considered a specific Nabataean territory. In contrast to the valorisation of homelands found for example, in Sumerian, Egyptian, Assyrian, or Jewish accounts, we have no evidence for a similar attachment to Raqamū-Petra or any other region of the Nabataean polity. It is remarkable to note that the majority of Nabataean inscriptions and the earliest in date are found in the periphery and not in the heart of the Nabataean realm. Sinai has scored the highest in number of inscriptions (7500 inscriptions), whereas the earliest texts come from Ḥawrān (50 BCE) and the Naqab (7BCE) (see Graf 2004: 147-48). Therefore, it is possible to partly consider the suggestion of Gawlikowski that Raqamū-Petra had played the role of a holy city or a *ḥaram* (see 1982: 303).[59] The absence of the term 'Nabataea' to denote a specific territory, again, seems to suggest that the link between a common or shared historical territory and the Nabataean *ethnie*, if not altogether absent, was at least very weak.

F. Sense of Solidarity

Limited evidence makes it difficult to determine the extent and depth of solidarity felt by Nabataeans towards Nabataeaness. There is, however, evidence from 312 BCE about Nabataean resistance to the advances of the 'Hellenistic' post-Achaemenid Diadochoi (Antigonids, Seleucids and Ptolemies) and Judaea. Since solidarity cannot be understood without having an antagonist, both in the case of measuring identity, and in understanding the validity of solidarity, it can only function in the presence of an enemy, a challenge, or a danger about to strike the community. Or as John Bartlett puts it in a broader way: A 'population fluctuates, changes its ethnic content, develops its culture, develops and loses its traditions, acquires a new sense of identity as it is affected by political events and internal pressures, but unless a major disaster strikes, it does not just stop' (1990: 34). It is at that point that the sense of solidarity can be tested and examined. Records show that Nabataea was involved in few conflicts with its (usually larger-if not stronger) neighbours. For example it was threatened by Antigonus (312 BCE), the Ptolemies (3rd-2nd centuries BCE) (Strabo 16:4:18) and Romans (1st century BCE). In addition there was a series of Nabataean-Judaean conflicts as recorded in *Jewish Antiquities* and *Jewish Wars* (Josephus Ant. xiv: 18, xv: 106ff., JW i: 126-127, 354-385, iii: 169). At a certain level, these conflicts must have helped to enhance the notion of a distinct Nabataean identity. This can be observed through the stand the Nabataeans took in 312 BCE to resist Antigonus' mighty army in his two attempts to conquer the Nabataeans. It was expressed in the letter that they sent to Antigonus and the message they dispatched to his court in Damascus in the person of their elderly men in an embassy (Diodorus XIX. 96-97). To this extent, one could argue that they also helped formulate a strong sense of solidarity. The problem, however, remains. It is also possible that the differential impact of conflict within Nabataean society may have weakened some bonds of solidarity. The question that arises is to what extent one could have a strong sense of Nabataeanness among some segments of Nabataean society due to these conflicts? And at the same time, how can an estrangement of some sections of Nabataean society from other sections affect this sense? Thus geopolitical events may have paradoxical affects on notions of solidarity in any given society.

G. Conclusion

In the presence of the currently available evidence, it seems that the Nabataeans lacked a common myth of ancestry in a shared historical territory. This would suggest that the Nabataean *ethnie* was weak in this respect. It is important, however, to leave room for the absence of evidence, or look for other ways of reading their identity. Interestingly, Smith makes a distinction between a demotic *ethnie* and an aristocratic *ethnie* (1987: 76-89). A demotic *ethnie* is characterised by a bond that tends to transcend class divisions, and as such is organised vertically, so that the sense of belonging does not exclude the lower orders. Examples of demotic *ethnie* are city-states, *amphictyonies* (city-councils), tribal confederations and Diasporas. An aristocratic *ethnie* is restricted to the ruling elite, but is fairly wide-ranging geographically. The Nabataean case seems to fit more that of an aristocratic *ethnie*, as all the available evidence suggests that the Nabataean *ethnie* was not deeply ingrained outside the Nabataean elite, contrary to what Smith argues that demotic *ethnies* are typical of urban-based traders and artisans. However, Nabataean *ethnie* is somewhat complicated. For example, Dushara (one of the main markers of Nabataeanness) was the god of the royal house and remained closely identified with the royal house. But still, this fact did not deter the *demos* in the middle of the desert from dedicating inscriptions to Dushara, such as in the Safaitic inscriptions (Graf 2003: 39), nor for each locality to have its own deity or deitess.

Even though it is possible to trace in the Nabataean case, many of the features that Smith would argue characterise an *ethnie*, it is difficult to find out how Nabataeans felt themselves to be unique and cohesive, or how deeply

[58] We do not know, however, the political position of settlements, such as Qaṣraweṭ and Tal aš-Šuqāfiyah.

[59] Gawlikowski suggests that Raqamū-Petra was a sacred city that had a rule of prohibition on building houses, that which would explain the anonymity of tombs in Raqamū-Petra in particular (1975-76: 39; 1982: 303). A few tombs in Raqamū-Petra, however, were found with names, such as 'Unays's tomb 813 (Zayadine 1974: 144; CIS, II, 351), and the bilingual Nabataean-Greek tomb at the entrance of the Siq (Gawlikowski 1982: 303; Milik 1976: 143-147). Gawlikowski's view, however, does not bear strength today after the uncovering of many residential areas and houses, see al-Zanṭūr for example (Bignasca *et al* 1996).

their fund of myths, memories, values and symbols had penetrated their social hierarchy (Smith 1987: 46). What is certain, to some extent, is the persistence of a particular style of Nabataean culture during the Nabataean kingdom. Its manifestation can be seen in pottery, architecture, arts, sculpture, numismatics, modes of hairstyle, dress, script and language, funerary architecture, characteristics of temples, religious ritual modes, deities, symbols, motifs, as well as their hydraulic technology and modes of economic activity. All of these manifestations of style, along with what is known about their polities, religion and social organisations within the political and geographical frame mark and identify a cohesive, unique and exclusive identity for the Nabataean *ethnie*. However, theirs was an identity constructed by the formation of a state with its administration, army, economy, and borders.[60] We could say that Nabataean identity was dependant on the existence of the state and, once it collapsed, that identity also dissolved and we know nothing of the royal Nabataean family after the Roman annexation.[61]

It is possible to conclude that the Nabataeans constitute an aristocratic *ethnie* formed, consciously or unconsciously, by the elite, through which the quality of Nabataeanness was diffused among the upper sections of the population. This ethnie was weak to the extent that it was not able to survive for long after the state was dissolved.[62] In the rest of the book, I will examine the role of women within this *ethnie*. In the next part, I will explore the society that shares the formation of the Nabataean *ethnie*.

[60] For an elaborate discussion on ethnicity see Smith 1987: 47ff.

[61] Note the hypothesis advanced by al-Otaibi regarding the date of annexation which he suggested was 111 CE and the Nabataean resistance (2005: 154-208).

[62] al-Otaibi disagrees with such conclusion and argues that Nabataean identity became stronger under the threat of dissolution and that they survived in different forms until the rise of Islam (2005: 64).

Chapter Three

The Composition of Society

In the preceding chapter I established that the Nabataeans formed an aristocratic *ethnie*, which seemed weakly articulated and therefore unable to survive. In this chapter, I want to deepen the previous initial analysis by trying to draw a fuller picture of the various constituent elements within the Nabataean *ethnie*. I will, therefore, discuss in some detail the forms that society took in towns and villages, going from the nomad-tribal to the urbanised. I will also discuss the shapers of Nabataean society, including the different groups that made up the Nabataean community. These groups will be divided into three categories, linguistic categories, scribal types, tribal groups and foreigners. Then this study will conclude with the treatment of other marginal groups.

A. Lingusitic Category

1. Aramaeans

The Aramaeans are conventionally classified as belonging to the problematic category of 'Semitic' peoples that was known in the form of a tribe, who immigrated, according to early theory, from Arabia to The Land of the Two Rivers and Canaan in the third millennium BCE (Moscati 1957: 168). Today, this view is disputed. Some scholars view the Aramaeans as nomadic hordes from the Syrian Desert, whereas others refer their origins to the Middle Euphrates from where they began to spread out south-west into Syria and south-east into Babylon (Pitard 1994: 208-210). The word 'Aramaeans' was known for the first time from an Akkadian text of the twenty-third century BCE (Moscati 1957: 168). But as for Aramaeans in Syria, they were first mentioned in Assyrian records in the twelfth century BCE (Pitard 1994: 210). They formed a part of the confederation known as *Aḫlāmū*, which spread beyond the Euphrates (Moscati 1957: 169). They established cities in Upper Land of the Two Rivers and Syria during the second half of the second millennium BCE and the first millennium BCE which included: Bit-Zamani, Bit-Baḫiani, Bit-Ḫalape, Laqu, Bit-Adinin, Yaḫan, Arpad, Sam'al (modern Zenjirli), Hamath, Aram Zobah, Aram Beth-Rehob, Aram Maacah, Geshur, and Aram Damascus. In central and southern Syria, during the 10th-8th centuries BCE, Aram Damascus was the most powerful Aramaean state in southern Syria (Pitard 1994: 212, 216). In the Land of the Two Rivers, the Aramaeans succeeded in establishing the Chaldaean kingdom in Babylon in 625-538/9 BCE (Moscati 1957: 54). Although their political career was not impressive, their civilisation's legacy was in language and script. Aramaic became the *lingua franca* for diplomacy and commerce, from the Assyrian Empire to the Achaemenid, covering the period from the beginning of the first millennium until the advent of Alexander. Under the Achaemenid's it became the standard for bureaucratic administration in the chancelleries of their various satrapies from the Aegean to India (Graf 2000: 75-76). With the establishment of the 'Hellenistic' post-Achaemenid kingdoms, each city developed its own form of Aramaic, which developed dialectical variations (Healey 1989b: 40; Pitard 1994: 226-8).

Aramaeans are assumed to have constituted most of Ḥawrān's Nabataean population. Although there is no direct evidence of Aramaeans in Raqamū-Petra or Ḥegra, and it was difficult during the Nabataean period to pin down Aramaeans. It is unlikely that there were no Aramaeans there and we can still consider most of Ḥawrān as populated by Aramaeans, since it was one of the major Aramaic centres before the Nabataeans (al-Fassi 1995: 9). The inclusion of some of the Aramaean pantheon's deities, such as Atargatis and Baḫal-Šamīn (see Tarrier 1990) in the Nabataean pantheon suggests a degree of assimilation or acculturation between these two peoples. Some scholars do not even consider Ḥawrān to have contained Nabataeans, only Aramaeans, Ituraeans and the Arab tribes of the Trachonitis (Peters 1977: 269). Since Aramaeans formed part of the Nabataean ethnie it became hard to distinguish them as such, knowing that Nabataeans were in Ḥawrān as early as the middle third century BCE. They were referred to in the Zenon archives dating from 259 BCE (Graf 1990b: 53).

B. Scribal Types

1. Liḥyān

Liḥyān was a prosperous kingdom in north-west Arabia for about five centuries (6th century-1st century BCE) (see plates XIV & XV). It was situated in the metropolis Dedan, known today as al-'Ulā. An important oasis/state on the Arabian frankincense trade route, it stretched its borders in the north-west as far as Taymā, where an Aramaic stele, dating from the sixth century BCE, was found mentioning the king of Liḥyān (Abu Duruk 1986: 62).

Although the theory of the existence of a 'Dedanite' kingdom that preceded Liḥyān was accepted for a long time (Albright 1953: 6-7), Abdelrahman al Ansari agreeing with Winnett (1937), believes it to be divided into three phases, a Dedanite in the 6th century BCE, a Liḥyanite kingdom from 5th century BCE and a Minaean-Liḥyanite kingdom from 3rd century BCE (1966: 28, 1970; 2005: 517). Fiorella Scagliarini contests it and argues for one kingdom and two phases. The first phase began when the kingdom was named after the town Dedan, and the second, and later phase, when it was named after the tribe Liḥyān (1995: 120). Saba Farès-Drappeau in a recent study takes the position of three phases two of which are Dedanites and the third is Liḥyānite. The Dedanite phase is marked by the Dedanite king's name and dates back to the 8th century[63] BCE, whereas the Liḥyānite phase dates to the fourth century BCE (2005: 116-125). The Liḥyānites built a strong state with Minaean help, and had strong diplomatic and economic relations with the new power in Egypt, the 'Hellenistic' post-Achaemenid state of the Ptolemies (Tarn 1929: 16-21; Caskel 1950; al-Khathami 1999: 129-134).

After a century of rivalry between the Liḥyānites and the Nabataeans over economic interests, Liḥyān was defeated by the latter in the first century BCE, though no details have survived. Gradually, Dedan was abandoned as a result of the Nabataean settlement in Ḥegra, which took Dedan's place as a main centre on the aromatic caravan route in north-western Arabia (Parr *et al* 1970: 214). The Liḥyānites, however, did not fade away. Some of them probably stayed back in Dedan, some moved to other towns. Werner Caskel believed that the Liḥyānites merged with other tribes and migrated to Iraq where they became part of the state of Ḥīra (1954: 44).[64]

It seems that Ḥegra was their first choice, because many Liḥyānite inscriptions and graffiti were found in Ḥegra (JS 6-34). Although these may be early inscriptions from the time when Liḥyān was controlling Ḥegra (Winnett 1939: 9), the Nabataean inscriptions that refer to a king of Liḥyān called Mas'udu (JS 334, 335, 337), whom Van den Branden believes was the last Liḥyānite king (1957: 14), show either a continuity of Liḥyānite presence after the formation of the Nabataean settlement on the one hand, or a sign of Nabatization of the Liḥyānites in their last stage on the other.

2. *'Safa' and 'Thamud'*[64]

Before going further it is necessary to clarify a few terms, namely 'Safaitic' and 'Thamudic'.[66] They are artificial terms that were given in the nineteenth century to inscriptions found in Syria in an area called Ṣafa. The inscriptions of this type of script have nothing to do with the Ṣafa area in name. The name appears only once out of more than 20,000 inscriptions found up to recently and was outside of Ṣafa (Macdonald 1998: 183). As for the Thamudic inscriptions, it was also a misnomer given to another type of script, not far from 'Safaitic' that has slight differences within itself that tempted many epigraphists into the trap of breaking it down to even smaller fragments of alphabets and other categories such as *Taymanite, Tabūkī, Hismaic*, etc. Thamudic is a label given to a version of southern Arabian script found all over the Arabian Peninsula, whereas Thamūd is a known historical people in ancient Arabia, but has no relation to the script named after it. Out of thousands of inscriptions, the tribe's name *ṯmd* was mentioned only six times. This is a classical example of the 'invention of ancient communities on the basis of modern misrepresenting epigraphic labels'. It is unacceptable anymore to use these terms and believe that they belonged to distinguished people with specific language, dialect and history. Some scholarly studies were carried out by following the misnomers without critiquing them to the extent of even writing a whole history of based on these inscriptions, such as Van den Branden in his *l'Histoire de Thamoud* (Van den Branden 1950; Macdonald 1998: 184). Abdel Rahman al Ansari introduced a new term for these two categories, the *Bādiah scripts*, means the script of the Bedouins, such script, he believes, has developed from the formal script of the centers or the cities, then taken up by the nomads of the surrounding areas and formed their version of writing (Public lecture, 1994) Here I shall not go into the technical differences between the two sorts of script nor shall I extend Ansari's argument. For the reading convenience I shall use the misnomers, since it will be hard to create a new category that is not finely defined. I shall keep it between inverted commas next to Ansari's term.

Briefly, these terms refer to two groups of nomads and urbanised tribes from northern Arabia mixed and interacted with the urban Aramaeans of the cities and villages of

[63] Khaled Eskoubi in his study on the Inscriptions from Rum region s/w of Tayma, suggests that they were Liḥyanite inscriptions that date to the 7th cent. BCE (1999: 507-508)

[64] Liḥyān comes into the scene in a later period at the dawn of Islam as a tribe living around Makkah(Ibn Ḥazm 196).

[65] Thamud is a known tribe in north Arabia from the eighth century BCE and is mentioned in different sources up to the fifth century of our era (Van den Branden 1966: 7, 30). They were mentioned in the Assyrian records, at the time of Sargon (Luckenbill 1926-1927: II: 17, 118). Most scholars use the ethnic name Thamud as a term for an ancient north Arabian script. 'Thamudic' inscriptions mention the Thamud as a tribe in six cases only, three of which were found around Taymā, out of a total of thirteen thousand inscriptions found up to 1966. ḏmd occurs only once in the nisbah form (Van den Branden 1966 : 17, 22). It was not until after the Nabataeans lost their independence and became subsumed into the Roman province of Arabia in 106 CE, that Thamud is mentioned again after a long absence. A bilingual Nabataean-Greek inscription and other Nabataean and Greek inscriptions were found in Rawwāfah, north-west of Ḥegra, dating to 166-169 CE, and referring to Thamud as a *šrkt* and ethnos (Milik 1971: 55-6). Milik interprets the Greek word ethnos as 'nation', and the Arabic loan-word *šrkt* as 'association, société, congrégation, fédération' (1971: 56-7). This is revised by Macdonald, who suggests it to mean 'une unité militaire' (1995b: 100). It is also an ancient Arab nation that is mentioned 13 times in the Koran to have lived in engraved (al-'a'rāf: 73, Hūd: 61, mountains and disobeyed their prophet Ṣāliḥ (68, 95, al-'Isra': 59, al-Šu'ara': 141, al-Naml: 45, Fuṣṣilat: 17, al-Ḏāriāt: 43, al-Qamar: 23, al-Ḥāqqah: 4-5, al-Šams: 11). According to Koran this people is dated to the second millennium BCE, however, no historical evidence was found yet.

[66] For the reasons given below, I shall keep these two terms between inverted commas.

Ḥawrān, many of which became sedentary tribes. In the case of the writers of Bādiah 'Safaitic' inscriptions, they dwelt in the whole area of northern Arabia and southern Syria, westwards up to Lebanon, the eastern Jordan valley and west of the Euphrates, where their inscriptions and graffiti are found. Those who wrote in what is called Bādiah 'Thamudic' were largely spread in south, east, west, central and northern Arabia (al-Rosan 1987: 34-37, 198-200).

Over 20,000 Bādiah 'Safaitic' graffiti have been found up to the present time and these are roughly dated between the first century BCE, and the fourth century CE. Their onomastica and pantheon names show a close connection with the Nabataeans, within whose boundaries they lived. The principle deities mentioned in their graffiti are Allāt, Dushara and Raḍu (Macdonald 1995a: 760-762). References to Nabataeans in Bādiah 'Safaitic graffiti'[67] are numerous and allude principally to military status in war and peace. There were also some bilingual inscriptions or complementing inscriptions Nabataean-'Safaitic', most famous are the ones found in Dayr al-Kahf (see Nehmé 2003: 242), and few other Greek-'Safaitic' bilinguals found south of Ḥaurān (Macdonald, al-Mu'azzin and Nehmé 1996: insc 11-12, J1-J2, Mg 1- Ms 29), which show the overlap and convergence of these groups. In addition there are references to kings who were probably Nabataean kings.[68]

Although some of the tribes writing in Bādiah 'Thamudic' lived within the borders of the Nabataean kingdom, no reference has been found so far to the Nabataeans in their inscriptions.[69] Deities similar to the Nabataean's were mentioned, such as Allāt and Dushara, as well as a number of 'basileophoric' compound names using the names of Nabataean queens and kings such as *'bd-šqlt* (probably 'Abd-Šaqīlah) (Harding 1952: no.311), *tm-'bdt* (Harding 1952: no. 190), *'bd-ḥrṯt* (Macdonald and King 1999: 438) *'bdmlk, 'bdmlkn* Harding 1971: 400). The relationship between the tribes of the Bādiah 'Thamudic' script and the Nabataeans can, however, only be suggested through the above evidence.

It is possible to gather that the tribes writing in Bādiah 'Safaitic' and 'Thamudic' would have participated in the Nabataean army, or at least would have taken part in the protection and patrolling of caravans and traders.

[67] See Macdonald (1993: 388) who finds that describing the 'Safaitic' epigraphical remains as 'inscriptions' is a misnomer, and suggests that they should be called 'graffiti' instead.

[68] See CIS,V: 220, 2670, 2820, 3680, 4866; Winnett 1957: no. 855, 705, 911; Khraysheh 1985: no.1; most of these inscriptions come from northern Jordan and southern Syria. See also the recent Bādiah 'Safaitic' inscription found on the Baghdad highway, a reference to a Nabataean King appears (al-Khraysheh 1985: no. 1, p.402).

[69] JS I, II 1909-1911; Van den Branden 1950; Littmann [1940] 1966: 148-153; Winnett and Reed 1970; Harding 1971; Parr *et al* 1972: 36-52; Winnett and Reed 1973: 62-94; al-Rosan 1987: 469-498; al-Theeb 1999.

C. *Tribal Groups*

The notion of 'tribe' is difficult to pin down, and is evident in the floating nuances of the words *'l, 'hl, bn, ḏū*, used to describe such ancient ethnic groups. They do not all convey the same monolithic meaning, like today's Arabic term *qabīlah*, which conveys controversial negative notions in anthropological literature, that tended to explain tribes 'primitive cultures', which is stagnant and inferior to the West (Graf 2003: 52-54). In attempting to describe and explain these community units in the ancient and modern world, no one definition has been accepted. There are, however, certain common denominators that have been agreed upon and emphasised. Firstly, there are common descent and kinship ties. Secondly, there are political functions of a tribe, exhibited in the internal communal maintenance of order and the external defence of the unit. One could consider as a maker of a group a combination of 'the local native ideology of tribal identity, the administrative notion, the implicit practical notion held by the people, and finally the analytical-anthropological notion of tribe' (al-Rasheed 1991: 17-19). This notion has been newly upgraded to assume that 'all societies, including nomadic ones, are not stagnant, but fluid and dynamic, with ruptures, breaks, contradictions, differences, discontinuities, paradoxes, disjunctures and punctuations[70] Macdonald, in his studies on the 'Safaitic' inscriptions, adds to the controversy of terminology, arguing that *'l* does not necessarily refer to a tribe, but can denote any social group from an immediate family to a 'people' such as the Romans (1993: 344).[71]

The tribal form of society recognises the tribe as its principal social and political unit. It has played the equivalent role of a state in desert communities, where affiliation to a tribe protects its members, with a special form of protection given to their women. A concept made the Arabians keen to preserve long oral and written records of their genealogies in order to prove their ancient and strong lineage as a tribal unity.

Ibn Khaldūn (14th century CE) correlated the dissolution of genealogy with urbanisation (n.d.: 122) and noted also by Caskel, linking this dissolution with the power of the state (1954: 40, 42, 44). Ḥegra is a good case in point. The absence of long genealogy in the Ḥegra names is clear. It is remarkable that the genealogies in Ḥegra tomb inscriptions are short. Most of them ascend to the second generation (x son of y, 38 times), and rarely to the third (x son of y son of z, six times). Only once does it extend to the fourth generation (CIS,II,213). Moreover, there are a number of names without even a parent mentioned, which may signify a sedentary trend and a weak tribal structure, where the tribe is no longer playing a central role for its

[70] M. Asher, *The last of the Bedu: in search of the Myth*, 1996: 22, after D.Graf 2003: 54.

[71] See other tribal complexities with the term *šrkt/ethnos* in the Rawwāfa inscription (Macdonald 1995b), or further below.

affiliates. Even the reference to the *šlmw* does not stand as evidence of a real tribal association, for it did not occur as a part of a genealogy. On the contrary, it shows that the tribe had developed a different function that is a kind of a code of practice that linked the Nabataeans to the Šalamū (Sulaymians) probably as an alliance (*ḥilf*), not a state. On the other hand, in Ḥawrān, where a large percentage of the population is made up of recently settled nomads, the inscriptions contain long genealogies. In Dūmah, 300 km south-east of Raqamū-Petra in northern Arabia (see plates XX & XXI), there seems to have been a strong tribal structure. An inscription dated to 27 CE with a long genealogy, similar to the 'Safaitic' inscriptions, was found: *dnh qbr' dy bnh šlymw br šlmw br mnyw br šlmw br maw xx br mwzy br tymw lnpšh wlbnwhy* (seven generations).[72] Despite the long genealogy, the inscription, however, does not include a single tribal name.[73] On the other hand, however, one finds that the 'Safaitic' inscriptions bear long genealogies, adding to that marking the name of the clan or the tribe. Some inscriptions have genealogies that mount eleven generations (e.g. CIS, V, 2988). The majority of inscriptions, however, keep three generations a minimum, whereas many among them have five generations (e.g. CIS, V, 59, 235, 250, 278, 329).

The nomads provided protection for the sedentary societies, who also gained revenue from passing caravans, etc. as well as regional security from the nomads. In return, they intervened in regional competitions and conflicts, and the nomadic leaders drew power, authority and wealth from their connections with the state (Beck 1995: 232). In addition, many of these cities adopted the nomadic life-style because, as Werner Caskel puts it, 'the inhabitants of these cities were themselves settled Bedouins, as is shown by their constitutions'. For in the process of de-bedouinization, as he called it, tribes or divisions of nomadic tribes would settle down (1954: 38, 45). In fact, both ways of life appear to have overlapped, as Michael Mann puts it, 'in a 'structural and ethnic continuum', exchanging material and cultural products, energising and transforming both ways of life and providing potentially powerful 'marcher' groups that could mobilise elements of both' (1986 I: 82). The nomads might have become sedentary and vice-versa according to political stability: 'Historians are inclined to view the rise and fall of nomadic societies as a direct consequence of the strengthening or weakening of the administrative grasp and military power of state governments... Anthropologists, on the other hand, have argued that nomadism can be viewed as a defensive adaptation to the state machinery' (La Bianca 1985: 252-3). There does not seem to be a difference between the two points of view. One is the result of the other. For when the state loses its power and military grasp, the tribe adapts or takes on the role of the state and emerges as the political and military unit in the form of a tribe. In other words, the tribe represents the preliminary form of the state, confirmed by Beck, who says that 'many states began as tribal dynasties from which emerged state-like confederacies and eventually empires, such as the Ottoman Empire' (1995: 232).

In the following, I will try to introduce, the principal peoples and tribes that composed part of the Nabataean *ethnie*, such as the Aramaeans, Liḥyānites, Sulaymians, Ḍaifites, Rawḥ, 'Amrah, 'Ubayšah and Muzaynah. Some of the tribes are known to have used Nabataean script, dated after the Nabataean kings; to have lived within the borders known to belong to the Nabataean Kingdom in different periods, and to have offered to the principal Nabataean deities.

1. Šalamū

This is a unique tribe with which the term *nbṭw* as a name of a tribe, or probably a *ḥilf*,[74] is associated. They are used together in reference to 'the traditional law which applies to the sanctity of tombs' of Ḥegra (JS1, 8, 19), and it probably refers to the main local tribe, although no inscription where a person is described as belonging to nbṭw or šlmw was found at the site. In Ḥawrān (Umm al-Jimāl,[75] Ṣalḫad), however, some persons are described as belonging to Šalamū. In Ṣalḫad, a Nabataean foundation inscription of a Šalamite (Salamite or Sulaymian) architect, *bny'*, called *'dynw br grm'lhy br 'bd'lh' šlmy'*, was found. In 75 he built a sanctuary for Dushara, the favoured god of King Rab'el (Milik 1958: 231, ins 2). The reference in the inscription to Dushara as 'god of Rab'el' is unusual in its exclusiveness for this king. The usual phrase was 'god of our lord' found in Ḥegra and elsewhere. The genealogy is triple. The tribe is probably the same as the one known in Ḥegra. We find the same tribe in Umm al-Jimāl,[76] where an individual called *whb'lhy br mn'mw* is said to belong to *'l šlmw* (Lit 44N).

Salamū was probably mentioned in Babylonian texts. Using some linguistic comparisons, Langdon, in an early article, drew some conclusions identifying the Salaymians and the Nabataeans with Babylon and the Aramaeans (1927: 530-533). In early Islam, a late tribe by the name of Banū Sulaym was well known for its large size and its natural fortified areas that extended from al-Ḥijr (Ḥegra) in Wādī al-Qurā to Khaybar and eastern Yaṯrib as far as the

[72] The reading given here is the latest reading by S. al-Theeb (1994: ins. 13; al-Theeb & al-Muaikel 1996 ins. 35) which is slightly different from the earlier reading by Starcky (1970 ins. 16; Healey 1993a: 246) see plate XXI, lower page.

[73] A long genealogy is found also in Palmyra, see Cantineau 1930: 548.

[74] It is possible that the Nabataean state derived its name from a main tribe in the state which was called *nbṭw*, or from the name of a confederation *ḥilf*. A confederation similar to some of the important Semitic and Arab groups in the area prior to and after the Nabataeans, such as the Aḫlamu, (which means confederation), of which the Aramaeans formed a part (Moscati 1957: 168-9), the Ismaelites, Ismael war eine protobeduinische Konföderation (Knauf 1985: 113), and the Tanūḫ, 'Tanūḫ was a people not a tribe' (Caskel 1954: 42; see below, *tnūḫ*).

[75] See plate XXX.

[76] For the Salamians in Ḥawrān see Graf 1989: 364-65.

two mountains of Ajā and Salmā (in present day Ḥā'il), and especially in the lava area of *ḥarrah* named after them, called *Ḥarrat Banī Sulaym* (al-Hamdānī 274), where the tribe still resides (al-Anṣārī 1977: 45-47). It is possible, therefore, that there is a link between that tribe and the *šlmw* of Ḥegra and Babylon (al-Fassi 1993a: 100-102). Hommel has already made this identification (in Langdon 1927: 530).

2. *Ḍayf*

The tribe of Ḍayf is considered the most prominent in the Bādiah 'Safaitic' inscriptions, and was the largest in terms of size (Macdonald 1992: 26). Reference to it is recorded in about fifty-four inscriptions, spread throughout a large area of Syria and Jordan. Their pantheon included the major Bādiah 'Safaitic' deities, i.e. Allāt, Dushara, Ruḍa and Šiya' al-Qawm, in addition to a special deity that belonged to this tribe called *gd ḍf*, Jadd Ḍayf (al-Rosan 1987: 328-332),[77] a patriarch who was probably their ancestor (Milik 1980: 41). Graf regards it as a 'large tribal confederation' (1989: 363).

3. *Quṣayy and Rawḥ*

qṣyw, a tribe known in Boṣra (see plate XXXI), is confused with the tribe Rawḥ which is presented in the long genealogy inscription from Ṣalḫad showing Quṣayy and Rawḥ as great-grandfathers of the inscribers (CIS,II,170; Milik 1958 : ins 1). These people were very much attached to the worship of Allāt, possibly as her servants and priests.[78]

Rwḥw was another important tribe found in Umm al-Jimāl and Ṣalḫad in Ḥawrān. They were possibly related to the Quṣayy by having mutual ancestors, as both were known to be connected with the worship of Allāt.

In Ṣalḫad, the tribe built a temple for Allāt in the middle of the 1st century BCE.[79] This temple was later renovated in 56 CE,[80] and renovated for a second time in 95 CE.[81] The last inscription gives a long genealogy according to the tribal system. Although the above inscriptions do not give a concrete answer as to whether Rawḥ was a tribe or merely a proper name, the inscription found in Palmyra, dating from 132 CE sheds some light on this point. The person mentioned in the inscription CIS, II, 3973; RES 285, carries the name of the writer, who calls himself 'the Nabataean from the tribe of Rawḥu'. Reference to this tribe is found in the Bādiah 'Safaitic' inscriptions from the same region, Umm al-Jimāl (CIS, II, 5162).[82] Rawḥ had probably continued in existence through the Islamic period, for the *Banū Rūḥ* or *Rawḥ* tribe in al-Šām were known at the eve of Islam (al-Rosan 1987: 313). Continued reference to Rawḥ from the middle 1st century BCE until the 7th century CE is quite remarkable. The connection to the Nabataeans is also significant and was discussed above, where it was suggested that the tribe took part in a Nabataean alliance as an important member of the Nabataean community, being both an urbanised and nomadic tribe.

4. *'Amrah*

'mrt is a major tribe known in Syria and Jordan, especially in Madaba, referred to in at least 18 texts (see Milik 1958: no. 6; 1980: 41-54; Graf 1989: 360; al-Khraysheh 1995: 401-414; Graf 2003:45), which prayed to Allāt and Dushara, and the Fortune of Ḍayf *gd ḍf*. The latter deity name links them to the tribe of Ḍaif.

They wrote in Safaitic, Nabataean and Greek. Few of the inscriptions are dated (Milik 1980: 46; Macdonald 1980: no. 36; al-Rosan 1987: 336-9; al-Khraysheh 1995: no.1).[83] They probably did not converse in Greek among themselves. They were able, however, to communicate with the communities surrounding them in that language.

al-Qalqašandī of the 9th/15th CE century refers to the Arabian tribe of banū 'Amr which was part of Ṣaḫr, which was a 'part of Juḏām of the Qaḥṭān. They lived in Ṣarḫad [Ṣalḫad] in Bilād aš-Šām, and were known as the Arabs of Karak' (1959: 375). It is possible that this Arabian tribe was related to the Nabataean *'mrt*, if we consider their location and the earlier sources to which al-Qalqašandī would have turned.

5. *'Ubayšah*

The *'byšt* is an important tribe in Sī' in Ḥawrān (plate XXX). Part of this tribe, however, lived also in al 'Īsāwi in Syria and in Wadi Muqat in Jordan (CIS, V, 3262, WH; 1725a) (al-Rosan 1982: 334-5). They are known in Sī' from two Safaitic inscriptions, one bilingual Nabataean-Greek, one Nabataean and one Greek inscription (Grushevoi 1985: 51-3; Graf 1989: 360-361). Milik believes that 'Ubayšah served some form of a military function for the Nabataeans in the second half of the first century CE in the Syro-Jordanian desert and Madaba as 'une organisation rigide, quasi militaire' (1980: 46). The bilingual inscription

[77] The tribe of 'Awḏ is the only other tribe that had a private deity named after it; *gd 'Awḏ* (al-Rosan 1987: 339-341).

[78] See the *kmr* of Allāt discussed in the chapter on Nabataean women.

[79] *dnh byt' dy bnh rwḥw br mlkw br mlkw br 'klbw br rwḥw l'lt 'lhthm dy bṣlḥd wdy nṣb rwḥw br qṣyw 'l rwḥw dnh dy 'lm byrḥ 'b šnt 'šr wšb' lmlkw mlk nbṭw br ḥrtt mlk nbṭw rḥm 'mh* (CIS, II, 182).

[80] *byrḥ tšry šnt šb' lqldys qysr dnh tr'' dy 'bd mlkw br qṣ[yw] kmr 'lt šlm qry* (CIS, II, 170).

[81] *dnh byt' dy bnh 'wt'l br qṣyw br 'dynt br 'wt'[lh] br 'klbw br rwḥw br qṣyw l'lt wwgrh b[-] ṭb' byrḥ sywn šnt 'šryn wḥmš lrb'l mlk' mlk nb[ṭw] dy 'ḥyy 'mh wš[yzbh]* (Milik 1958 : ins 1).

[82] *[whb bn šmt ḏ'l rwḥ.*

[83] Recently Bādiah 'Safaitic' inscriptions from Jordan were published, written in 'the square or monumental script', belong to 'Amrat (al-Khraysheh 1995: nos. 1, 2, 5, 6). One is dated after the death of a Nabataean king, *lḥnn bn 'ḏr'l ḏ'l 'mrt wġls mn 'dmt snt mt mlk nbṭ*, 'For Ḥunayn son of 'Aḏir'el from the tribe of 'Amrat and he stayed home to recover from the fracture on his head, the year of the Nabataean king died'(al-Khraysheh 1995: no.1).

commemorated the person who made renovations in the temple of Ba'al Šamīn, which was a site of pilgrimage to the tribe (Graf 2003: 49-51). He was Mālikah, s. of Aus, the son of Muġayr, and the text dates from 33/32BCE (Lit 100N). The Greek inscription reads 'the community of inhabitants of Sī' erected the statue to Mālikah, s. of Aus, the son of Muġayr, as he built the temple and all the adornment surrounding it' (Cantineau [1930] 1979 II: 14; Grushevoi 1985: 53). A relative or descendant was known from another inscription as belonging to the tribe of 'Ubayšah. He commemorated the achievement of Mālikah, for giving the temple the new enlargement,[84] by erecting a statue in his honour (CIS,II,164).

Alexander Grushevoi argues that the tribe 'Ubayšah became settled in the first century CE that is at the time of the composition of the inscriptions from Sī'. Although not enough sources are available to determine whether the mode of life of this tribe in the preceding epoch was nomadic or semi-nomadic, Grushevoi suggests that the tribe 'Ubayšah made up, in whole or in part, the civil and sacred community of the people of Sī', and they borrowed, like other Bādiah Safaitic peoples, the cult of Ba'al-Šamīn, who was the principal deity worshipped in Sī' (1985: 53-4) as well as the goddess Allat (al-Rosan: 334-5)

6. Muzaynah

It was possible to learn of this tribe, to which a woman belongs, from a funerary inscription found in Ḥegra: *škynt brt mrt mznyt'*, Sukaynah d. of Murrah the Muzniyyah (JS 23). *mznyt'* could be a *nisbah* derived from the tribal name Muznah, Muzaynah or Māzinah, the preferable parallels are to Muzaynah (al-Fassi 1993a: 133). It was a tribe known at the dawn of Islam. Their lands were to the south of the tribe of Balī, whose lands were near Taymā ('Ali 1980: 4: 263). It is probable that the lands of Muzaynah were further to the north in the first century CE, because of the traditional direction of tribal movements after the arrival of Romans in the northern parts.

In addition to the Nabataean sedentary and nomad tribes, other social groups shared with the Nabataeans their social structure and some of them even made up part of the Nabataean *ethnie*.

D. Foreigners

What is meant by the term 'foreigner' here is any individual or group of people who do not come from the town or area where their name occurred, despite, possibly, being of the same ethnic group. The economic importance of Arabia in the ancient Nile to Oxus came from frankincense, myrrh and aromatic production and trade, which caused the Arabian towns and oases to attract foreigners, as merchants or entrepreneurs, and also as priests who took care of small shrines or temples established to serve the different transient groups. These towns received foreigners from inside and outside Arabia proper.

[84] For the temple's excavations, see Dentzer 1981.

Arabian society, even in the central parts of the desert, was not isolated from the outside world, whereas Syria was of a more complex nature. The mobility of caravans was constant through the cities, towns, villages and oases, throughout the centuries. The caravans not only transported commodities, but also people, ideas, culture, trends, religions, news and diseases, in short, everything.

1. Egyptians

The Egyptian presence in Raqamū-Petra was to be expected. First, because of the geographical approximity and the long Egyptian history in the region ever since the ancient Egyptian dynasties, and secondly, because of the economic operations with the Levant and Phoenicia, especially in the process of importing wood and silver from Lebanon and frankincense from Arabia to Egypt.

The relations between the Nabataeans and the 'Hellenistic' post-Achaemenid states varied according to the circumstances of the period and the strategy undertaken by each ruler and his/her state's interests. In the second century BCE, the Ptolemies, with the help of the Nabataeans' rivals, the Liḥyānites in Dedan, tried to seize control of the incense traffic by diverting part of it to Egypt by sea, thus preventing it, partially, from reaching Raqamū-Petra (Tarn 1929: 23).

Despite this history of hostility, Egyptians and Ptolemies had intensive trade relationships with the Nabataeans, and it would be expected that a few of them would have lived in Raqamū-Petra as merchants to look after their interests. The influence of the latter can be seen in some of the Nabataean facades in Raqamū-Petra and Ḥegra, such as the obelisk tomb at the entrance of the Sīq in Raqamū-Petra, the Ḫaznah (plate XXIII), which shows affinity to Alexandrian architecture. Isian motifs (see Wright 1962; 1973; Lyttleton 1990: 19-29) and more detailed influence can be found there and on the Ḥegra facades by the architect Aftaḥ who introduced the Egyptian architrave (see McKenzie 1990: 17). Being influenced by Egyptian art, however, does not necessarily mean they were built, engraved, or carved by Egyptians.

The Egyptian cults are also attested in Raqamū-Petra, especially that of Isis[85] and possibly also, of Osiris (Parr 1962; Hammond, Ph. 1981 and 1990). On the other hand, we find that Nabataean colonies were established in eastern Egypt, southern Sinai (Rothenberg 1970: 18-19) and northern Sinai; namely in the towns of Tal al-Šuqāfiyyah and Qaṣraweṭ, dating from the first century BCE (for eastern

[85] The presence of the Isis cult in Raqamū-Petra has been discussed by many (see Meza 1993 and 1996; Takács 1995; Parlasca 1998). For the relationship between Isis and the Nabataean queen see al-Fassi: forthcoming/b.

Egypt see Littmann 1914: xviii; 1954: 280; Littmann and Meredith 1953: 1-28; 1954: 211-246; for other details see Strugnell 1959: 35; Zayadine 1990: 151-174, for Qaṣraweṭ see Strugnell 1959; Oren 1982 and map II).

2. *Persians*

The Persians, especially the Parthians, were in contact with the Nabataeans, as they were their contemporaries. Although in the available sources we do not have much evidence of direct contact, such relation were unlikely not to have taken place. The evidence available refers to a Nabataean military assistance to the Parthians in their war against Jerusalem during the reign of King 'Malichus' in 54 BCE (Dio Cassius 48.41.5), probably King Mālik I who ruled between 60-30BCE. The Parthians, like the Nabataeans, were involved in caravan trade, and the previous Achaemenid administration in the region would have had established economic and cultural contact. It has been reported, however, that Nabataeans had direct routes with Forāt city of Misān on the Persian Gulf, which was under the protection of Parthians.

The Achaemenid Empire emerged and prospered from 550 BCE until Alexander's conquest between 334 and 323 BCE, which overthrew them and the Chaldaean-Babylonian Kingdom (Kuhrt 1995 II: 659). Under Cyrus the Great (559-530), the Achaemenid Empire became 'the largest empire the world has seen, spanning the territory from the Hellespont to north India, including Egypt (for most of its history) and extending into central Asia up to the frontiers of modern Kazakhstan' (Kuhrt 1995 II: 647). Their empire replaced the principal powers of the ancient world for nearly two hundred years, ruling through a strong and effective administrative system that later enabled the Seleucids to link the Achaemenid institutions with their own dominions (Kuhrt 1995 II: 701).

The Arabians had good relations with the Achaemenid rulers, first through helping the troops of Cambyses to find their way in Sinai during their invasion of Egypt (Herodotus 3: 88; see for an identification of the Arab King Lemaire 1974: 63-67, 71; AbdulAlim 1987: 13). Later, however, instead of paying the usual tax, they presented the king with a gift of 1000 talents of frankincense (Herodotus 3: 97). That was in return for keeping control of the caravan frankincense trade between southern Arabia and the Palestinian ports under Persian control (Kuhrt 1995 II: 690).

The Arsacids emerged in the historical records for the first instance as vassal kings for the Achaemenids and later for the Seleucids until they captured the Seleucid capital of The Land of the Two Rivers, Seleucia-on-the-Tigris in 141 BCE and controlled the Iranian plateau in 147 BCE, which they took also as capital. By the end of the century, the Parthian kings controlled Babylon and, partially, Armenia and formed what is known as the Parthian Empire, lasting until they were overturned by the Sasanians in the early third century CE, circa 228 CE (Kawami 1987: 1, 5, 7, 16). By the beginning of the first century BCE Parthia had become one of the major powers in Western Asia (Koshelenko and Pilipko 1994: 131-33). Parthian expansion eventually succeeded in conquering the trade routes with the Romans. Small states like caravan cities, such as Palmyra, Ḥaṭra or Dura Europos, played an important role in this conflict as buffer states (See Colledge 1967: 36ff.). They were in direct contact with Raqamū-Petra's traffic of frankincense trade.

King Artaban III (16-40 CE) was a contemporary of Ḥāriṯah IV, from the time he married Queen Šaqīlah until his death. During his reign, Parthia, though it continued fighting with Rome in The Land of the Two Rivers and Syria, witnessed economic prosperity, as indicated by King Artaban's coinage (Kawami 1987: 12). The decline started after his death with the disintegration of some parts of Parthia, such as Charax in southern Babylonia at the head of the Persian Gulf (ibid. 12-13). By the end of the Nabataean Kingdom, the Parthian contemporary was the important king Pacorus II (78-105 CE) (Kawami 1987: 14).

During these two hundred years, displacement and movement of individuals and families was common, particularly in the case of the Empire's *satraps* and their provincial courts. Contact between the two realms seems evident within the frame of the international economy and trade network, which covered in part the Parthian lands and part of the Nabataean, from Susa to Raqamū-Petra via Palmyra, and necessitated the displacement of merchants. Some other contacts could be seen in the artistic traditions in Nabataea and Parthia, especially in stone sculpture, which shows obvious evidence of Parthian patronage, in the Parthian skills of imagery (see Kawami 1987: 149) when compared with the stone sculpture and rock carving in the Nabataean art and architecture (see Mackenzie 1990). Sullivan considers Syria to have been populated at the time by Semites as well as Iranians (1990: 80) and Littmann believes that some Persian merchants lived in Ḥegra and Raqamū-Petra as they used to come and frequent Makkah and Yaṯrib at the dawn of Islam in the 6th-7th century CE (1914: xviii). A few Nabataean inscriptions can be attributed to Persians, such as the one which belongs to phkwrw (Pacorus) (Lit 24N) and *'škrs br prs'*? (JS 170 N)[86] and the female name *'rsksh brt tymw* (CIS,II,213) found on one of Ḥegra's tombs. These were either names of Persians or influenced by Persian onomasticon.

3. *Greco-Romans*

The contact between people of the Nile to the Oxus and the Greeks goes far back in the annals of history and archaeology (see Bernal's argument on those links, which, according to him, started from 2100 BCE with Egyptian

[86] *'škrs* was considered as a Greek name from Areskousa (Milik 1976: 148), it could, however, be the Persian name Xerxes and the PN *prs'*? Derived from Persia rather than 'horseman' (al-Fassi 1995: 10).

and Phoenician colonisation of Greece, [1987] 1991: 17ff., 110, 337ff.). A Hellenic political presence in the region, however, begins only with Alexander at the end of the 4th century BCE. By the 3rd century BCE two Macedonian political entities, replacing the Achaemenid governors, were established in the form of 'Hellenistic' post-Achaemenid states, the Seleucids in The Land of the Two Rivers and northern Syria, and the Ptolemies in Egypt and southern Syria. During which, they were in constant economic contact with Arabia.

The first historical reference to the Nabataeans was about the first Hellenic[87] contact with them in 312 BCE, incorporated in Diodorus' history (20: 100). The relations between the Hellenes and the Nabataeans were not stagnant. It was intermittently peaceful and hostile throughout their mutual coexistence, until they were all overrun by the Romans, the Seleucids in 64 BCE, the Ptolemies in 30 BCE, and the Nabataeans in 106 CE. Accordingly, there was a great deal of contact and a need for a peaceful relationship.

The Nabataeans refused Hellenic political domination, as was attested in the resistance to Antigonus' son in 312 BCE, when they were expelled from the Dead Sea asphalt business by the Nabataeans (Diodorus 20: 100). Apart from that, we do not know how the Nabataeans reacted towards the Hellenic presence among them, or towards their cultural influence. On the other hand, there is evidence from the Jewish community of that same period, showing conflict with its Hellenized religious leaders and the higher ranks of society, and also there is evidence of difficulties between the peasants and urban masses, who did not wish to compromise their religious traditions. The Hellenization of Palestinian Jews was so deep that they would have been absorbed, had it not been for Antiochus Epiphanes (175-164 BCE), the Seleucid persecutor, whose actions instigated resistance. Hellenization was demonstrated in many aspects, by the substitution of Aramaic by Greek, the adoption of Greek personal names, the adoption of Hellenic educational institutions, such as the gymnasium, the growth of Hellenistic literature and philosophy, in culture, theatres, amphitheaters, and most serious of all, religious deviation and syncretism as seen in legal institutions and in art (Feldman 1986: 295). Such a controversial relationship in the neighborhood must have extended to the Nabataeans, or at least they must have known of it. Initially we can say, according to the archaeological finds in Raqamū-Petra, that no gymnasium had been uncovered, which could be significant in denoting a different attitude towards Greek or Hellenic culture.

On the other hand, there is some indication of an attempt to 'nationalise' the Nabataean coinage after it had copied Greek coinage for some time. This policy started at the time of 'Obadah II (62-60 BCE), who was the first Nabataean King to strike coins bearing a Nabataean inscription in 62 BCE (Meshorer 1975: 3). And it was extended during the time of Ḥāriṯah IV (9BCE- 40CE), who dropped the Greek epithet that his predecessor had used philhellenos and adopted a Nabataean epithet with a distinct 'national' implication, *rḥm 'mh* 'lover of his people', philopatris.

The struggle in the Red Sea was at its peak during the second century BCE, at the time when the Ptolemies were first establishing their state. It was then that they started to make inroads into the frankincense trade by trying to shift the trade routes from land to sea in order to gain control. They founded ports and stations all along the west shore of the Red Sea (Tarn 1929: 21-22; Nuṣḥī 1976 I: 59-60). The Nabataeans, who were the principal partners in this trade with South Arabian kingdoms, felt threatened by the Ptolemies' attempts, so they resisted by inciting maritime wars and skirmishes, and that was interpreted by the Roman authors as 'piracy' (Strabo 16:4:18). In spite of the resistance and the Nabataean keenness to maintain their own culture, it was inevitable that they would have to communicate with surrounding cultures and peoples, both influencing them and being influenced. In this regard, the Hellenes were successful in implanting their culture within the indigenous cultures. The present interest, however, is not the influence of the Hellenes, but rather whether Hellenic groups were living among the Nabataeans and making of themselves part of the Nabataean social structure.

Finding Greek personal names in the Nabataean onomasticon does not necessarily prove a Hellenic population there. Among male names there are remarkable features, such as sons with Greek names, whose fathers' names, can be recognised as Nabataean: see *tyṭys br 'bdw* (Titius s. of 'Abdū) (CIS, II, 303). On the other hand, the opposite is also found, a man carrying a Nabataean name appears from his genealogy to have a father with a Greek name, e.g. *'nmw br dmsps* (Ġanimū s. of Damasippos) (CIS, II, 234). Both can be considered as Nabataeans. A similar situation is found in Egypt under the Ptolemies and was suggested to have been introduced as a result of mixed marriages. In later centuries, Greek names in Egyptian onomasticon did not have, however, any ethnic significance, for Egyptians bore Greek names and vice versa (Pomeroy 1984: 124).

Interestingly, however, this feature does not appear to be the case among Nabataean women. No Nabataean woman is found carrying a Greek name, however, many women's names were found in Greek texts from the Ḥawrān. Women were not seen to be part of the Hellenization process, either by intention or by tradition. In Palmyra, a very Hellenized-Romanized city, where the men and deities, male and female are dressed *à la Hellène* and carried Greek names and titles, women were never portrayed in Hellenic dress nor were given Greek names as far as evidence available (see the funerary portraits of Palmyrene women in Sadurska and Bunni 1994).

[87] By Hellenic I mean Greek and Macedonians.

Keeping women out of the Hellenization process shows how Nabataean women were, like women in general, considered being representatives and preservers of their culture, tradition and the values of their ancestors.[88]

Not far from Ḥegra, however, there was the Greek Milesian[89] colony of Ampelone, which is known only from Pliny (6:32:159); archaeological or other classical evidence is yet to be found. It was W.W. Tarn who identified the city with the enigmatic 'White Village',[90] believing it to have been founded by Ptolemy II, who was active in Arabia between 277-260 BCE (1929: 21-23). If Pliny's story is acceptable, Ampelone, or the White Village, should have had constant interaction, for at least two centuries, with the local people. One wonders whether this Greek presence could be one of the reasons for Hellenic influence on the Nabataean choice of proper names in Ḥegra, bearing in mind that Ḥegra itself had not been founded by then. The other major town and state nearby was Liḥyān in Dedan, which in fact had some Egyptian influence on their art and king's names.

How far this interaction went on is unknown. Speculation on social relations, such as marriage, would be possible. In the middle of the 2nd century BCE Agatharchides mentioned that an Arab tribe in western Ḥijāz, called the Debae, had a legend of intermarriage between Greeks and Arabians. He said this is why they treated Peleponnesians and Boeotians well (Strabo 4:16:18). The Debae could have been a neighbour of Ampelone, or had some kind of special relationship with them. This colony would be expected to have played a role in transferring Hellenic culture, or at least, artefacts, to the centre of ancient Arabia. This story, however, until some more evidence is available, will neither be accepted nor rejected.

As for the Romans, their presence among the Nabataeans is similarly attested through different types of relationships of war and trade. They started to expand in the eastern Mediterranean region after eliminating their main rivals in the western and eastern Mediterranean, such as Spain (Spanish Wars), Carthage (Punic Wars) and Macedonia (Macedonian Wars), by the middle of the second century BCE (Cary and Scullard 1975: 113-160). After spreading their hegemony over Asia Minor, they directed their strategies eastward towards defeating Parthia principally, and the remaining 'Hellenistic' post-Achaemenid states, such as the Seleucids, the Ptolemies, Pontus, Armenia, Commagene, Judaea, the kingdoms of northern Asia Minor and The Land of the Two Rivers and the Nabataeans (Sullivan 1990: 22-24), in order to control world trade and the centres of the precious products of the 'East'. By the middle and end of the first century BCE they had conquered most of the Nile to Oxus. They succeeded in annexing Syria by 64 BCE, forming the Syrian Province, then Egypt in 30 BCE, and squashed the Nabataeans in the middle.

After capturing Egypt, Octavius ordered his prefect over Egypt, then C. Aelius Gallus, to invade Arabia Felix and try either to capture the land of the Arabian kingdom, mainly of southern Arabia, or to make good friends with them, 'For he [Octavius] expected either to deal with wealthy friends or to master wealthy enemies' (Strabo 16:4:22). He carried out his expedition in 26/25 BCE (Jameson 1968: 77), but returned defeated (Strabo 16:4:24). Thus the only alternative that remained to Octavius was to establish relations on a diplomatic friendly basis in southern and northern Arabia (Periplus 23; Pliny 12:31:57).[91] During the period from 26/25 BCE until the annexation in 106 CE, relations between the Romans and the Nabataeans were unstable.

Rome never conquered Raqamū-Petra. The Nabataean political status, however, was questioned; it is disputed whether it was autonomous, a vassal state or an independent polity. Some scholars believe that the Nabataeans became subjected to Rome or as Bowersock suggests, that by 1st century CE, and after the Gaius Arabica expedition, Nabataea was reinstated for Ḥāriṯah IV (1983: 56-7). Others consider Nabataea as an independent state (for example Sullivan 1990: 213). It is possible, however, that Nabataeans, not given very much choice, chose a policy of realistic co-operation (Paltiel 1991: 26), which allowed them a special kind of relationship hovering on the borders of autonomy and clienthood. Their assertion of independence was tested further by Ḥāriṯah IV, a situation of power relationships that needs independent study.

Many Romans, among other foreigners, were attested to have lived in Raqamū-Petra during the first century BCE. Strabo relates that his friend Athenodorus (74 BCE-7 CE), who lived in Raqamū-Petra for a short time, 'found both many Romans and many other foreigners sojourning there' (Strabo 16:4:21).

In Ḥegra, a considerable amount of Greek and Latin inscriptions and graffiti have been uncovered (JS 4-8,10-20G), containing proper names and some titles. Historians have a problem dating these inscriptions, principally because of the various possible reasons for finding Greek inscriptions, which depend on their date. Some

88 An exception in this regard is found in Hellenic women in Ptolemaic Egypt who 'appeared more Egptianized and men more Hellenized'(Pomeroy 1984: 124), which is mostly exemplified in the case of Cleopatra VII.

89 For the Milesian colonies and their expansion in the Mediterranean see Ehrhadt 1983: 87-92 esp. 91.

90 This was translated into Greek as Leuce Kome (Strabo, 16:4:24; Periplus, 9), present-day 'Aynūnah, or Wajh (see Ingraham *et al* 1981: 77; Sayed, 1981: 54-55; Kirwan, 1984: 55-61; Gatier and Salles, 1988: 187; Sidebotham 1991: 21) (see map II and plate XIX for 'Aynūnah).

91 For details about the expedition see Sprenger 1873: 121-141; Jameson 1968: 71-84; Bowersock 1983: 46-49.

hold that they date to the Nabataean period; others date them to the provincial period, i.e. the 2nd century CE[92] (Bowsher 1986: 25-27; Graf 1990c). Others date them to the expedition of Aelius Gallus (Seyrig 1941: 220). And a fourth group views them as of a later date, having been made by native soldiers serving in the Roman army, who had now returned to their homeland (Seyrig 1941: 220). More discussion of these inscriptions, graffiti, Greek and Latin names, archaeological finds etc. is given by other scholars (Sartre 1982; Bowersock 1983; and Graf especially 1990c, appendix).

Having a Roman presence as individuals among Nabataeans seems to have become common by the first century BCE onwards, as merchants and mainly as soldiers. It is not possible to speak of soldiers, however, until the annexation. Many Nabataean merchants wandered in the Greek islands, such as Rhodes, Tinos, Priene, Miletus, Delos, Kos, and Athens (Roche 1996: 73-99; for Miletus see Ehrhardt 1983; for Kos see Della Vida 1938: 140-142 and Sherwin-White 1978: 246, 370-71), and Roman cities, mainly Rome and Puteoli (Roche 1996: 73-99). They have even established temples or sanctuaries for Dushara, such as the one referred to in Puteoli (CIS,II,158; 157; Lacerenza 1988; 1994; Roche 1996: 86-89).

Friendly relations were shown in a few cases, such as the Nabataean help sent to Octavius at Actium in his battle against Cleopatra and Antony (Bowersock 1983: 43) and to Vespasian and Titus in their siege and war against the Hasmoneans (Bowersock 1983: 72), as well as offers to help in the Roman expedition against South Arabia. Relations on this level were official and formal, as well as on the level of the soldier community, either Roman or Nabataean. A few Roman merchants, however, would have resided in the principal Nabataean cities to maintain their trade interests.

It is not possible to consider the Romans as part of the Nabataean *ethnie*, for they did not settle in civil communities, like the Greeks for example, nor were they perceived as absolute friends, for they would always be suspected as potential invaders.

4. Jews

The Jewish presence in Arabia is known in the sixth century CE through Islamic sources. Modern scholars, however, try to argue for a Jewish presence in Arabia that dates from the sixth century BCE (see Ben-Zvi 1961: 143-190; Noja 1979: 283-317). Some scholars rely in their arguments on later historical evidence.[93]

The Nabataean period provides more substantial evidence of interaction. Jewish-Nabataean relations were active and constant, according to the accounts of Josephus' two works, the *Antiquities* and the *Jewish War*. These relations generally swung between war and peace. In war they were sworn enemies, and in times of peace they intermarried.

Within the Nabataean realm Jews, who lived mainly to the west of the Dead Sea, near Judaea, are considered to be part of the Nabataean *ethnie*. Most of our information about that region comes from the Babatha archive in Wādī Ḫabra, dating from 93 until 132 CE (Yadin 1963: 229). It demonstrates the mixed population which lived on the frontiers and which was encouraged to move more towards the Nabataean border during the restlessness that resulted in Bar Kokhba's revolt in 132 CE (Yadin 1971; Bowersock 1983: 88). It shows a community maintaining its legal rights by means of Nabataean law and the Raqamean court. Integration with the Nabataean community is evident, for example, from their location (Yadin 1963: doc 3; 2002: 1, 2, 3). Secondly, there were shared legal obligations. For example, Babatha's child's guardians were a Nabataean and a Jew (Yadin 1963: doc 11; Lewis 1978: 108; Cotton 1994: 96). And thirdly, there were Nabataean witnesses in Jewish legal disputes and law-suits (Yadin 1962: 238). Some lived in Ḥawrān, having moved there during the fluctuating expansion of the Hashmonean state in the north. Little evidence of Jewish settlements, however, is found there throughout the Nabataean period (see Frey 1952: 90-105; Sartre 1985: 158-159). Henna Cotton summarizes the relationship between the two people according to the papyri, by saying :'The papyri show the well-off Jews of Arabia having excellent relations with their neighbours the Nabataeans, who serve as guardians, witnesses and subscribers in the Jewish documents' (2001:154).

At Ḥegra in Arabia some Hebrew graffiti (JS1- 8Heb)[94] can be found and one Nabataean inscription on a tomb belonging to someone from Judaea or a Jew (JS4). A few other short Nabataean graffiti have been found with Jewish personal names, most of which date to a later period (see Altheim and Stiehl 1968: 310-316; Noja 1979: 294-306).[95] One graffito refers to 'Natan who is from Jerusalem, peace' *ntnwy dy mn 'wršlm šlm* (CIS, II, 320b), which points to

[92] The only dated Greek inscriptions belonging to that period are those of Rawwāfah dating from 166-169 CE. Those are a bilingual inscription, two Nabataean inscriptions, and two Greek. The bilingual Nabataean-Greek mentions a Thamudic *šrkt*, which built a sanctuary and dedicated it to the Roman Emperors Marcus Aurelius Antoninus and Lucius Aurelius Verus, and the Governor of Arabia Antistius Adventus for bringing peace among the Thamudaeans (Parr *et al* 1971: 55-58; Bowersock 1978: 513-22; Macdonald 1995b: 93-101).

[93] For instance, C.J. Gadd introduced the view that there was a Jewish community that was introduced to Taymā accompanying the Chaldaean army in the sixth century BCE. He was relying on the later Jewish presence in some Arab towns thirteen hundred years later, during the seventh century CE, including Taymā, Dedan, Fadak, Khaybar, and Yaṯrib, which were among the towns Nabonidus had conquered (1958: 86-8; Ben-Zvi 1961: 143-149; Noja 1979: 284).

[94] Milik and Starcky (1970: 163) had two Hebrew inscriptions from al-'Ulā, one of which was published partly by JS no. 223.

[95] Sergio Noja, in an attempt to establish an evidence for an early Jewish presence in northern Arabia, looks for Jewish or semi-Jewish proper names found in Nabataean, Liḥyānite or Greek inscriptions (see 1979: 289-316).

a possibility of this person being one of the immigrants, travellers, merchants or soldiers from among the 500 Jews who participated in the expedition of Aelius Gallus in 26/25 BCE. (Strabo 16:4:23). Two Nabataean inscriptions, dating from a post-Nabataean period (307, 356 CE), one from Dedan (JS 386) and one from Ḥegra (Altheim and Stiehl 1968 V/1: 305-309; Stiehl 1970: 87-90), bear personal names that correspond with Jewish ones. A sundial with personal names correlates with possible Jewish names was found in Ḥegra (Healey 1989a: 334).

In Arabia we hear in later periods (6th-7th century CE) of Jews in Wādī al-Qurā, which includes Dedan and Ḥegra. Arab traditions mention a Judaean immigration into Arabia after the Jewish revolt and the Roman destruction of Jerusalem in 70 CE (al-Ṭabarī 1:346-7; al-Andalusī 1: 57). They came to Ḥijāz, in groups, such as banū an-Naḍīr, banū Qurayẓah, banū Bahdal, banū ʻIkrimah, banū ḏaʻlabah, banū Maḥmar, banū Zaqūra, banū Qaynuqāʻ, banū Zayd, banū ʻAwf, banū al-Faṣīṣ, and banū Murānah (al-Iṣbahānī 19: 95). Some Arabian tribes neighbouring the Jewish tribes of Khaybar and Yaṯrib became in part Jewish.[96] According to early Islamic sources, these tribes were considered to be a mixture of Arabians and Judaeans, where it was difficult to draw a definite line between the two groups.

E. Clients and Slaves

The unusual term gr is found in a female Taymānite tomb in Ḥegra belonging to *wšwḥ brt bgrt*, Washuḥ d. of Bajrat (JS11, 12). Dating from 34 CE, Wašūḥ's inscription included in the will for the tomb her 'clients', grhm,[97] male and female, *dkr 'wnqbt'*. The word *gr* or *jār* probably refers to persons under protection, 'clients', '*protégés*' (Healey 1993b: 256). Under the old tribal system of Arabia, strangers (whether they were freed slaves, or refugees ostracised from their own tribe) would be freely admitted to 'protection' under the aegis of a powerful chief or another influential man (or woman), who would then assume the responsibility of protecting the person and property of his/her 'client'. The one claiming protection, or *jiwār*, would then belong to the family of his/her protector or patron, and would be spoken of as *jār al-bayt*, 'the *jār* of the house'. The house in which the protected stranger lodges was called *mujāwir*. The sense of solidarity was such, however, that the obligation of protection, once assumed by a member of the group, was equally binding upon every other member of the tribe (Schaeffer 1915: 152). The client also could be a man settled in his wife's tribe, or with his mother's people, *aḫwāl* (Smith 1903: 50). The word *gr* is mentioned three times in the inscription, indicating a strong commitment to this aspect of social relations.

It may seem unusual for a non-Ḥegran woman to play the role of protector. Such a role was usually limited to local men of power in a tribe or city (see the discussion by Jawād ʻAlī 1970 4: 360-365); let alone a woman from another town. *Jiwār* was known, however, and recognised by ancient Arabian society. Ibn Hišām, writing in the 3rd century H /9th century CE, gives several examples of women taking this role in early Islamic history, one of which was when the Prophet recognised the word of protection or 'honour' that Zaynab, the Prophet's daughter, announced in the mosque of al-Madīnah for her ex-husband Abū al-ʻĀṣ s. of al-Rabīʻ s. of ʻAbd al-ʻUzzā s. of ʻAbd Šams, who was still an infidel (mušrik) (ii: 218). Another example arose while the Muslims were surrounding Makkah before capturing it in 9 H/ 630 CE. Umm Hāni' d. of Abī Ṭālib gave her 'word of protection' to her husband and her brother-in-law who were non-Muslims and this received the acceptance of the Prophet (ibid. iv: 46). A third case, was when Umm Ḥakīm d. of al-Ḥāriṯ s. of Hišām took under her protection ʻIkrimah s. of Abī Jahl, her husband, and this was also recognised (ibid. iv: 45). The Prophet blessed the act of taking into the jiwār saying: *innahu yujīru ʻalā al-muslimīn adnāhum* 'any Muslim (the average) can take anyone under the Muslims' protection' (ibid. ii: 218).

It is interesting to notice that the cases of *jiwār* in early Islam raised by women were specifically for their husbands and relatives. A person who accepts such a responsibility has to have a legitimate reason, such as being a husband or relative. It is, however, not certain whether a foreign woman or man could exercise such a position in Nabataean society. Apart from this incident, no other reference to this practice is found, which would suggest that the group of people taken into Wašūḥ's protection as clients were of her own tribe or city (Taymā), or even her husband's and his family. On the other hand, the recognition by Ḥegran society for Wašūḥ's clients shows that Nabataean women were capable of taking groups of men and women under their protection, and shows the status that the Taymānite woman had gained among Ḥegraeans. It also indicates the legal power a Nabataean woman enjoyed, not only as a native in her city but also as a settler from a different town (al-Fassi 1997: 54).

A discussion will be useful about whether slaves constituted part of the Nabataean *ethnie* or how strongly they were represented in Nabataean society. As seen above, Nabataean *ethnie* was aristocratic and elitist; it is unlikely that slaves were considered as part of the Nabataean ethnie. Like average people, belonging to the state was not as strong a tie for them as was the city or town or even the tribe. A quick overview of the concept of slavery and its historical position at the time will also be useful.

The earliest reference to slavery comes from Sumer, where records give description of slaves as 'males of a foreign

[96] Such as a clan from as al-Aws and al-Ḫazraj, a clan from al-Ḥāriṯ bin Kaʻb, from Ġassān and another from Juḏām (al-Yaʻqūbī I: 257), as well as most of Kinda, Kinānah and Ḥimyar (ʻAlī 1980: 6: 514).

[97] This cannot be a reference to jawārī, i.e. 'female slaves' as suggested by S. al-Theeb (1998: No.201, p.235-236) since the inscription specifies the male and female members of the gryhm.

country' and 'females of a foreign country', indicating that the first people to be enslaved in Sumer were captive foreigners (Mendelsohn 1949: 1). Slavery was considered a normal practice in ancient societies. Many of the ancient law-codes in The Land of the Two Rivers, Egypt, Greece and Rome mentioned slaves, their position in society, their duties, and rights (if they had any). The law-codes also treat of matters of owning, selling and buying slaves, and the penalties applied to them (see Woodhouse 1920a: 612ff., 1920b: 621ff.; Mendelsohn 1949: 34ff.).

The society of ancient Arabia also practised slavery, but information about the treatment and life of slaves is only sparse. From the fragmentary evidence available it is understood that the usual supply of slaves came principally through war (booty), and in addition unpaid debt, theft, or kidnapping. Slaves were then traded in established markets. Arabian pre-Islamic inter-tribal wars were known, and booty was always taken, mostly, however, to be ransomed for money (see al-Nasif al-Dosari 1998).

In the second century BCE, with the increase in agriculture, the need for slaves increased and the trade of slavery in the Mediterranean became prosperous and was at its peak. In western Asia, Ġazzah was the biggest market and the main centre for exporting slaves (Browning 1989: 14). Delos was the centre of this trade and its biggest market in the Mediterranean, where many nations participated and encouraged by the great revenue they received. In a detailed account, Strabo, who qualified it as an 'evil business', wrote,

> 'The exportation of slaves induced them most of all to engage in their evil business, since it proved most profitable, for not only were they easily captured, but the market, which was large and rich in property, was not extremely far away, I mean Delos, which could both admit and send away ten thousand slaves on the same day, whence arose the proverb, 'Merchants sail in, unload your ship, everything has been sold'. The cause of this was the fact that the Romans, having become rich after the destruction of Carthage and Corinth, used many slaves, and the pirates, seeing the easy profit therein, bloomed forth in great numbers, themselves not only going in quest for booty, but also trafficking in slaves. The kings both of Cyprus and of Egypt co-operated with them in this, being enemies to the Syrians' (14:5:2).

The Ptolemies were involved in slavery as were the Seleucids and, to a lesser degree, the Nabataeans. The Zenon records report the role of Zenon, the treasurer of Ptolemy II (285-246 BCE) in this trade. Residing in the Fayyūm village of Philadelphia, Zenon was the business agent for Apolonius in slaves' trade, and the manager of his large private estate in Fayyūm (Graf 1990b: 53). His records produce information on the Greek drovers (slave traders) from Ḥawrān to Ġazzah, covering Phoenicia and Palestine (Nuṣḥī, 1966 iii: 124). His men were notorious for kidnapping free women from Transjordan and Syria. They were always being stopped by the Nabataean troops (Starcky 1966: 904; Graf 1983: 566). Graf gives a new reading of the document describing it as a 'memorandum from Herakeides ..., concerning the activities of two renegades named Drimylus and Dionysius, who were engaged in selling slave-girls as prostitutes to temples, border guards, and residents of the region. Their 'business' extends along the Palestinian coast between Jappa (Joppa) and Ptolemies (Acco), and then across the Jordan valley to Amman and north into southern Syria. After selling a slave girl for 150 drachmas in the Syrian Ḥaurān, on their return, the document indicates, they encountered the 'Nabataeans'. When they attempted to contrive a deal with them, there was an immediate outcry of protest, resulting in the slave traders being placed in fetters and guarded for seven days. After their release, they continued their enterprises, but the geographical references for their activities and other details cease' (1990b: 53-4).

This source raises many questions about the role of Nabataeans in slavery trade; however, answers are to be sought. For the Nabataeans to arrest the dovers and jail them does not explain why this happened in the first place. Did the Nabataeans arrest the dovers because Nabataean authorities were upset with Zenon personally? Or because Zenon's men did not present a legal document to authorise them to pass, if such a document existed? Was it because Zenon's men did not behave themselves, or did not pay certain taxes? The reason may be that they did not get a piece of the action, or simply, they disapproved of the slavery trade in general.

In the Nabataean inscriptions and graffiti there are quite a few references to slaves, male.[98] Other references are found in Liḥyānite[99] and Bādiah 'Thamudic'.[100] A couple of graffiti mentioning slaves were found in Ḥegra[101] and one in the Sarbūt al-Ṯalīla mountain to the south-west of Tabūk. The latter reads *šlm 'ytw br twts 'qṭyr 'l'lm* (al-Theeb 1993: no.56). Al-Theeb argues that *'qṭyr'* is a Nabatization of the Latin (Greek) profession actor publicus, who was responsible for the slaves and public property (1993: 132). If this is a correct reading, we are dealing here with a profession concerning slaves imported from the Roman world.

---

[98] *'lym* i.e. *ġlym* [JS 1909 I: 211 or *qn/qyn* [Lisan, *qyn*], [also means 'smith' or 'singing' in north-west Semitic see Lisān, *qyn*; Hoftijzer and Jongeling 1995 II: 1008-1009]) and female (*'mh*).

[99] See JS 59, for a slave in Liḥyānite (*'bd*).

[100] From Manṭar banī 'Aṭiyyah north of Taymā, a graffito reads: *ḥmyt bn tmṯ' qn mnf*, 'Hamiyyah s. of Taym-Tha', slave of Manaf' (Parr *et al* 1971: ins 23) (see Plate XXII).

[101] From Maq'ad al-Jundī, between Ḥegra and Dedan, a graffito reads *dkyr ynss 'lym mry tk'*, 'Remembered be Yunassis servant (slave) of the master TK' '(JS 257), and from Ḥegra another graffito reads *šlmw tymw 'lym ḥlpw*, 'Peace on Taym slave of Khalaf' (CIS, II, 276). See also JS 53 and 85.

Two more inscriptions, one from Iṯrā in Wādī al-Sirḥān and the other from Ḍumayr in Ḥawrān, are worth noting and comparing. The first reads *dy 'bd nšrw 'bd' br ḥrmw dy mn 'l qmyrw*, 'this is what Nashru, the slave, son of Ḥarām who is from the tribe of Qumairu, made' (Milik and Starcky 1970: no. 130). The second, dating from 94CE, reads:

I, 1-*[dnh m]sgd' dy hqym*
2-*[h]n'w br ḥry gdlw brt*
A *hn'w*
II, 3- *bgrt 'm 'drmw 'srtg'*
4- *wnqydw mn 'l ṭ'm'* [102]
5- *bny 'bd mlkw*
B *'trmw br m..*
III, 6- *'srtg' byrḥ 'yr*
7- *šnt 405 bmnyn 'rhwmy'*
8- *dy hw šnt 24 lrb'l*
9- *mlk'*
C *nqydw brh*
F *...lhnw 'tth*
(Sachau 1884; CIS,II,161(1893); Cooke 1903: no. 97).

[This is the c]ippus which Hāni' set up, the freedman of Jadalū, d. of Bajarah, mother of Adramu the Strategos and Neqīdu, by adoption sons of 'Abd-māliku the Strategos, in the month Iyar , in the year 405, by the reckoning of the Romans, which is the 24th year of King Rab'el.

If the readings are accurate, both inscriptions illustrate the tradition of associating slaves with their owners, be it a tribe or an individual. The tribe that Nashru belonged to, Qumairu, is mentioned thirteen times in the Bādiah 'Safaitic' inscriptions, and thought to reside in Ḥawrān and spread through to Wādī al-Sirḥān (Milik and Starcky 1970: 160; Graf 1989: 365-366). In the second case, which refers to a freed man or a former slave who erected a stele or cippus, he is identified by the name of his former owner, Jadalū d. of Bajarah, a known woman whose husband and son, Adramu, were both strategoi (see Hammond 1973: 110). She is the central figure in the inscription, related to all the personages mentioned as mother or spouse or ex-mistress, regardless of the prominent position of her husband and son.

What is of interest in this inscription is the relationship between freed slaves and their former owners. It shows, on the one hand, women holding ownership of slaves and, on the other, their power to free them. It is curious, however, for the freedman, instead of identifying himself by his own father's name, he uses the name of his ex-mistress. It is not certain whether keeping the name of former owners was an elective or intentional decision. It could either follow the tradition of adopting the master's tribal name, or mean that he was genuinely proud of his ex-masters. This pride, however, cannot be attributed to mere personal liking as much as wanting to be associated with a distinguished woman within a Ḍumeirian family, which was politically and, probably, economically prominent.

In brief, the two inscriptions from Wādī al-Sirḥān and Ḍumayr illustrate the relationship that evolved between the freed person (in the second case) or the slave (in the first case) and their (ex-) owner's tribe, a tradition that apparently prevailed from southern Syria to northern Arabia.

It is suggested that the Nabataeans had concubines besides their spouses. In a funeral inscription from Raqamū-Petra, a wife and a concubine are mentioned with their jewellery, *...bt 'prw 'ntt ...'w 'srt' [dh]b' w'dyt' dy tḥth, ... 'ty dy 'l'...* 'Bet-'Afro wife of ..'w, and the concubine, gold and jewellery that is under.., my corpse (at rest) above ...'. Zayadine dates it to the second century CE (1982: 366-7). *'srt'*, known also in Official Aramaic, also means 'prisoner' (Hoftijzer and Jongeling 1995 I: 91) similar to Arabic, asīr means 'war prisoner' (Lisān 'sr). The association between the word for concubine[103] and female booty can be taken to explain the origin of concubines. Probably they could also be traced to those bought in the prosperous trade that was reported in Zenon's archives.

II. Conclusion

In this chapter I have tried to show how multi-cultural, cohesive and complex is the nature of the Nabataean society. The Nabataean *ethnie* comprised a collective name for the ruling family, distinct culture and a strong sense of solidarity. I have tried to trace the features that constitute an *ethnie* and reached the conclusion that these were the major components in distinguishing Nabataeanness, which in its turn became strongly associated with a specific class, the elite. This factor, together with the nature of their religious system, resulted in a weak sense of ethnicity that faded with the annexation of the Nabataean state. This *ethnie* managed to encompass all differences and absorb them in a homogenous texture.

Tribal structure probably differed from one place to another within the Nabataean realm. It included nomads and sedentary inhabitants from different tribes and towns, and different ethnicities and linguistic categories, each having its own characteristics as well as its script. It seems, though, that the urbanised areas witnessed interchange and interrelations with the nomads. The relationship between the two forms of society was derived from a common social background and mutual interest, especially economic, between irrigation-based agriculturists and manufacturers,

[102] *ṭ'm'* known in Official Aramaic with many meanings, in this inscription, according to Hoftijzer & Jongeling, it means 'on account of decision sons (i.e. adoptive sons)' (1995 I: 427).

[103] Laïla Nehmé does not agree with Zayadine on interpreting *'srt'* as concubine and prefers to stick to the real etymology of prisoner or slave (2003: 213-216, MP16).

on the one hand, and cattle herders and caravan merchants, on the other.[104]

It is probable that Nabataeans had two sorts of writings, Aramaic-Nabataean and Nomadic Bādiah 'Thamudic' and 'Safaitic', which represent the combination of the two forms of Nabataean society. Such a rigid division of society, however, is not a reliable ground for drawing conclusions, for the reciprocal process is more complex. On the other hand, the Nabataean inscriptions known in Bādiah 'Safạitic' inscriptions form, written by members of Arabian tribes, present evidence of the change that occurred in the tribal society once it mixed with the settled Nabataeans. The nomads learned the Nabataean script, and even had new functions or jobs. An individual from the *'mrt* clan had the title *bny'* 'architect', an unusual job for a nomad. In contrast, the Ḥegran social structure is relatively urbanised, judging from their houses of the dead still extant and the absence of long genealogical lineage or tribal affiliation.

The interaction between Nabataeans and the different groups of people residing in, settling in or visiting their lands, on missions, for trade, war or personal interest, was dynamic. In this process, Egyptians, Persians, Hellenes and Romans left their mark on Nabataean culture and society.

Certain features are to be noted regarding family structure, where women were not hidden and did not take a back seat. The finding that women made magnificent and expensive tombs to their family members, male and female, confirms a Nabataean social norm of a legitimate place for elite women. This fact was not limited to the specific elite of a town, but prevailed among women expatriates of a community, as was the case with the Taymānite woman in Ḥegra. Not only did Wašūḥ the Taymānite enjoy the position that Ḥegran women were occupying, but also she was able to proclaim her protection over strangers both male and female, who joined her jiwār, and be recognised by Ḥegran society. Women also enjoyed, as will be seen in detail in the following chapters, legal rights that extended to owning slaves and freeing them. Looking at clients and slaves, however, show the presence of diverse minority groups in Nabataean society, but it is important to realise that these groups can hardly be considered as formative or influential for the majority of the society.[105]

After examining Nabataea from the point of view of its identity and the overall picture of the people who composed its society, in the following chapter, we shall be focusing on one aspect and side of Nabataean society, that is, women: their presentation and perception across areas of exposed power and their visibility.

[104] See the case of the Steppe nomad society in Mongolia which bears similarities to Arabia, in Morgan 1986: 34-37.

[105] Suggested by D. Graf.

Chapter Four

Nabataean Woman

In the preceding chapter, I have illustrated how the Nabataeans demonstrated various cultural facets. Also how they were a complex community on the one hand and a social entity on the other, combining the tribal and the agrarian, the native and the foreigner, and how they accommodated the latter. In this chapter, I will try to establish whether and how Nabataean women attained a particular high status, and to examine the relevant evidence. Starting at the first moment Nabataean women appeared in the historical arena, which was represented by the queen, I will then proceed to describe the condition of women and explain their social status, religious beliefs, and how legal practices affected them.

I. Engendering Power: Women and the Royal House

Public life for women in the ancient world was usually restricted to certain defined religious activities, as priestesses or worshippers, whereas other spheres of public life such as the legal or the political were usually strictly male domains. What the 'public' term can refer to, is the juridical representation and authority of women's activity in the public domain, which includes control over people, resources and property (Linnekin [1990] 1993: 2), and according to Gerda Lerner, control over sexuality (1986: 7, 8). The public domain was always the core for the question of women by which the status of women is sometimes assessed. In this part of the chapter, the issue of woman's participation in public life through political channels will be explored.

There is a common opinion among Greek authors that the decadence of the state is directly associated with the rule of queens, queen-mothers and others, which is a Greek historiographical perspective on 'Oriental' states (Sancisi-Weerdenburg 1987: 33), however, it was not something necessarily specific to Greeks, it was a common attitude among historians to seldom see women as political actors but rather as pawns to be used in the political manoeuvres of men or traded to create and cement male alliances (Collier, 1974: 89). In fact, it is found that in the Nabataean kingdom, when women appear to be influential, or have a presence in the political arena, it was at the peak of the Nabataean state and thus the most prosperous period, in the sense of expansion and inclusion of land and population, as Nabataean power had reached Damascus by the end of the first century BCE (Schmitt-Korte 1990: 131).

A. Queens and Coinage

Nabataean women do not appear clearly until the end of the first century BCE. They continued to exercise a public role until the end of the kingdom in the early part of the second century CE. During this time, inscriptions were written in abundance and references to women in different roles increased. It is interesting, though, that the first significant evidence of woman's status in Nabataean society came in the form of the representation of queens in coinage. A queen's appearance on coins provides one of the most important indicators of the process that women went through until they were to achieve a presence in the public life of the kingdom.

The date of the beginning of Nabataean minting was disputed for a long time (see Meshorer 1975: 5-16; Bowsher 1990: 223-225). Bowsher follows the idea that Aretas II (Ḥāriṯah II) set the stage to expand his realm by minting coins dating to late second century BCE, and that the earliest coins of Nabataean minting that were found in Petra belonged to Aretas II (1990: 223) However, Bowsher does not claim that there was an inscriptional evidence to this belief. However, in the latest trilogy of studies carried out by Karl Schmitt-Korte and Cowell and Price used new methods of x-ray fluorescence analysis on coins, he came to the conclusion that there were no Nabataean coins prior to Ḥāriṯah III (83-71 BCE) (Schmitt-Korte and Cowell, 1989; Schmitt-Korte 1990; Schmitt-Korte and Price 1994), and that it was this king who introduced minting when he seized Damascus in 84 BCE (1990: 131). The coins of Ḥāriṯah III and those of 'Obadah II (62-30 BCE) and Mālik I (60-30 BCE), carried the image of the king's laureated head, or bust, or the king standing. The obverse varies in images of Tyche, Nike, eagle, cornucopiae, and a palm or palm branch. The script started with Greek lettering, in an imitation of the Seleucid coins during Ḥāriṯah III's time, then became Nabataean by the time of 'Obadah II. Bronze and silver coins were struck, and one incidence of a lead coin has been found.

Queens appeared for the first time on the coins of 'Obadah III (30-9 BCE), who was, according to Meshorer and Schmitt-Korte, the fourth king to strike coins, in 29/28 BCE (Meshorer 1975: 89, No. 20) and the fifth king, according to Bowsher. A woman's bust that is probably the queen's appeared next to the king on the obverse of silver coins until 25/24 BCE. Later in 18/17 BCE, she appeared on the reverse, standing and wearing a long mantle and a girdle, and raising the right hand with palm extended. That continued until 10/9 BCE (Meshorer 1975: No. 31-39). In 16 BCE, 'Obadah struck a unique type of coin, which Schmitt-Korte calls the 'Dushara type', because it has the name and invocation of the god, Dushara, and is inscribed *brkt dwšr'* 'benedictions from Dushara'. On its reverse, it carries the first depiction of a woman whom we are more certain it was for the queen. It is, however, anonymous (1990: 110). The following year, a coin was minted bearing the bust of a queen veiled on the whole reverse side of the coin, with only the name of the king *'bdt mlk'*, 'Obadah the king (ibid. 1990: 110).

In summary, during the reign of 'Obadah III the queen appears on coins anonymously. Only the king's name appears in the three forms of *'bdt mlk' mlk nbṭw*, *'bdt mlk nbṭw* and *'bdt*. In the year of Sullay, 9 BCE, we do not find any queen on the hastily struck coins. The first coins that Ḥāriṯah IV struck were very interesting, for he struck more than one form in one year, all in silver. From Meshorer's list three types can be distinguished:

1. The first type (Meshorer 1975: No. 47, 47a) is very peculiar and stands out because it has the bust of a woman, who is probably the queen, in front of Ḥāriṯah's bust on the obverse, showing her veiled (Plate XXVII). The reverse shows the king alone diademed. Although she has here a remarkable appearance, similar to that of 'Obadah's Dushara type coin, the queen is still anonymous.

2. The second (Meshorer 1975: No. 46) shows the jugate bust of Ḥāriṯah and a woman, who is probably the queen, both diademed on the obverse, and an eagle standing on the reverse, with an inscription referring to the king only, by his common title *ḥrtt mlk' mlk nbṭw*. In this type, the queen is still anonymous, and no different from the 'Obadah coin No. 20.

3. The third type is the turning point as far as reference to queens is concerned, for it is the first to bear a name. On the obverse Ḥāriṯah is shown alone diademed, while the queen occupies the reverse by herself, with her name and title *hldw mlkt nbṭw*, 'Queen of Nabataeans' (see plate XXIX), she looks similar to the previous anonymous coins. This coin bears also the first reference to Ḥāriṯah's official Nabataean title, *rḥm 'mh*, 'lover of his people' (Meshorer 1975: No. 48 ff.).

Although all three types appear in the first year of Ḥāriṯah IV's reign, one might have expected this series of coins to continue. Coins were, however, not struck uniformly. This is evident from the different types of legends and inscriptions on coins of the same year and later. From information on other coins published by Schmitt-Korte (1990: No. 52-57) the full title of Ḥāriṯah does not appear on coins struck in 8, 6, and 5 BCE. Similarly, the queen's name disappears from these coins until 4 BCE. This shows an inconsistency in official titles, at least on coins, or could indicate an instability in his early years as a conflict or co-existence occurred between Ḥāriṯah and Sullay (Syllaeus) who was executed in 6 BCE.

This interesting moment of history needs closer scrutiny, for this turning point could not have happened automatically. There must have been some factors allowing the change, supporting it and encouraging it. For that reason, this section will focus upon describing the material available in order to be able to analyse it in the final chapter.

To describe the evidence, the following section will deal with the dynastic genealogy, names of the queens, their titles and a description of their appearance.

B. Genealogy[106]

Twelve 'genealogical' pieces of evidence are so far available. They are inscriptions and a papyrus that mention the Nabataean royal house and together form the basis for a genealogical tree.[107]

It appears that there are two separate trees, but only one inscription related to the first tree. It refers to *'bdt br ḥrtt*, 'Obadah son of Ḥāriṯah[108] and dates from 96/95 BCE. The kings mentioned are identified as Ḥāriṯah II (120/ 110-96 BCE) and 'Obadah I (96-85 BCE) (Starcky 1955: 89-90; Wenning 1987: 202; 1994: 38). Then there is the second branch which starts with Ḥāriṯah IV (9BCE-40CE), *ḥrtt mlk nbṭw rḥm 'mh* 'King of the Nabataeans, Lover of his People'. He appears on coins and in inscriptions.[109]

Ḥāriṯah IV appears in 18 CE with a queen called Hājar. She is suggested by Starcky to be his mother (1971: 157). No other reference to her is found anywhere else. He had a wife called Ḫuld,[110] suspected to be the daughter of 'Obadah (Zayadine 1999: 52). She is portrayed on Ḥāriṯah coins from the first year of his rule until 15 CE. She appears also in inscriptions as *ḫldw 'tth mlkt nbṭw*, 'his wife, Queen of Nabataeans' (CIS, II, 158; Savignac 1937: No. 1). Ḥāriṯah IV's second wife was Šaqīlah, who appears on coins from 16 until 39 CE as Queen of the Nabataeans. On inscriptions she appears as Queen of the Nabataeans and as his sister *'ḫth mlkt nbṭw* (CIS, II, 354; Khairy 1981: 22).

[106] See Nabataean royal genealogy tree in plate V.

[107] CIS, II,158; CIS, II, 351; CIS, II,354; Dalman 1912: No. 92 (RES 1434); Savignac 1933: No.1; Savignac 1937: 405, No.1; Negev 1961: No. 1; Yadin 1963: 230: doc.2 (updated and elaborated in Yadin 2002, doc 2); Starcky & Strugnell 1966: 244, No. 2; Starcky 1971: 151-59; Milik & Starcky 1975: 112-115; Khairy 1981: 22 (Milik commentary p. 25); Wenning 1994.

[108] I will follow an Arabic transcription of the Nabataean proper names.

[109] CIS, II, 158: 5 CE; CIS, II, 354: 20 CE; Khairy: 25 or 35 CE; RES 1434: 71-106 CE; Yadin 1963; 2002: 99 CE; Savignac 1937; Starcky 1971.

[110] This will be discussed in full later.

Ḥāriṯah IV had at least eight children,[111] *mlkw*, *'bdt*, *rb'l*, *pṣ'l*, *š'dt*, *hgrw*,[112] gmlt, and šqylt (Khairy, CIS, II, 354) (Mālik, 'Obadah, Rab'el, Faṣīl, Sa'īdah, Hājar, Jamīlah and Šaqīlah). Three of the children appear together in an inscription from 'Abda: 'Obadah, Faṣīl and Sa'īdah (Negev 1961: No. 1). The short list of Ḥāriṯah's children may signify a certain unity between these three children, such as being full brothers and sisters of the same mother, their mother to be either Queen Ḫuld or Šaqīlah, or that they were the three eldest of the eight children. The evidence of coins, which shows that a commemoration at Faṣīl's birthday was made in Ḥāriṯah's fifth year (4/5 BCE) (Meshorer 1975: 45-49, nos. 60-64A; Schmitt-Korte & Price 1994: 104) shows that these children were probably the eldest of Ḫuld's children. Worthy of noting in this regard is the fact that the commemoration of the first born was for a girl named Faṣīl,[113] who was also given the title of malikah.[114] Therefore, knowing that Mālik succeeded Ḥāriṯah to the throne might suggest that 'Obadah, the eldest son, had died earlier. Some children are given specific titles, as in *šqylt brt ḥrtt*, who is called *'ḥt mnkw*, Manku's sister. A possible explanation is that among the sisters, there was 'full' and a 'half' sisterhood, which needed to be specified in this way. Jamīlah on the other hand was given the title *mlkt nbṭw*. What is known about Hājar is that she has a son named after his grandfather Ḥāriṯah,[115] who is, remarkably, referred to in his matrilinear lineage.

The third generation starts with *mnkw*,[116] who had five children: *gmlt*, *hgrw*, *š'wdt*, *rb'l*, and *qšm'l* (Savignac 1933; Yadin 1963; 2002). Rab'el carries his royal title, *mlk nbṭw dy 'ḥyy wšyzb 'mh*, (who brings life and deliverance to his people). The three daughters were given the royal titles *'ḫth mlkt nbṭw* (His sister Queen of Nabatu). The Wādī Ramm inscription mentions *qšm'l*, *š'wdt*, Qāsim'el and Sa'īdah, without titles (Savignac 1933). From this generation comes the above mentioned Ḥāriṯah s. of Hājar d. of Ḥāriṯah *rḥm 'mh* (Khairy). It is interesting to note the matrilinear reference to the female royal children. Both genealogies were recognised: the patrilinear and matrilinear.

The fourth generation consists of Rab'el's children who number either four or five: 'Obadah (Yadin 1963; 2002: doc 2), Ḥāriṯah, Mālik, a daughter or son whose name starts with *š* (Savignac 1933), possibly *šqylt* or *š'wdt*, and Ḫuld, whose relation is not very clear in the eroded inscription. Yadin, missing Ḥāriṯah, considers 'Obadah to be the 'Crown Prince' who did not rule (1963; 2002: doc 2). In rereading RES 1434, J.W. Eadie suggests another crown prince, Mālik. He considers him to have succeeded his father Rab'el for at least a year. An inscription from Ḥegra refers to his first year reign (CIS 218) (1985: 412-413). To this generation also belongs Qāsim, s. of Sa'īdah d. of Mālik s. of Ḥāriṯah *rḥm 'mh* (RES 1434). Here again the matrilinear genealogy is noted. To the fifth generation belongs only Qāsim'el s. of Qāsim s. of Sa'īdah d. of Mālik s. of Ḥāriṯah *rḥm 'mh* (RES 1434).

C. *List of the Nabataean Queens*

1. *Hgrw (Hājar) I*

An inscription of Wādī Mūsā, edited by Starcky, presents a queen called Hājar in relation to Ḥāriṯah and Mālik. It dates from the 18th year of Ḥāriṯah reign.[117] The problem of this text is that Hājar does not appear in the early genealogies. The Hājars known are: the daughter of Ḥāriṯah IV and mother of a Ḥāriṯah (who was not a ruler's spouse) (CIS, II, 354). The second is Hājar, Rab'el's second wife and daughter of Mālik (RES 1434).

Ḥāriṯahs who are possible candidates for this inscription are the third and fourth. Starcky elaborates on the hypothesis of this being Ḥāriṯah III, who is associated with Mālik I, probably his son, and that this inscription may suggest co-regency about 67 BCE, for it would be the 18th year since he assumed the throne in 85 BCE. Starcky argues, however, for a second hypothesis, for Ḥāriṯah IV. He supports the account by Josephus about Aeneas, who changed his name to Aretas (Ḥāriṯah) when he claimed the throne. He suggested that Ḥāriṯah was not 'Obadah's son. He had, however, a right to the throne by being partially royalty, probably through his mother, who is the one mentioned in this inscription, Hājar daughter of Mālik I (1971: 157). She was called Queen of Nabaṭū until the date of this inscription, the 18th year of Ḥāriṯah's reign, i.e. 8/9 CE. There is no reference to this queen elsewhere so far, either in other inscriptions, or in coins. It is possible to assume that it was this queen who was depicted on the first coin to be struck by Ḥāriṯah, which shows the queen, veiled, dominating the foreground of the obverse (Meshorer 1975: No. 47, 47a) (plate XXVII), which will be discussed below.

---

[111] Dijkstra counts six children only(1995: 59): *mlkw*, *'bdt*, *rb'l*, *pṣ'l*, *š'dt*, and *hgrw*.

[112] Dijkstra assumed she was the daughter of Mālik, 1995: 58.

[113] Faṣīl (*pṣ'l*) appears as a male name in the Idumaean house of Herod. The son of the Arabian (Nabataean) princess, Cypros, is known under this name (Josephus Ant. xiv. 121). Today it is a very common name in modern Arabic, in the male form of Fayṣal (Khairy 1981: 23).

[114] See the inscriptions found in al-Habis at Raqamū-Petra (Milik & Starcky 1975: 1. a,b,c).

[115] Or hn'ktbs'lw (see Milik 1981: 25-6).

[116] This is the name of Mālik at it appears in some inscriptions and coins. Possibly, it is the original one or that there was a fluctuation between the two names.

[117]
1- [*'lh q]ṣry' dy bnh*
2- [... *b]r dydwrs rb pršy'*
3- [..] *'l ḥyy ḥrtt*
4- [*mlk nb]ṭw whgrw mlkt'*
5- [....]*mnkw mlk nbṭw*
6- [...]*šh wdy bnwhy*
7- [*byrḥ šb]ṭ šnt 18* (Starcky 1971: 157).

2. *Ḫldw* (Ḫuld)[118] *(9 BCE-15 CE)*

Ḫuld was mentioned in two inscriptions, one from Ḫirbet Tannur (Savignac 1937: No. 1) and one from Puteoli in Italy (CIS, II, 158). In both inscriptions, she is referred to as Queen of the Nabataeans and wife of Ḥāriṯah (*'tth*), the only queen referred to as 'the wife'. There is no reference to the title 'sister' of the king in the inscriptions. Ḫuld was a strong queen. I believe she is the one who forced her name to be inscribed on coins, linking it with Isis (Parlasca 1998), and also managed to save the throne for herself, putting the Queen Mother aside, if Starcky's hypothesis were to prove true.

It is probable that Ḥāriṯah was married to her prior to 9 BCE. She could also be related to the royal house. Zayadine supports this and suggests her to be 'Obadah III's daughter (1999: 52). This could have been the way by which Ḥāriṯah claimed his right to the throne, and enabled her to have the right to implement new rules, which were to be the guidelines for the queen's privilege in the Nabataean household. Zayadine adds to Ḫuld's role and suggests that it was she who commanded the Khaznah to be carved in memory of her divine ancestor, 'Obadah I, portraying herself in the Ptolemaic queens' image as Isis-Tyche, the relief found on the facade of Khaznah (1999: 52).

Earlier studies on the Khaznah's iconography showed that the Khaznah was a heroon (temple for the cult of Isis) as much as it was a funerary monument of a large scale (see Wright 1962; 1973; Lyttleton 1990: 19-29). Margaret Lyttelton, contrary to Zayadine's, believes that the Khaznah is the tomb of King Ḥāriṯah III (1990: 23). One could still ask what is the proof for Ḥāriṯah III's burial there? Or what is the reason behind Ḫuld commemorating her great-great-grandfather with such an edifice? In addition, if this monument is dated from the mid-first century BCE (ibid.), then she could not have had anything to do with building it. It is unlikely that it was made for a lesser reason, but it still needs stronger evidence. Taking Lyttelton's view about the role of the monument into consideration, I find that the point of Zayadine should be taken further once more. It has been established that the image of Isis-Tyche identifies with the Ptolemaic queens (Lyttelton: 1990: 21-22; Zayadine 1999: 52) (see plate XXXVII). Regardless of the disagreement about which Nabataean queen is represented in that monument, it is possible to accept, however, that the image of Isis making an icon of the queen. It seems that she represented the qualities of Isis synchronised probably in one of the major Nabataean goddesses.

Ḫuld was the first queen to appear on coins by name in the first year of Ḥāriṯah's reign 9/8 BCE, in joint busts (Meshorer No. 48). The titles appear as follows: obverse *ḥrtt mlk nbṭw rḥm 'mh*, reverse *ḫldw mlkt nbṭw*. From then onward she appears in almost all Ḥāriṯah's coins until 15 CE.

One must seek a reason for Ḫuld's disappearance after 15 CE. The only possibilities are either that Ḥāriṯah repudiated her, or that she died before 16 CE, the date of the commemorative coins of Ḥāriṯah's union with Šaqīlah (Schmitt-Korte 1990: 130). The same situation occurs about the same time in the reign of Rab'el II, who also married two wives, one after the other, without evidence to explain whether the first one died or was repudiated, or a second was taken later.

3. *Šqylt* (Šaqīlah) I *(16-40 CE)*

Šaqīlah's name could be derived from the root meaning 'weigh out' (Hoftijzer & Jongeling 1995 II: 1187) which is transcribed as Šaqīlah. Her name, however, have possibly been derived from the goddess Allāt means, 'who longs for Allāt'. It could be also that the original form was as ŠawqīLāt. It is more probable that the second possibility was the case. Knowing the traditional tendencies in choosing proper names affiliated to gods or goddesses, it is possible that her name is derived from an affiliation with Allāt. Abbreviation, though, over the years has doubtless developed the name into the form of Šaqīlah.

She was Ḥāriṯah's second wife, judging from the way she appears on coins next to him in the same fashion that Ḫuld used to. She bears the queen's title mlkt in addition to the title *'ḫth*, 'his sister',[119] for the first time, though not on coins. She is mentioned twice in inscriptions (CIS, II, 354; Khairy), from al-Numayr and Wādī Mūsā. In both, she is referred to as Queen of the Nabaṭū and sister of the King.

Coins commemorate Šaqīlah joining the royal family, or her marriage to Ḥāriṯah, as suggested by Meshorer (1975: 57) and affirmed by Schmitt-Korte. The latter solved the enigma of the X-sign on bronze coins introduced after Ḥāriṯah and Šaqīlah's marriage. He believes that this sign marks the year four of Queen Šaqīlah's joining the throne and that was the year of the currency reform, when the new silver and bronze coins were altered (1990: 130). Šaqīlah appears on coins of the year 24 of Ḥāriṯah's reign (16CE) that shows the queen standing with raised hand, and only her name inscribed, *šqylt* (Meshorer 1975: Nos. 112-121; Schmitt-Korte 1990: Nos. 66, 77-81; Hašim 1996: No. 63).[120] It is found in the bronze collections studied by Schmitt-Korte (1990: Nos. 96ff.) and Hašim (1996: Nos.

[118] Her name is found in this form, in a Bādiah 'Safaitic' inscription from the eastern Jordan Desert: *ldb bn 'ṣm tl wwjm 'l ḫld 'ḫth mtt trḥt w'bs wrġmt mn mmt*, 'by Ḍabb s. of 'Āṣim of the tribe of Taim. And he laid a stone on the tomb of Ḫuld, his sister. She died, she was grieved for, and he frowned, and she was reluctant against death'. Enno Littmann comments on this inscription by saying that 'Khuld is undoubtedly the Nabataean Khuldu' (in Harding 1952: No. 522). It is also found in the famous Minaean inscription of the 'Minaean wives, formerly, the Hierodulentisten, from *wg'* (al-Said 1995: 199, 213).

[119] The question of sister-wife will be discussed later.

[120] The commemorative coin which can be traced now to 16 CE depicts the statue of the new queen with a royal wreath, the only issue of this type in the whole numismatic history of the Nabataeans (Schmitt-Korte 1990: 130).

63-80). She appears on silver coins from 17 CE onwards with the title *šqylt mlkt nbṭw* (Meshorer 1975: Nos. 96-111; Schmitt-Korte 1990: No.70-76). Queen Šaqīlah appears on two inscriptions: one dated 20 CE (CIS, II, 354), and the other dated 25 or 35 (Khairy 1981).

4. *Šqylt* (Šaqīlah) II *(40-76 CE)*[121]

The rule of Mālik II (40-70 CE) starts with a queen with the same name as the previous queen's name, who was probably Šaqīlah's daughter. Šaqīlah II is known to have outlived her husband and ruled with her son, Rab'el II (71-106CE) for six more years, which means a span of over thirty-six years in all. Assuming she was about 13-15 years of age when she got married, then by the end of her rule, in 76 CE, she was about 49-51 years old An indication of age expectancy can be useful in future studies on demography.

Šaqīlah II appears on coins, for the first time in 40/41 CE, the first year of the reign of Mālik II (Meshorer 1975: No. 123 ff.; Schmitt-Korte 1990: No. 82)(see plate XXIX). It was not until 64/65 CE in a single bronze coin that she appears again with her husband/brother in jugate heads on the obverse (Meshorer 1975: No. 140). It has been suggested that there was a political and economic decline under Mālik's reign especially in the last seven years of his reign (Meshorer 1975: 67-68). She is the only queen to bear the title *'m mlk'* 'mother of the King' during the reign of her son, Rab'el II. Šaqīlah appears to be a strong queen, who left her name on Nabataean remains. After ruling beside her husband/brother Mālik for thirty years, as a widow she assumed the throne beside her son Rab'el as regent.

The coins refer to her from the first year of her son's reign as 'Šaqīlah his mother, Queen of the Nabataeans' *šqylt 'mh mlkt nbṭw*, until the year 6 of Rab'el (Meshorer 1975: Nos. 142-146; Schmitt-Korte 1990: no 84; Hašim 1996: Nos. 85-87). During her reign, as a queen consort, she was depicted on coins alone on the reverse until the year 75/76 CE (Meshorer 1975: Nos. 123-139,142-145), and once in a jugate portrait with Rab'el (Meshorer 1975: No.146).

A magnificent tomb, 20 metres in height, which occupies a prominent place in Raqamū-Petra at the western facade of the Ḫubṯa cliff, bears a short inscription with the title of Šaqīlah's brother-vezir (tomb 813, of Hegr type, see plate XXV and map of Raqamū-Petra, map III) (Zayadine 1974: 142, 144). It reads *'nyšw 'ḥ šqylt br ..* "Unays brother of Šaqīlah, son of ... '(CIS, II, 351). Strabo relates that 'the King has as administrator one of his companions, who is called brother' (16:4:21). Although the inscription is not clear about the identity of Šaqīlah, whether she was the first or the second queen, or just another Šaqīlah, it is possible to eliminate some possibilities. If this was a blood brother of Šaqīlah first or second we would have found his name in one of the royal genealogy lists discussed earlier, The sentence showed that Šaqīlah was an important woman, much important than 'Unays, he was identified by associating himself with her. Therefore, she cannot be an ordinary Šaqīlah; it should be an important figure. Since he is not referring to a blood sister, and this woman is an important figure in the Nabataean society, then he would be the brother in the political sense known in the Nabataean system; a Vezir. By comparing the status of the two Šaqīlahs in the Nabataean known history, it is more probable that he was the Vezir and Administrator of Šaqīlah II during the time when she became the effective ruling monarch between 71-76 CE during the minority of her son Rab'el II. He was probably King Mālik's vizier who continued in position under the regency of his widow.

Šaqīlah's name appears in two inscriptions. The first dated from 25 or 35 CE, i.e. before her reign with Mālik. She is referred to in the genealogy of the royal family in the inscription from Wādī Mūsā, as the sister of Mankū (Khairy 1981: 22). The second inscription, undated, found on a statue of Ḥāriṯah IV in Qaṣr Bint Far'un,[122] refers to her and to Mālik as the two kings, (*'l ḥyy* mlkw [*wšqyl*]*t mlky nb*[*ṭw*]), i.e. king and queen, of the Nabataeans (Starcky & Strugnell 1966: 244 No.2).

5. *Gmlt* (Jamīlah) *(76-101 CE)*

Queen Jamīlah, daughter of Šaqīlah and Mālik, was the first wife of Rab'el II (71-106 CE) and his sister, who reigned with him from 76 until 102 CE (Meshorer 1975: 40). Her name on coins appears without titles. She appears on the al-Ḫubṯa inscription (RES 1434) and in the Babatha papyri (Yadin 1963; 2002: doc 2). In both, her name is followed by that of Hājar, as they are both sisters of Rab'el and the Nabataean queens.

6. *Hgrw* (Hājar) II *(102-106 CE)*

Hājar was the second wife of Rab'el II and his sister, who reigned with him from 102 CE (Meshorer 1975: 41) until the Romans annexed the state in 106 CE. She appears on coins in a similar way to Jamīlah, without titles. She appears in the same two inscriptions with her sister Jamīlah, referred to in the same way (RES 1434; Yadin 1963; 2002: doc 2).

7. *Others*

There are also Faṣīl d. of Ḥāriṯah IV (Yadin 1962: 239; Milik & Starcky 1975: 112-115; Khairy 1981: 19-26) and Sa'īdah, *š'dt*, 'the queen' and sister of Rab'el (RES 1434), and others.

Two other remarkable royal women were those known from Josephus' account, since both of them were married

[121] See the Epilogue.

[122] This inscription was decisive in dating the temple of Qaṣr al-Bint (Bint Far'un) (Parr 1967-8: 5-6).

into the royal house of Judaea. The first, Cypros, perhaps a Nabataean, married to Antipater, the Idumaean who was an adviser and friend of Hyrcanus II, the Hasmonean (63-40 BCE). He was also a friend of the Nabataeans. His closeness to the Nabataean king may have allowed him to be tied to King Ḥāriṯah III by marrying Cypros, who bore him Herod (40-4 BCE) and other children (Salome, Phasaelos) (Jos. Ant. XIV: 121). This constituted, perhaps, an alliance between the Idumaean house and the Nabataeans. Cypros was referred to as a woman from a very prominent Arab family[123] and assumed to belong to the Nabataeans since reference to Arabs interchanged with Nabataeans in Josephus accounts. One may wonder, however, why is it, had she been a Nabataean princess that no reference was made to her connection with the Nabataean kings. There are, though, many references in the Antiquities of Josephus to the communication of the royal women in both houses. Remarkably, some Nabataean names are found in the Idumaean royal family genealogy, such as the name of Herod's brother and Cypros's son *pṣ'l* (in nab a girl's name), transcribed into Phasaelos (Ant. XIV: 121; Milik & Starcky 1975: 114), Moreover, Herod was the son of an Idumaean father, which render him, ironically, Arab (Nehmé and Villeneuve 1999: 138).

The second royal woman, not known by name, was the daughter of Ḥāriṯah IV, who married Herod Antipas, the Tetrarch (4 BCE-39 CE), grand-son of Antipater. The marriage alliance was repeated, but it did not prevent wars. Josephus is the only source referring to the ill-fated marriage of Ḥāriṯah's daughter. She found herself a deserted and unwanted wife when Herod, her husband, s. of Herod the Great, fell in love with his sister-in-law and niece, Herodias. He decided to marry her in spite of his brother still being alive. When the Nabataean royal wife found out, she decided to escape to Nabataea, and asked Herod for an escort to a castle on the borders, known as Machaerus (Maqawir today, see plate XXXI) from where she fled with the help of her father's governors, probably during the time of the governors 'Abd'abdah and his father Itaybel (CIS, II, 196).[124] When she arrived in Raqamū-Petra, Ḥāriṯah, although Josephus says he declared war, did not in fact do so until ten years later, which minimises any direct connection between the two incidents. Since Herod II ruled between 4 BCE and 39 CE, he was a contemporary to Ḥāriṯah during his whole reign. This does not help in finding out when he was married to Ḥāriṯah's daughter. And it is left to speculation to know whether she bore him any children, but it seems that this was one of the aims of such diplomatic alignments. Evidence concerning her identity is to be found among the four daughters that are known of attributed to Ḥāriṯah: Faṣīl, Sa'īdah, Hājar or Šaqīlah. In the 'Abda inscription (Negev 1961) that refers to the eldest three children of Ḥāriṯah two daughters are encountered: Faṣīl and Sa'īdah. It is most probable that the bride was one of these two. Although Starcky suggested Sa'īdah to be the one, he did not present an argument (1966: Col 914). What one would argue is that the daughter in mind was Faṣīl. The care with which the inscriptions of Faṣīl were inscribed and preserved in a high place in al-Ḥābis in Raqamū-Petra (see the details in Milik & Starcky 1975: 112) would make it more probable that they were made for their queen who had left her court in Jerusalem to save her dignity as a Nabataean queen.

The reference, however, to the beginning of war, which coincided with Tiberius' death[125] is helpful. If Tiberius died in 37 CE, Ḥāriṯah's daughter fled Jerusalem around 27 CE. If she was married for a few years, then it is expected that her age will be about twenty years. In this case, it would not have been possible that she was the daughter of Queen Šaqīlah who reigned from 16 CE. It would be more likely that she was Ḫuld's daughter. One may wonder, in this event, how much of her mother's character, charisma and ambition was in her, and how far Ḫuld played a role in marrying her to the Judaean king. Unless the princess was married for over ten years, it would be improbable that Ḫuld was alive to play any part in it. Nonetheless, Ḫuld must have been aware of the importance of raising daughters so that they would be fit for their future role in a foreign court, but would not lose their loyalty to their mother land (for a general view on such alliances see Parsons 1994: 75).

It is important to add a note on Sullay's attempt to marry Herod I's sister, Salome.[126] This incident dates to the time of Cypros, who was the mother of both Herod and Salome. It is possible that Cypros was a facilitating factor, in addition to the diplomatic relationships that were intensified by the end of the first century BCE and the need of the Nabataeans to maintain relationships at a time when the Romans were trying to swallow what remained of Syria. Sullay's attempt at marriage did not, however, succeed because of the religious difference, as stated by Josephus. Sullay refused to convert to Judaism, for fear he would be stoned by his people. His offer of marriage was declined.[127] The surprise with which Sullay received this condition shows that this type of union had not been considered before. That is, Nabataean men marrying Jewish women. It is noted in this regard, that Nabataeans royal men, especially kings, did not marry from the Herodian house, but rather they

[123] 'From among whom he took a wife of a distinguished Arab family, named Cypros (variant, Cypris); and by her he had four sons, Phasael, Herod, who later became king, Joseph and Pheroras, and a daughter, Salome' (Josephus Ant. xiv: 121).

[124] See translation in Healey 1993b: 247-48.

[125] After defeating Herod, the Romans decided to invade Raqamū-Petra. They did not, however, carry out the campaign after the news had reached them of the death of Augustus Tiberius in 37 CE (Jos. Ant. XVIII: 109-125).

[126] Found in the incidents of the year 10 BCE or earlier (Jos. JW I: 184-487).

[127] 'But when they asked Syllaeus to be initiated into the customs of the Jews before the wedding – otherwise, they said, marriage would be impossible – he would not submit to this but took his departure, saying that if he did submit, he would be stoned to death by the Arabs' (Jos. Ant. XVI: 220-226).

gave their daughters in marriage to the Edumaeans. It is possible to say with confidence that Nabataean kings only married within the royal family. Sullay was about to break this rule by marrying Salome, but finding out the price of such a bond, he refused.[128]

In this respect, it is intriguing to ask what the situation of the Nabataean royal women was. Were they also compelled to convert, or were women exempted from that? I would take the second position, supported by the biblical evidence of Jewish kings marrying with foreigners who keep their gods and goddesses. Most famous of all, was King Solomon with his Phoenician (Sidonian) and Canaanite (Moabite, Ammonite, Edomite) wives (1 Kings 11: 1). Furthermore, it is unlikely that Ḥāriṯah, the proud king of Nabaṭū, would allow his daughter to abandon Dushara and the other gods and goddesses of her own people. Furthermore, the fact that these marriages were operating with both failure and success is important in looking at the role that royal women played in these alignments. The fact that the Nabataeans gave their women in marriage abroad, but did not take foreign wives, shows how they relied on the power that the Nabataean royal women could generate even in a foreign context. Even if Josephus did not tell enough about Cypros and Ḥāriṯah's daughter's activities in the Jerusalem court, one cannot ignore the fact that Cypros' son, Herod, was one of the major Judaean kings, who ruled for a long time and had a strong grasp on his state (see Richardson 1996). Being the mother of a king at this level of power and strength would have generated a great deal of authority on her part. This is probably shown in the fortress Herod built to honour her near Jericho, and his dedications to Nabataean temples and gods especially in Sī' in Ḥawrān (Richardson 1996: 4). Similarly the fact that Ḥāriṯah's daughter lived in Jerusalem during the peak years of the Nabataean glory must have had an effect on the attitude in the court towards her, and must have generated respect. In this regard, the incident of Herod's relationship with Herodias can better be explained in the context of Ḥāriṯah's daughter becoming so powerful that Herod felt it was about time to diminish that danger, accepting her request to move to Machaerus castle. It is curious, though that she did not initiate some kind of a vengeance attempt from there, but instead withdrew to her father's domain.

Even though the historical record does not tell a lot about these women and their activities, it is likely that their closeness to power in both courts formed their ambitions or directed their lives towards making a political mark.[129]

[128] It is possible that Sullay did not consider marrying Salome as breaking the rules. Since Jewish religious identity is inherited through the matrilinear side, he might have regarded her as half Nabataean from her mother's side, which in this case means she was not a complete Jew.

[129] For similar instances in the history of royal marriages and the role that royal women play and develop, see Parsons 1994: 63ff.

D. Titles

1. mlkt

The title *malikah* or *šarratu* was used only for goddesses such as Innana-Ashtarte or 'Anat in the Babylonian and Syrian records. *Šarratu* was also used of the queens of the Arabs in the Assyrian records (Oppenheim 1964: 104; Hoftijzer & Jongeling 1995 II: 639), a significant specification that shows the link between the two roles. *Mlkt*, however, is used in Arabia to designate the female consort of a *mlk*, who is called 'king' in English. It has commonly been accepted that the term that expresses the absolute hereditary ruler is *mlk*, or *šarru* in Semitic languages, and this has been translated conveniently as 'king'. This word, however, is problematic. 'King' is found originally in Anglo-Saxon *cyng* and *cing* and means 'chief man of a tribe', literally, 'one of noble kin'. He was usually elected or selected, and then became a sovereign who ruled with hereditary rights. This does not necessarily cover or mirror the meaning of *mlk*. According to Lisān, *malaka* (v.) means 'to own'. As a noun the word *malik* means 'he who owns people and things', i.e. a property of God. Therefore, a *malik* (n.) is he who owns everything. Usually 'owning' is coercive (Lisān: *mlk*). And *mlkt* is similarly problematic, translating it to queen is too simplistic. Though this translation is commonly accepted, it also needs challenging. There is a need to specify whether *malikah* is a consort in marriage, or sisterhood, and whether it includes power as well. In other words, it is imperative to know whether it is possible to consider the female version of the title as the female of the absolute ruler with all his entitlements. This is an open question. But for the present study, it is suffice to raise awareness of the problem.

It is important to mention that, Nabataean queens were not the first Arab queens known in history. A phenomenal period of Arab queens who ruled northern Arabia at Dumat al-Jandal *Adumatū* for two centuries 8-7th BCE was the first precedence, in addition to the famous Queen of Sheba as well, however, no historical evidence is found in south or northern Arabia to document her existence as yet. A detailed discussion of this background would be a digression here and I would reserve it to an independent study.

In Nabataean, the title *mlkt* appears for the first time, as seen above, with Queen Ḫuld, who was called *mlkt nbṭw* on coins and later in inscriptions in Ḥāriṯah's first year 9/8 BCE. This title appears with the Nabataean women who appear next to the Nabataean kings on coins, who are taken as their wives, Ḫuld, Šaqīlah I, Šaqīlah II. The first and second wives of Rab'el and his sisters, Jamīlah and Hājar, were not given the title malikah. Other royal women, were given the same title in addition to the title 'sister of Mālik', such as Faṣīl and Jamīlah ds. of Ḥāriṯah IV were given the title *mlkt nbṭw*, and Sa'īdah d. of Mālik. It is noted, however, that a few royal women were not given the title, such as Sa'īdah and Hājar ds. of Ḥāriṯah and Ḫuld? d. of Rab'el. For Meshorer, the title malikah seems to be given to the members of the Nabataean royal house (1975: 79). But the question will remain whether giving titles to some royal women and not others signifies a difference in ranking, meaning more than we understand from the word ('Ajloony 2003: 158-159), or if it is just used at random.

It is significant that the male royal members were not given a similar title, but were known by their first names. The situation of having one word to mean a queen and a princess is confusing and impractical. On the one hand, one would ask why this title which is the feminine version of mlk was used, and on the other, why was it that many of the female members of the family bore it even when they did not marry a king. And lastly, why were the male members not given any sort of title, at least in the inscriptions?[130] For the purpose of this study, however, I shall regard mlkt as meaning 'female member of royal family' not merely 'queen'.

2. *Sister of the King, 'ḫt mlk'*

The Nabataean queens were also given the title *'ḫt* mlk', 'sister of the king', an epithet that has aroused much interest. Although it was assumed that the Nabataean consorts of kings were called 'sisters' as a general epithet, scrutiny of the coins and inscriptions shows that this title was not given to all queens or royal women.

The *'ḫt* title appears for the first time with Queen Šaqīlah I in inscriptions from Wādī Mūsā and al-Numayr (Khairy 1981; CIS,II,354). This title does not appear on coins until the time of the following queen, Šaqīlah II, during the reign of Mālik II (40-70 CE), in 40/41 CE, the first year of his reign (Meshorer 1975: No. 123 ff.; Khairy 1981; Schmitt-Korte 1990: No. 82). Jamīlah, Hājar and Sa'īdah, the daughters of Mālik II and wives of Rabe'el, were called sisters of Rab'el II in addition to having the title of mlkt (Yadin 1963; Savignac 1933).

The main question that this title raises is: did the Nabataean kings marry their blood sisters? This will be addressed in two ways. Firstly, there will be a discussion of the facts of this kind of marriage, and then an analysis will follow.

In the case of Šaqīlah I, and similarly of Ḥāriṯah, the genealogical tree (see plate V), does not provide her father's name to tell of whether she was Ḥāriṯah's blood sister. Šaqīlah II is described as the sister of Mālik and she is, according to genealogy (Khairy 1981), also the queen of the Nabataeans and the mother of the king. Jamīlah and Hājar, who were the consorts of Rab'el respectively, appear to be also his sisters, ds. of king Mālik. Although it is possible to argue that the kings married women with the same names as their sisters, or that the consorts changed their names into dynastic names when married with kings, as it is known from Ḥāriṯah IV's changing name from Aeneas. The question would remain, why did these queens choose dynastic names that happened to be the same as those of their sisters-in-law? It is unlikely that such a coincidence repeats three times. It is more probable that they were their blood sisters.

With regard to the suggestion that the Nabataean dynasty of Ḥāriṯah IV started after a breach which established a new branch of the Nabataean royal house, and in relation to the opinion that there was an attempt to create a certain sanctity around the Nabataean house, especially through the female line (al-Fassi: forthcoming/b), it seems appropriate, in the framework of the era of Alexandria and Egyptian culture and mysticism, to accept that they then could have adopted Egyptian tradition, revived by the Ptolemies, of incestuous marriage (Pomeroy 1975, 1992: 123)[131] as an assertion to the sacredness of the Nabataean blood. Incest marriage is much older and was also traced to the pre-Aryan social system, based on a belief that all the pre-Aryans originally worshipped the great fertility goddess of Asia and the companion god who was both her son and consort. W.W. Tarn held the view that in fact the custom of marriage of a full brother and sister belonged to that religion of fertility beliefs, a custom that was not exclusive to the Egyptians or 'Hellenistic' post-Achaemenid period, but was found also in the ruling families from Nile to Oxus, and the house of Maussollus in Caria (1952: 138). Erns von Kornemann, though an old study, traced this type of marriage and found it widely practised in the ancient world. His inclusion of some peoples in this marriage is not accepted anymore, such as the Sabaeans. He came to the conclusion that the way it came to the Hellenistic or 'Hellenistic' post-Achaemenid world was mainly through the Achaemenids, who apparently link this concept to the Mazdaic religion, where Bel, the king, takes his sister, who is 'beautiful like a goddess', as his wife (1925: 235-360; for a recent study on the biology of brother-sister marriage in Roman Egypt see Scheidel 1996: 9-51). It could be a remnant of an ancient tradition of matrilinearity, where only the maternal line is recognised, which would explain the half sister-brother marriage.

The attempt of Nabataeans to present themselves in a sacred image was also demonstrated in the link that Nabataean kings created between themselves and certain deities i.e. claiming their patronage of the Nabataean dynasty. Two gods were associated with the royal house. The first was Ba'l Šamīn, who was adopted by Mālik I as 'his' god (Khairy 1981). The second was Dushara, who became the marker of the Nabataean dynasty from the time of Ḥāriṯah IV (for the association between these two

[130] Except for Sullay who had the title *'ḫw*.

[131] Arsinöe II's and Ptolemy II's marriage was the first between a full sister and brother. Among the Macedonians, this is regarded as an incestuous marriage, contrary to the half-brother sister marriage from different fathers, which was recognised. They were both, Arsinöe and Ptolemy, worshipped as divine during their lifetime, and this became a custom with their successors (Kornemann 1925: 358; Pomeroy 1975, 1992: 123-124).

deities see Tarrier 1990). In support of this point, one finds King Ḥāriṯah portrayed on coins with the sign of a horn on his head. Queen Šaqīlah appeared with a similar horn, a sign unique to the Nabataean coins (see Meshorer 1975: No. 60). This was merely described by Meshorer as a 'V'-shape decoration (1975: 43) without giving clarification. The explanation I give would not go beyond an intentional attempt to create or invent a divine image that can deploy power and might throughout the kingdom wherever the coins were used.

Moreover, Nabataeans were not unexposed to the mythological influences from the cultures surrounding them, which enforce such ideas of the mother goddess[132] and queens, who were known in myth to marry with their brothers (see Diodorus writing on Isis' myth, I: 27: 4-5). Taussig associates this practice with politics, saying that the 'Hellenistic' post-Achaemenid queens married their brothers 'as an assertion of their divine status and political power', associating these marriages with those of the sibling divines, Zeus-Hera/ Isis-Osiris. By doing so queens such as Arsinoë II (282-246BCE) or Cleopatra VII (51-31BCE) who wanted to exploit this image, were able to transcend the title 'sister' to denote 'The Divine Sister of Osiris', transforming their sibling marriages into divine marriages (1997: 268) (see plate XXXVII).

Although it is possible to find an indigenous interpretation for this custom, one cannot avoid considering the incestuous marriage practised by the Ptolemies, Seleucids and Parthians.[133] According to the Pharonic concept,[134] such marriage is a custom to keep the royal blood 'pure'. Following on from there, this striving for 'purity' was the establishment of a special legacy of the 'royal' by linking it to the divine (see Taussig 1997: 268) through the medium of myth and ritual. Other rare evidence shows other examples of incestuous marriages, such marriage between mother and son (Parthia: Mūsā and her son Pharaatices V) (Colledge 1967: 47), and father and daughter (Sasania: Queen Atur-Anahit, daughter and wife of Shapur I) (Perikhanian 1983: 644).

Having established the concept behind sibling marriage among the royalty, which puts the Nabataean practice in perspective, it is appropriate to look at the role of the terms 'brother' and 'sister' among the Nabataeans and their implications.

The words *'ḫ* and *'ḫt* are kin words that can easily stretch to a large number of kinship and relations in Nile to Oxus culture, like *'b* and *'m*, where the members of a family, a clan, or a tribe considers itself as brothers and sisters, the elderly as fathers and mothers, and the youngsters as sons and daughters. In Nabataean, the term *'ḫ*, could refer to both physical sanguine brotherhood could and have other broad meanings. It is found to refer to a vizier or prime minister, who occupies, it seems, the position of the second man in the state (Hoftijzer & Jongeling 1995 I: 31). We have two cases of 'brothers', that of Sullay (Syllaeus) *'ḫ mlk'*, brother of King 'Obodah III (RES 675) and, 'Unays, *'nyšw 'ḫ* brother of Queen Šaqīlah II (CIS, II, 351), in addition to Strabo's comment that 'the king has as Administrator one of his companions, who is called brother' (16:4:21). It has been noted that, like the title 'king', the title *'ḫ mlk'* is reserved for one male person at a time, a position that is employed in relation to the king only and not simultaneously to other members of the royal family, which means that the title confers the highest status (Dijkstra 1995: 318). Accordingly, when the Mother-Queen, Šaqīlah II ruled as a regent for her minor son, fulfilling the king's duties, she appointed an *'ḫ* for herself, which corresponds with her position as malikah.

Returning to the term 'sister', it is possible that there was a broad meaning for the title. Although one cannot imagine her as prime minister in that context, the title could indicate closeness to the king, her husband. Between the view that considers the title 'sister of the king' as a blood title of a physical sister (Meshorer 1975: 79), and that which is uncertain as to whether the title was real or metaphoric (Hammond 1973: 107), Klaas Dijkstra does not discard the possibility of incestuous marriages, though he considers the title *'ḫt* to be used broadly in the context of the Nabataean royal house (1995: 317). Though the title of sister could be considered as honorific, it seems more likely that the Nabataean royal house practised sister-brother marriages.

If it is accepted that Nabataean kings married with their blood sisters, the question arises whether or not this was an alien tradition. It is most probable that the first king to marry his sister, attested on *inscriptions*, was Ḥāriṯah IV in 16 CE, whereas the title is not found on *coins* until the time of Šaqīlah II and king Mālik II in 40CE. Whether the absence of the sister title on Ḥāriṯah's coins was intentional or accidental, one cannot tell. But certainly, inscribing the title on coins is a much more effective method of publicising an image. This did not happen during the time of the strong king Ḥāriṯah, but waited for almost thirty years to appear on the coins of his son and daughter. It is possible, however, that the king and queen, realising the novelty of this type of marriage, tried to invent or at least revive ancient myths and legends that affirm incest as divine unification, such as that of Isis and Osiris in a gradual manner.

3. *His Wife, 'tth*

Queen Ḫuld, consort of Ḥāriṯah IV, was the only queen referred to as 'his wife', *'tth*, though not his sister. It is

[132] It has been noted that Nabataeans, based on a study of a group of 182 terracotta figurines from Raqamū-Petra, did not appear to have given mother goddess figurines an attention. No emphasis found to have been made on the sexual fertility parts of the female figurines (see Parr 1990: 80).

[133] There is evidence that a Parthian king married two of his maternal sisters. Among the Sasanians, evidence is found where Ardashir I married his sister Queen Denak (Perikhanian 1983: 644).

[134] Lise Manniche regards incest among ancient Egyptian royalty as the exception, as it does not occur anywhere with reference to ordinary Egyptians (1987: 29).

interesting that the 'wife' status does not appear anywhere else afterwards in relation to kings. It is possible; however, to suggest that Queen Ḫuld was not a sister-wife, and that, as it was the beginning of the new Ḥāriṯah's rule, the establishment of the sacred blood was not implemented until Ḥāriṯah's second marriage, took place at Šaqīlah's time.

4. His Mother, 'mh

This title appeared only once when Šaqīlah II was regent. She had coins struck with her title as the king's mother (Meshorer 1975: Nos. 142-146; Schmitt-Korte 1990: no 84; Hašim 1996: Nos. 85-87).

E. The Queen's Physical Appearance

The information on the queen's physical appearance comes only from coins. The statues so far found in Raqamū-Petra and elsewhere unfortunately do not explicitly represent queens. Most are of goddesses, mythological Hellenistic women, or unidentified terracotta (see Lyttlton & Blagg 1990; Parlasca 1990; Parr 1990; the great temple excavations). Since coins are the principal source, information is limited to what coins would tell in terms of what pictures are preserved on both sides. Appearing either in full length, standing, or only a head or bust. Their features are dominated by the long straight nose that distinguishes the Nabataean kings as well. Standing queens are mainly depicted draped in a long garment girdled at the waist. Queens in general are portrayed veiled, laureated, or wearing jewellery. Earrings appear sometimes, especially when a queen is depicted alone (Meshorer 1975: No. 49A). Sometimes she is adorned with a necklace of beads, spiral and pendulum shaped (ibid. 1975: 43). An additional decoration in the form of a V in front of the laurel wreath was also found. Similarly, the king had such a decoration ((ibid, 1975: 43), which has been identified as a shape of a horn that was possibly a marker of divinity, as mentioned earlier.

The major characteristic of the Nabataean queen's external appearance is her veil, which most frequently shows the front of her head and laurel wreath. The veil covers her hair and the nape of her neck and hangs down onto the robe wrapped around her shoulders (Meshorer 1975: 43). This was a feature that the queens of the 'Hellenistic' post-Achaemenid states shared with the Nabataeans, as much as it seems to have been the custom (see plate XXXVI). Morris Jastrow argues that veiling originated in Assyria, and the Babylonian-Assyrian influence was strongest in Palestine, Syria, Arabia and parts of Asia Minor (1921: 233). Although the origin of the veil is still disputed, it is known from the Assyrian legal codes dating from the mid-second millennium BCE (Jastrow1921: 210; De Vaux 1935: 411; Roth 1997: MAL40-41), and in Persian Achaemenid art, where royal women especially appear veiled (Brosius 1995: 86). In Parthian Iran, Mesopotamia and Ḥaṭra, queens and princesses appear veiled (Homès-Fredericq 1963; Kawami 1987: 144). In Syria we find later examples of Palmyrene women who apparently veil the face when they are outside their homes (De Vaux 1935: 399) and cover the hair in different styles underneath (see for Palmyra's example Sadurska & Bounni 1994). This can be seen in the splendid high-relief funerary figures (see plate XXXIV). Similar decoration is seen in Dura-Europos (Cumont 1926: 64ff. Pl. xxxv) (see plate XXXV). In Arabia, the veiling of women is known from pre-Islamic Arabia, regardless of religion (De Vaux 1935: 403-405). In ancient Greece, women were known to have worn a head-dress called a *chaluptra*, which is a sort of veil (ibid. 1935: 398). Moreover, references to veiling women in Greek mythology and elsewhere show a custom of veiling, e.g. Penelope in the Odyssey. Roman women, however, used veil as a fashion accessory, not strictly, as was the custom in Greece (Jastrow 1921: 230-32). Nonetheless, the Syrian queen, Julia Domna,[135] can still be seen in her Syrian veil in a sacrifice scene (Cumont 1926: 66, fig. 14). It is remarkable that the city goddess, depicted on the coins of Raqamū-Petra after its annexation by the Romans, and in Hadrian's times, appears veiled (Hill 1922: 35, pl. v: 11).

The initial relation between the veil and women can be seen through the connection made between the veil and the goddesses of fertility, like Ishtar and Demeter. They veil in the cycle of the seasons, marking their mourning, as a symbolism of hiding during the dead or mourning period, and unveil when they revive in spring following the rhythm of changing of seasons and life. An interesting discovery in Tall Ḥalaf of a veiled sphinx, identified by Oppenheim as Ishtar, links this veiling with the veiling and unveiling of day and night (Jeremias 1931: 9; De Vaux 1935: 398-399, 408-410). This analysis can explain the tradition of veiling brides in many parts of the old and modern world, until the wedding night, which is regarded as the celebration of fertility. In some cultures, such as the Greek, only married women wear the veil (Cassimatis 1985: 23).

Some unidentified statuettes found in Raqamū-Petra and the surrounding area which were attributed to the Nabataean queen, principally, Ḫuld or Šaqīlah (Parr 1960: 134-35; for identification with queens see Negev 1974: 87; Khairy 1986: 107; 1990: 55). The statuettes have some interesting features. They do not; however, seem to belong to official monuments. No statue or statuette that is attributed definitely to the king or the queen has been found.[136] During the 'Hellenistic' post-Achaemenid period, it seems that the veil prevailed over the region from Nile to Oxus; a sign of cultural continuation.

[135] Note that this same queen appears unveiled on coins.

[136] The only definite reference to a king's statue is lost. The inscription that was found on the base that describe it to belong to King Ḥāriṯah VII (Starcky & Strugnell 1966: ins 1). A bronze head, found in Raqamū-Petra's street, however, is suspected to be of a Nabataean king (Murray & Ellis 1940: pl. xli), see plate XXXVII.

II. The Legal: Woman's Personhood

Examining the legal aspect will explore Nabataean women's status, since it is one of the areas where evidence permits this. The legal aspect will include a discussion of women's legal qualification, by which I mean, what would qualify women of ancient Arabia, for example as in Nabataea, to have legal status that would allow them to initiate and participate in different legal practices without an agent or a guardian. I will argue that Nabataean women were able to initiate legal documents without the need for a guardian.

Before proceeding further, some terms need elaboration, starting from the definition that links legal status to personhood. Judith Romney Wegner states that 'personhood means the legal status as defined by the complex of an individual's powers, rights, and duties in society', where her 'legal power' includes a 'capacity to act in a way that produces a legal effect', such as the power to transfer property, the capacity to own, buy and sell property and to testify in a court of law (1988: 10-11), i.e. she claims there is no personhood without a legal status. This enforces the idea of distinguishing a human being by the recognition of his or her legal status. In the documents, whether inscriptions or papyri, from northern Arabia, women at times participated a great deal in daily public life. There is more information about their involvement in transactions, owning property and inheritance. These three elements will help to shed some light on the role that women played in Nabataean society, and are suggested as a marker of high status for women in the above sections. It is essential to allow for variables such as class: an elevated juridical status must go hand in hand with upper-class, wealthy women who come from influential families. The age variable is significant as well, for it is not possible to equate young girls with adult women or grandmothers. The state of freedom is another variable that shows a distinction between free and slave women, whose legal status differs accordingly. Additionally, marital status is also significant. In some societies, women's relationship and attachment to their fathers as guardians is different from when they are married, divorced or widowed, with children or without. These differences will be noted in different levels in the following sections, in which some general legal references relevant to Nabataeans will be introduced.

Law, which is about the authority that codifies social relations, is defined as 'the body of rules which are recognised, interpreted, and applied to particular situations by the courts of the state. It derives from various sources, including custom, but it becomes law when the state, which means in the last resort the courts, is prepared to enforce it as a rule binding on citizens and residents within its jurisdiction' (Maciver & Page 1961: 175). On the other hand, custom means 'a group procedure that has gradually emerged without any constituted authority to declare it, to apply it, to safeguard it. Custom is sustained by common acceptance... Customs are so intimate that, until we reflect on them, we do not realise how they attend nearly every occasion of our lives' (ibid. 1961: 176). There were, however, other traditions in Nile to Oxus, which interacted and produced what is called 'common law', and this applies to this area and period. Muffs believes that 'there can be little doubt that subsequent Near Eastern legal documents written in Aramaic, Syriac, or Hebrew are all reflections of the older Aramaic common law tradition represented by the Assyrian and Babylonian dockets and by the Elephantine papyri' (1969: 193). This statement gives a wide range of possibilities for interdependence among these societies, adapting and modifying law for their own convenience. In the Nabataean case, although no proper written codes are available, the difference between what was law and what was custom can be distinguished. Therefore, one is left with an attempt to fill the gaps with what is known from the Aramaic common law. Even if this aim and method is remote from any final achievement, it is enough, I believe, at this stage, to address the subject and look for the signs of such a law.

Historical accounts of the Nabataeans refer to a main court in Raqamū-Petra. It seems that the city remained as a juridical centre after the collapse of the Nabataean state, since it had been the 'metropolis of Arabia' before the capital moved to Boṣra[137] at the time of Rab'el. In another document of the Babatha[138] archive, dated from 12 Oct 125 CE, Babatha refers to the case in which she prosecuted one of the guardians of her orphan son before the legate at Raqamū-Petra. The document says: 'Therefore I summon you to come and be judged before the judgement seat of the governor Julius Julianus at Petra, the Metropolis of Arabia' (Yadin 1963: 237). This shows that Raqamū-Petra was, and probably continued to be, a juridical centre of Nabataean courts and law.

The newly published papyri of this archive show that a woman could testify in court in support for a sale she made of her property. Abi'adan, a Nabataean woman, states in her sale document that she sells her palm-garden, and that the owner has all rights to it, to buy and to sell it, to pledge and to bequeath, and to grant as gift and anything that he wishes. She adds that if this transaction was to be subject to any lawsuit, contest, or oath, she will clear the purchaser or his descendants forever (Yadin 1963; 2002: do. 2, L 9-10; doc. 3, L 10-12). A text that is showing the legal capacity of the woman, that is to stand up, probably, in court, on behalf of *'rkls* or *Šm'ūn*, in case of a lawsuit to claim the garden (see Healey's comment 2005: 3-4),

[137] See the argument of J. Eadie(1985: 413-414), and the excavations by Tondon in Blanc *et al* (2002: 86).

[138] A Jewish woman lived in the Nabataean Kingdom by the Dead Sea in the first and second centuries CE, and left a rich archive of papyri written in (cursive) Nabataean, Jewish Aramaic and Greek. Her archive is mainly private family documents of marriage, inheritance, law-suits, guardianship, sale and other legal documents (for details see Yadin 1963).

as well as signing contracts on her own behalf, as will be shown below.

The main court is also described as a temple. A document found in Wādī Ḫabra (Naḥal Ḥever), dating to the year 124 CE, says that it was issued in the temple of Aphrodite in Raqamū-Petra (Yadin 1963: 235). The document is an official copy of the 'record of the city council of Petra' (ibid. 243). The temple of Aphrodite was discussed by Hammond and identified with the temple of winged Lions.[139] Aphrodite, on the other hand was identified with Allāt by some (Hammond 1990: 120-24) and al-'Uzzā by others (Zayadine 1981: 113-117; 1984: 167-169). Another reference to issuing documents in temples comes from Ḥegra (JS 36) (see plate XII) where it reads that a copy of the text is kept in the temple of Qəysah *qyš'*, which is probably where fines were also collected.[140]

From Athenodorus the friend of Strabo, who lived in Raqamū-Petra and told him about his stay there, we have some information about the legal situation in Raqamū-Petra. Strabo writes 'he [Athenodorus] saw that the foreigners often engaged in law-suits, both with one another and with the natives, but that none of the natives prosecuted one another, and that they in every way kept peace with one another' (16:4:20), a statement that can be read at many levels. On the one hand, it shows how foreigners were treated, or treated each other. On the other, it can indicate a special order specific to Nabataeans that forbade them to raise law-suits against each other. This order, which is represented by Athenodorus as Utopian, could, in fact, indicate the existence of another more subtle legal system that organised quarrels between Nabataeans: their customary law.

The search for Nabataean legal practices can begin in the funerary inscriptions (see Healey 1993a), which are mainly found in Ḥegra, the second biggest city (see plates VII, VIII). These inscriptions have been observed as being, in reality, legal documents, which contain clauses similar to those found in conveyance documents from the neo-Babylonian period and later (Greenfield 1991: 222). Moreover, these documents can be considered to be wills as well as declarations of ownership and rights involved. Babatha's archives provide an additional range of legal documents about the Nabataean Jewish community, rich source for legal practices that shows a combination of Nabataean and Jewish legal practice within the Common Law.

How were women represented in the legal traditions of Nabataea and how can that demonstrate their status? This is what I will try to answer below.

[139] An important and unique legal inscription was found in the excavations of this temple (Hammond *et al* 1986: 77-8).

[140] Discussion of fines comes later in the chapter.

A. Owning Property

Owning property is an important element of legal power that is relatively informing. Reference to ownership among Nabataean women is repeated in inscriptions and papyri. One of the signs of this ownership is shown in the demand written in the funerary inscription of denying the right to bury someone in a tomb except by presenting a valid document, *tqf* (Healey 1993b: 90; Hoftijzer & Jongeling 1995 II: 1229), written (or signed) by the owner or owners[141] (JS 3, 5, 7, 8, 33, 34, 37). One example comes from a female tomb (JS 34) and another is from a tomb shared between a husband and wife (JS 33). Owning property was not a novelty in Nabataean society for it is known to be a right that women enjoyed since the third millennium in The Land of the Two Rivers and Egypt. It is also known to have existed in the neighbouring Liḥyānite society at Dedan south of Ḥegra, and in Ḥaḍramawt in southern Arabia. It follows then that according to this right women should be required to pay their duties as well, i.e. their taxes.[142] In Nabataean Ḥegra, the tombs owned by females reveal that women exercised the same rights as males, authorising burial, prohibitions, curses, fines, etc. Bearing in mind that there are many tomb stones that belong to women were found mainly in the rest of the Nabataean land,[143] other engraved in funerary tombs were also found in Raqamū-Petra, however, they were not as elaborate and informative as the Ḥegran ones, though interesting (for details see Nehmé 2003: MP16, MP325.2).

Seven of these tombs were owned completely by women (B19:[144] JS 16, B10: JS 11-12, C1: JS 23, B11: JS 13-14, C14: JS 26, E14: JS 34, E16: JS 35).[145] Three more tombs were owned jointly by a man and a woman (C6: JS 24, E1: JS 30 and E6: JS 33). The owners are man and wife or sister and brother. Some of the female tombs were also owned jointly between two or more women, mainly a mother with her daughters (JS 12(with 2 ds.), JS 14(with her aunt), JS 16 (with one daughter)).

[141] In an example from South Arabia, in a Sabaic funerary inscription, the owner does not allow anyone to be buried in the tomb, with or without a document *'lm* (CIS, IV, 619; al-Naim 2000: 241).

[142] One wonders if there is any relationship between the obligations for women owners to pay taxes and the women collectors of alms in the Liḥyanite Dedan, *slḥt*?

[143] For example: CIS, II, 173, 175, Lit: 4, 9, 15, 17, 20, 21, 29, 68, 76, 79, 80, 81, 82, 84, 85, 89.

[144] Tomb and inscription numbers are according to Jaussen & Savignac unless otherwise indicated.

[145] One more female tomb is attested in Ḏāt Rās, southern Jordan (Zayadine 1970: 131) (from a tomb à puit, at Shuqairah 4km s/e Ḏāt Rās) *ca* 9 BCE-40 CE

1. *bdnh ḥyt brt 'mrt*
2. *br 'ngsdms br*
3. *'mrt*

In this (tomb), Ḥayāt d. of 'Amrah s. of 'Angsmds s. of 'Amrah.

List of Female Owners of Tombs in Ḥegra

1. Kamkam d. of Wā'ilah d. of Ḥarām and her daughter Kulaybah

JS 16/ 1BCE (see plate IX)

2. Wašūḥ d. of Bajrah with her daughters Qayn and Naskawiyyah

JS 11-12/ 34CE (see plate X)

3. Sakīnah d. of Murrah, the Muzniyyah

JS 23/ ?

4. Hājar d. of Ḥafy and Maḥmiyyah d. of Wā'ilah (a burial niche for her br. Salamū (Sālim or Salīm etc.) (see plate XI).

JS 13-14/ 58CE

5. Haynah d. of Wahab

JS 26/ 61CE

6. Haynah d. of 'Abd 'Obadah

JS 34/ 72CE (see plate X)

7. 'Amah d. of Kamūlah

JS 35/ 74CE

List of Shared Ownership between men and women in Ḥegra Tombs

1. Man'ah and Hājar children of 'Umayrah s. of Wahab JS 30/ 7CE
2. Ġanam s. of Juzay'ah and 'Arsaksah d. of Taym JS 24/ 36CE
3. Šabb s. of Muqīm and Nubayqah d. of .. JS 33/ 39CE (see plate IX).

List of Shared Ownership between women in Ḥegra Tombs

1. Kamkam d. of Wā'ilah d. of Ḥarām and her daughter Kulaybah

JS 16/ 1BCE

2. Wašūḥ d. of Bajrah with her daughters Qayn and Naskawiyyah

JS 11-12/ 34CE

3. Hājar d. of Ḥafy and Maḥmiyyah d. of Wā'ilah

JS 13-14/ 58CE

Apart from the above practices, tombs were dedicated to several members of the family, especially the nuclear family, of a husband, wife, children and their offspring. A few of them included other family members, such as mothers, fathers, brothers, sisters, and aunt, or clients. The fact that women shared tombs with men, either husbands or brothers, is significant in demonstrating their legal capacity to share and to have equal rights to a substantive property such as a tomb of Ḥegran type. Moreover, the significance of owning a tomb does not conclude with the ownership, it involves many other activities, which can be publicly or privately done, such as hiring an architect, a sculptor, and a writer to design the facade, carve it, then inscribe the text.

One of the ownership markers that were also shared is the right to include in the tomb whomsoever they wish according to a deed of entitlement signed by them and, literally, taken from their hands. This was found in all the shared tombs as well as in one male tomb which was made for the owner's father, step-mother and two sisters, who shared the deeds of entitlement (JS 7). The fact of owning tombs does not mean that women's ownership was limited to property of this kind. Nabataean women, as we have seen earlier, could own slaves as well as having the right to free them (CIS, II,161). It follows that they will have had their own movable property of jewellery etc. From other evidence, it is possible to ascertain that they were owners of real estate.

On the edge of the Nabataean state to the west of the Dead Sea, in the Archive of Babatha, two deeds (Yadin 1963; 2002 doc 2-3) from Galgala'[146] dated from the year 28 of Rab'el II reign, i.e. 97/98 CE, refer to a certain *'by'dn brt 'ptḥ br mnygrs* (Abi'adan daughter of Aptaḥ son of Manigares). She appears as a Land Owner or a Land Lady, who is selling her own land, palm-grove including all types of trees, wood, wet and dry, arid land, and assigned watering periods, sunny and shady areas. She is selling either two pieces of land to two people within a month's time difference or one piece to the second person after the first sale failed (Healey 2005: commentary 11).

According to the papyri, her land is bordered from one side by the land of another Nabataean woman called *tḥ' brt 'bd ḥrtt* (Taḥa' daughter of 'Abd-Ḥāriṯah),[147] and another boundary abuts the garden of the king. These houses (Yadin 1963: 232), owned by Nabataean women were not just any houses; they neighboured the King's gardens. The significance underlining it is the fact that these women owners were publicly and officially registered as such owners in the legal documents, which define the grove that the father of Babatha bought. To suggest that they were the heads of their households would not be an exaggeration.

Transaction practices are discussed in the next section.

B. Transactions

In an early study, Peggy Sanday selected four dimensions for coding female status in the public domain, one of which is relevant here, that of 'female material control', which involves females having the ability to act effectively on, to allocate, or to dispose of – things land, produce, crafts, etc. – beyond the domestic unit (1973: 1694; 1974: 192). This includes activities such as transactions, which are public economic and social practices that transfer property from one person to another. These activities, such as selling, buying, renting etc. are shown directly in the Nabataean papyri of Babatha's archive and indirectly in the Ḥegran tombs. This is considered by Sanday as the first step on the ladder in the scale towards a high female status (see 1973: fig.2, p.1695).

Two sale deeds were found in Babatha's archive written in Nabataean and were mentioned above. They concerned Abi'adan daughter of Aptaḥ son of Manigares, the Nabataean owner of land in Galgala', who is selling it to two men. Her first buyer was *'rkls br 'bd'mnw/'bd'mw* (Archelaus son of 'Abd'aman/'Abd'Amu), the strategos, for the amount of 112 Sela' (Yadin 2: L. 3, 5,9, 10, 11, 13, 14, 21, 25, 32, 34, 37, 39), but it seems that this transaction was not fulfilled, since the same palm plantation with modification was sold after a month to *Šm'wn br ..*, (Šam'ūn son of ..) for a higher price of 168 Sela' (Yadin 2002: 3: L. 2, 6, 13, 15, 16, 23bis, 28, 32, 35, 37, 41, 43, 44, 49, see introduction Yadin 2002 pp. [201-204]; Healey 2005: commentary 11).

Abi'adan states, in her sale documents, that once she sells her palm-garden, the purchaser has all rights to it, to buy and to sell it, to pledge and to bequeath, and to grant as gift and anything that he wishes. She adds that if this transaction was to be subject to any lawsuit, contest, or oath, she will clear the purchaser or his descendants forever (Yadin 2, L 9-10; Yadin 3, L 10-12). This statement shows another sign of legal capacity the Nabataean woman had. That is to stand up, probably in court, on behalf of her party (see Healey's comment 2005: 118-119),

In Hegra, the different transactions, seemingly carried out by women, are shown from the funerary inscriptions found inscribed on the Ḥegran tombs – especially the female tombs. Below, two lists are deduced from the funerary texts, one is related to the prohibited transactions and the second is the transactions carried out by women.

[146] This is in *mḥwz 'gltyn* Maḥoz 'Eglatain, at the southern end of the Dead Sea, in the Nabataean Kingdom, later Provincia Arabia. It was the second only to Jerusalem in Judaea in the fertility of its land and in its palm groves (Pliny 5: 15).

[147] In 1963, Yadin read in this document two women owners of houses situated on the boundary abuts of the sold land. First was Ḥabībah d. of .. 'Ilah and the second was the same Tāḥah with a different father's name.

1. The Vocabulary of Prohibited Transactions

The glossary list in the transactions is important in itself, for not only does it show what kind of transactions the tombs might have been involved in, but also provides essential information about Nabataean society. The prohibitions that the owner asks to be respected seem to be agreed upon by most of the tomb owners, male and female. Some, however, have less detail than others, depending on different conditions. The general prohibitions are as follows (translation followed by the Nabataean word and the inscription number after Jaussen and Savignac):

These legal terms indicate what kind of transactions was common in Nabataean society. In the context of the tombs as the object of these transactions, research found that they became prohibition acts. Moreover, the texts show that there were some heirs who breached elements mentioned above. It is not clear; however, to what extent specifying the prohibitions was a deterrent or how far the state participated in enforcing them. Inscription JS 36 mentions that a copy, *nsḥt'*, of the inscription is deposited in the temple of the god *qyš'*, who could be the god of law or deeds. This god could be related to qos, the Edomite god (Milik 1958: 235-236). Another copy was probably kept by the administrators of the state in the metropolis, Raqamū-

• To sell (the tomb)	*zbn* (JS 1,5,8,9,10,12, 16,19,26,28,30,31,32, 34, 36, 38)
• To buy	*zbn* (JS 1,8,16)
• To give	*ntn* (JS 8, 16);
	yhb (JS 1, 27, 36)
• To lend, grant	*š'l* (JS 19)
• To pledge	*mškn* (JS 1, 9, 12, 19, 26, 30, 38);
	rhn (JS 8, 16, 28, 31, 32)
• To lease (lease)	*wgr* (JS 1, 8, 9, 10, 19, 31, 32, 34);
	'wgrw (JS 5, 26);
	'gr (JS 1,8, 9, 10, 19, 31, 32, 34)
• To change	*'yr* (JS 9, 12, 19, 31);
	šn' (JS 12)
• To raise on a tomb	*'ly* (JS 17, late inscription)
• To compose, draw up a document	*t'lf* (JS 8, 13, 34 , 26?)
• write a deed	*ktb tqp* (JS 3, 4, 5, 19, 26, 38)
• To write a deed of entitlement	*tqp* (JS 3, 5, 7, 8, 33, 34, 37)
• To open	*ptḥ* (JS 11, 13)
• To bring out (the body etc.)	*npq* (JS 2, 9, 11, 16)
• To bury a stranger	*qbr 'nwš rḥq* (JS 3)
• To bury s.o. not mentioned above	*qbr 'nwš 'dyn* (JS 4) (JS 8, 16, 4, 5)
• To dispose of, alienate	*'n'* (JS 1)
• To bury s.o. who is not a legitimate heir	*qbr 'ṣdq b'ṣdq* (JS 4) (JS 3, 4, 28)

(Taken partly from Healey's index, 1993b)

Petra. Other attestations of depositing copies of funerary texts in a special archive house or public record office are found in Palmyra, called *byt 'rk'*. A public record was also attested in Dura-Europos (Cuissini 1995: 237-38).[148]

2. Gendered Transaction (Inscriptions specific to Female Tombs)

In contrast to the general terms used above, some of these terms are specific to female tombs, or imply different applications:

Prohibitions	In Nabataean	# Times	# Inscriptions
to sell	*zbn*	6	16,30,11,12,26,34
to buy	*zbn*	1	16
to give	*ntn*	1	16
to pledge	*mšk*	4	30,11,12,26
	rhn	1	16
to lease	*wgr*	1	34
	'gr	1	26
to change	*'yr*	2	11,12
	šn'	1	11
to draw up	*t'lf*	2	34
to bring out	*npq*	2	16,11
to open	*ptḥ*	2	12,13
to bury s.o. not mentioned above		2	16,30

The full list of prohibitions or transactions is not represented on the female tombs. I shall list them, then discuss them, taking into consideration that these prohibitions are not essentially prohibitions, but that they acquire this quality by being pointed out in a funerary inscription. The main concern here is with the general transactions open to women in addition to the specific actions or prohibitions restricted for women. Below, is a list of the actions available to women concerning their tombs, starting by being able to define the persons who could exercise transactions over their tombs? Thus:

Burial without authorisation
Burial of non-family members, strangers
Burial of non-legitimate heir, not *'ṣdq b'ṣdq*
Burial of someone not mentioned in the will
Writing a deed
Drawing up a deed of entitlement
Lending money *š'l*
Giving *yhb*
Alienating *'n'*

[148] Detailed study of the prohibitions is found in al-Fassi, forthcoming/ a.

The fact that these actions and transactions are also found in the female tomb inscriptions is significant. It shows an element of egalitarianism concerning women's rights to build their own tombs with all the usual conditions. There are, however, some limitations. The main one is about bequeathing inheritance to descendants. Apparently women were not allowed to have legitimate heirs to their tombs or that they were not recognised as such. The sentence *'ṣdq b'ṣdq*, which means 'by hereditary title' (Healey 1993b: 91-92), is absent. It appears on tombs shared between men and women, but not on tombs owned completely by women. It is significant though, for family lineage, that women could not claim a legitimate lineage of their own for their children, even though some inscriptions link women to their mothers and not to their fathers, as in the case of *kmkm brt w'lt brt ḥrmw* (JS 16), *mḥhmyt brt w'ylt* (JS14), and *'mrt brt kmwlt* (JS 35) and others. Although women were known to pass inheritance and lineage to their children, mainly daughters, it seems that their daughters were restricted from owning their inheritance by heredity title, *'ṣdq b'ṣdq*, which may be a formula related to male inheritance.

With the scarce evidence available, it is not possible to say definitely that women did not have access to certain transactions, such as giving loans or gifts, for absence of evidence is not evidence of absence. Although causing a deed of entitlement to be drawn up was a prohibition that is not found in the female tombs, women were given the right to write deeds of entitlements to others, like any other owner or heir (JS 34). Opposed to this, there was an emphasis on women not having non-family members in their tombs as found in further sources. It is also possible that these are certain beliefs about the purity of the tomb, which prevented the inclusion of strangers[149] because the gods might not appreciate having to give mercy to someone who was not legitimate family. Male owners could have strangers buried in their tombs if they had an assent document from a particular owner or his heirs. As for 'alienating' or 'disposing of', I would suggest that this was not a limitation specific to women's transactions, but a specific transaction that could be Taymanite. It might be a Taymanite dialect loanword, since the owner is Taymanite (al-Fassi: forthcoming/ a).

In addition to the transactions expressed in tombs, a few others are attested from the papyri contracts found in the Dead Sea caves, showing transactions contracted between Jews and Nabataeans. One is *krz* and *krwz'*. Though not a proper transaction, it deals with selling. *krz* denotes an offer of sale announced publicly and *krwz'* is a herald or auctioneer (Starcky 1954: 168-69; Healey 1993a: 209), or a proclamation (see Yardeni 2001: 132 in her rereading of the papyrus).

[149] This is apparently not taken into account by the owner of the Taymanite tomb, who included her clients, who were possibly strangers.

C. *Guardianship*

Guardianship is a concept that was encountered above. In the Assyrian Codes, women are known to need their fathers to take them into marriage, but there is nothing to suggest that they needed guardians for their contractual practices. It was similar for the woman in Egypt (Ahmed 1992: 30), and Jewish women in certain periods and contexts (Isaac 1992: 71; Cotton 1993: 68).The guardian is mainly known in Greek legal practice and legal documents written in Greek as *kyrios*[150] from old Attic law which means 'the master of a person who could not won property' (Cotton 2002:131). In the Roman Codes it was known as *tutor*, and is usually the father if the woman is not married, or the husband. If a widow, her guardianship transfers to her son[151] (Gardner 1986: 5; Bremen 1996: 205-08). This was why Greek women in Egypt preferred to follow Egyptian law. An act was accepted within Ptolemaic Egypt since the state was unbiased and accepted legal actions in both Greek and Egyptian traditions (Pomeroy 1984: 119-120). In the Aramaic texts a guardian of a woman is called *'dūn* (Cotton 2002: 132).

Acting with a guardian implies that women did not have rights of their own or were not independent agents, a situation which shows that certain Greek and Roman women were not perceived to have legal standing or capacity in public affairs. The Roman court expects women to be represented by a guardian. Some of Babatha's documents of her archive from the Roman period show the assignment of guardians who were not necessarily her husband or relative. One time she had Yohanna son of Makoutha son of 'abd'abdat, whom is suspected to be a Nabataean himself (Yadin 22), and another time she used Babeli son of Menahem (Yadin 27), in Yadin 25 she uses Maras son of Abdalgos of Petra (in Greek) as her guardian. (Ilan 2001: 172, 174). On the other hand, the need for a guardian, which seems to have been justified by the need to protect women or by some 'deficiency in their innate faculties', means that they were not in control of their resources even if they were to inherit or to bequeath inheritance, and that their male relatives, or any male, were given the chance to be in charge of their financial affairs. The legal condition of some of the Greek and later the Roman women in courts contrasts strongly with the legal conditions concerning women's involvement in trade, transaction and contracts in Egypt, The Land of the Two Rivers, Syria and Nabataea.

Reference to fathers or brothers, as candidate guardians, in the Ḥegran female tombs, cannot be spotted easily, as guardianship or the presence of a potential guardian seems to appear only once in the form of a father (JS 34) and once a brother (JS 13), in comparison with Greek funerary inscriptions of Athenian women, where it appears that they had to have their father's or father and husband's name added in the epitaph (McClees 1920: 34). If agreed that funerary inscriptions can demonstrate whether or not the guardian relationship existed among the Nabataeans also, it is possible to state that since the female tombs lack any mention of principal male kin, it is improbable that Nabataean women needed any guardian to own a tomb or to pass it to their heirs. In fact, the question of whether Nabataean women needed to have their father as *kyrios*, there is the significant case of a woman making a tomb *for* her father (JS 34) and *for* her brother (JS 13, 24). On the other hand, having an agent or guardian seems difficult to implement in a society where men are involved in activities that keep them far from home most of the year. For Ḥegra, as will be seen in the last chapter, was the proper candidate from which to deduce patterns, as a caravan city involved in intensive trade activity which forces men to leave their women managing their own affairs by themselves for long periods of time. Whether one should take the example of Ḥegran women as a sign of women's independence or as a result of their specific economic activity, cannot say for certain. It is possible, however, to assume that they were not very different from their sisters in Egypt or Palmyra. The fact that the Ḥegran female tombs were independent of fathers, uncles or brothers clearly indicates a certain legal independence that women enjoyed in that period, i.e. the first century CE.

The recent publication of the Nabataean papyri in Babatha's archive (Yadin 2002: 1, 2, 3) gives an evidence to that Nabataean women had the legal capacity to appear in court, to contract in transactions without the need for a guardian of any sort.

In a 66 lined-papyrus classified as a debenture, or a written promise to repay a loan within a specified period of time, drawn up by the debtor (a husband) addressed to his wife, the creditor. His wife *'mt'ysy brt kmnū br 'mrū* ('Amat'aysy daughter of Kamnū son of 'Amr), lender of money, drew up a brief agreement, stating consents to the above loan and her right of foreclosure. She is loaning her husband Muqīm her own dowry *mhr*, dated after the year 23 of Rab'el II (Sept. 10th, 93-94 CE). In two years time Muqīm should repay his wife 150 Sela's. If he fails he will be charged interest as well as the remaining stipulations. (More details in the document, see Yadin 1: L 2, 9, 13, 18, 42, 47; in Yardeni 2000 p. [87] and Yadin *et al* 2002 p170-200) Text: 178-182). This document states a fact that the Nabataean woman had a legal capacity that allows her to draw up contracts and give loans on her own capacity without the need of a guarantor or tutor or agent, or at least, she could do that in the situation of dowry money (al-Fassi, forthcoming/ c).

In the sale documents Yadin 2 and 3 mentioned earlier, they end up by a signature of the parts of the contracts as well as the witnesses. The name of the Land Lady Owner Abi'adan appears clearly in the second document (Yadin 3) saying *'l npšh* 'on her own behalf', confirming that Nabataean

[150] In the Greek society until 212 CE, a woman needed her father or husband to witness any public act (Thurston 1989: 10-11).

[151] This practice still survives in modern Saudi Arabia.

women represented themselves without a mediator in contracts. It is remarked; however, that Abi'adan did not write her name in her own hand as is emphasized with some witnesses, nor were there any women witnesses.

According to the above, the Nabataean woman appears to be the subject of her contracts. In the first papyrus she is the one who owns the money and who is acting as a debtor and in the second as a Land Lady Owner who is selling it. Nowhere in the documents there was a reference to a guardian or the need for a representative. These are situations in which a woman is having the upper hand and representing herself by herself once against her husband and two times against other men in a direct process expressed in the documents with all the usual formalities in such contracts.

These contracts affirm that Nabataean women had a legal capacity that allows them to draw up contracts, give loans, own property, do with it what they wish, such as selling it up, on their own capacity without the need for a guarantor or tutor or agent. She has her own money and property, taking into consideration the limitation of the evidence. However, it must be noted that in no Hebrew, Aramaic or Nabataean papyri from Palestine do we find a woman represented by a guardian. It is only found in the documents written in Greek under the Roman authorities after the annexation of Arabia. It is very clear therefore that Nabataean or Jewish women did not need a guardian to represent her in court (Cotton 2002: 132-133). In the following section the light will be shed on her capacity to inherit and bequeath inheritance.

D. Inheritance

The funerary inscriptions of Ḥegra, if accepted as quasi-wills, show a scheme of inheritance in which women make a part. The word *yrt* designates 'to inherit' in Nabataean, and was found in Ḥegra, in the inscription of Kahlān the doctor (JS 19), and in a Dead Sea document (Starcky 1954: Fragment A: 6; Yardeni 2001: line 20, 21). Since one operates with few ancient legal codes[152] there is no alternative but to rely on indirect references to legal arrangements regarding inheritance, one of which is a funerary inscription. It is true that this is not the perfect way. It is, however, the only available one at present. It is possible to suggest that these tombs show some kind of a pattern that can parallel an inheritance succession. In the following, research is concerned with two things. Firstly, to trace the heirs or line of succession, especially related to women. Secondly, to see how the objects of inheritance, the tombs, were divided among the heirs.

1. In view of the involvement of females in the tomb relations, it is possible to claim that women were able to inherit and also to bequeath inheritance to whom so ever they wish. The fact that women were those who bestow rights to their close relatives demonstrates their legal power of ownership and inheritance. The male tomb inscriptions show that rights are not handed down in a family in a systematic way, but according to a written document. Accordingly, wives, children and their offspring would be allowed to be buried in tombs, and to have the right in the tomb itself. The situation in the female tombs was similar; they needed to specify who are to inherit their house of eternity. Although there is no evidence showing a specific responsibility for preparing a tomb, and for whom, there seems to be a pattern of some kind, which will be discussed in the following section. In this case, however, inheritance of tombs will be taken up as the example available.

2. Taking a closer look at the funerary details, as well as the architecture of the inner tombs, may reveal some relationships. From the inscriptions, it is known that inheritance was collective. In other words, the whole group of people who are mentioned in the deeds owns the tomb legally after the death of the original owner. Therefore, one is faced with the problem of abiding by the rules and conditions of the owner, as well as being confined by the penalties. A clue can be found in the specification that some owners made for each heir in the tomb. There are three examples demonstrating this practice (JS 14, 24, 33), one of which is a female tomb and the other two have women as partners.

The female tomb B11, dated from 58 CE, adorned by two inscriptions, inside and outside the tomb (JS 13-14), belonged to Hājar d. of Ḥafy and Maḥmiyyah d. of Wā'ilah, their children and offspring. It is in fact, a tomb jointly owned by two women, who are a niece and aunt. They have included in it, Hājar's brother, Salamū (Sālim, Salīm or Sulaym). The inscription divides the tomb equally between the niece and aunt, five cubits each, which means that the brother was not involved in the tomb, or that the outside inscription was written earlier than the inner one or before the arrangement of including Sālim, who probably shared the portion of his sister (Healey 1993b: 150). This arrangement does not express inheritance as much as it expresses ownership by women, and shows the sister taking charge of supporting her brother and allocating to him a space in her property. The inscription shows an aspect of women in charge of their household.

The shared tomb C6, dated 36 CE, belonged to Ġanam s. of Juzay'ah and 'Arsaksah d. of Taym, the governor, and their children (JS 24). The partners are probably a husband and wife, as suggested by the mention of *yldhm* i.e. their children. They made the tomb for 'Arsaksah's brothers, Rūma and Kalba, sons of Taym. The arrangement was for this tomb to be divided in thirds, a third for Ġanam and two thirds for his wife. Other details are added to designate the sections that are for 'Arsaksah to have the eastern part and her husband the south-eastern or right side. It is apparent that the double portion of 'Arsaksah's share is

[152] Most of the ancient legal codes are found in Sumer, Babylon and Aššur.

due to including her brothers within it, a similar situation to the previous one, where a sister is to take care of the burial arrangements of her brother(s).

The second male and female shared tomb E6, dated 39 CE, belonged to Šabb s. of Muqīm and Nubayqah d. of ... (JS 33) (see plate IX). The partners are probably wife and husband, as suggested by their dedicating the tomb to their children by legal inheritance. The inscription includes another woman among those who have the right to bury in the tomb, called Talam d. of Mālī, whose relationship is not defined. The arrangement implies that the tomb will be divided between Šabb and his wife, half for each, with an extra burial-niche for Šabb on his own. Since the balance is broken by the extra portion for the husband, it is possible to suggest that that part was left for the woman, Talam, whose relationship might be to Šabb rather than to Nubayqah, similar to the situation we found in the first shared tomb.

These division arrangements, which were probably used in all tombs, do not explain directly how people inherit. They can, however, be used to show who inherits from whom. In this respect, it is noted that there is no definite pattern, that fathers can make tombs for their daughters and vice versa, as well as sisters and brothers. What can be derived from the little evidence which exists, is that the head(s) of a house-hold be it a man, a woman, or a couple, according to their choice and probably financial ability, would take responsibility for making a tomb for the rest of the family. It is possible that whatever they owned, of movable and immovable property, they would pass to their children, female children in the case of a female tomb, and both in the case of male and shared tombs.

The archive of Babatha is also of great help in clarifying this aspect of Nabataean women's life. In her documents, Babatha refers explicitly to the property she inherited from her mother, and from her first and second husbands. She was able to inherit from both her husbands even in the presence of her children and step-children (Yadin 1963: 228). It is unlikely that these documents reflect rules of the Jewish community which were separate from the common law known and practised in the Nabataean kingdom's courts. To be able to trace some more of the Nabataean law of inheritance, it is possible to look at similar funerary inscriptions in a society where rules of inheritance are known, in order to compare the laws with the practice of tombs. This would have been possible if Palmyra is to be taken as an example, except that it is a large subject that should have an independent study. Alternatively, the possibilities of inheritance can be discussed in the context of female parentage and single mother's tombs in what follows.

E. Custody & Parentage

Strabo mentions that Nabataeans built costly houses of stone: 'Their homes, through the use of stone, are costly' (16:4:26). Although dealing with tombs, whereas he referred to houses,[153] they can give an indication of the extravagance in their building styles and materials, which are witness to wealth and status. These demonstrate that represented here is the upper class in Nabataean society. Despite that, the sepulchral inscriptions of Ḥegra represent the natural family structure of parents, children, husband, wife, etc. regardless of whether they were specific to the elite, for they show general social patterns that prevailed in Nabataean society.

The inscriptions clearly show that a father or a mother takes responsibility for making a family tomb, with certain limitations, which will be clarified by the following tables and commentaries. This section will highlight the evidence for a patriarchal society by investigating the parental duties towards the household and vice-versa. In surveying the Ḥegran funerary texts, it is possible to allocate inscriptions and references to certain kin in a fashion that will reveal degrees of relationships, as far as the limited epigraphic data will allow. This table of kinship of funerary dedications was drawn following a model of Saller & Shaw (1984:147). The relationships are divided into six categories: conjugal family, descending nuclear family, ascending nuclear family, siblings, extended family and others. Under each category, the number of times such a relationship is expressed in the inscriptions will be specified.

	From	**To**	**No.**	**Inscription**
1. Conjugal family				
	Husband	Wife	6	JS 4,7,20,27(*hiba*),32,38
	Wife	Husband	none	
2. Descending nuclear family				
	Father	Son	2	JS 36,38(2)
	Father	Daughter	2	JS 9,36(5)

[153] Strabo's friend Athenodorus who lived in Raqamū-Petra was blind; therefore, most of his account and description lack any reference to the magnificent rock tombs and elaborate façades.

	Mother	Son	none	
	Mother	Daughter	2	JS 11,12(5)
	Mother	Offspring	7	JS 11-12,13-14, 16,23,26,34,35
	Parents	Children	23	JS 3,4,5,8,9,10,14,16,20,22,23, 26,25,26,28,29,30,31,33, 34,35,38
3. Ascending nuclear family				
	Son	Father	2	JS 7, 29
	Son	Mother	5	JS1,17(268CE),20,33?,37(3 brothers for their mother)
	Daughter	Father	1	JS 34
	Daughter	Mother	none	
4. Siblings				
	Sister	Brother	2	JS 13, 24(2)
	Sister	Sister	none	
	Brother	Sister	2	JS 3(2),7(2)
	Brother	Brother	3	JS 1(2),36,37(3)
5. Extended family				
	Woman	Aunt	1	JS 13 (*ḫlt*)
	Man	Son-in-law	1	JS 36(*ḫtn*)
	Man	Father-in-law	1	JS 36(*nšyb*)
	Man	Brother-in-law	1	JS 24(2)
	Man	Step-mother	1	JS 7
6. Others				
	Woman	Clients	1	JS 12 (*gr*)

Kinship patterns and their frequency in tomb makings, show that in six instances, attested within the conjugal family table, a husband makes a tomb to wife. No wife made any tombs for her husband, the reasons for which will be discussed at length below. In the descending nuclear family table, equity between fathers making tombs for their sons and their daughters, though mothers are more concerned with daughters only. The ascending nuclear family table shows sons preoccupied with their mothers and rarely with their fathers, whereas daughters feel the opposite. They were probably concerned with fathers rather than mothers. In the sibling table, brothers are more concerned with their other brothers and sisters, whereas sisters might be concerned with brothers but not with sisters. The extended family table shows a mild concern with some extended family members, such as aunt, father-in-law, son-in-law, brother-in-law and step-mother. Lastly, although the Taymanite female tomb is small in size, Wašūḥ the Taymanite, had, uniquely, included in it her clients, male and female.

The available data suggests that the man in Ḥegra was responsible firstly for his wife, then for his mother followed by the rest of the family, whereas the woman was more concerned about her offspring, as is found in all the female inscriptions, with special reference to daughters. The many references to men making tombs for their brothers and sisters would suggest that one of the brothers in a family takes the initiative in making a tomb for the family, most probably the eldest brother. Making tombs for other members of the family, by adding them to the principal party, is found in most of the funerary inscriptions.

The absence of the tombs made by certain family members for other family members, such as by a wife for a husband, by a mother for a son, by a daughter for a mother, and by a sister for a sister, might be related to prevailing economic or religious traditions. A father, husband or son who was financially incapable of having a tomb cut for him and his family would presumably not have one. One might wonder what would happen to their social status, honour or pride, if heads of family failed to have a tomb of their own. There are not enough data, at present, to determine these factors for certain. Probably a family would depend on the financially better off members. Otherwise, they would cut out a modest grave, or dig an ordinary earth grave or ground-burial (see plate XIII), of which many have been uncovered around the sedentary area of Ḥegra. On the other hand, it shows that to whom one makes a tomb generally signifies the assertion of responsibility, generated from the male members in the family towards their household members, be they male or female.

Women made tombs mainly for their offspring (7 tombs), their father (JS34), brother (JS13), daughter(s) (JS11, 12), aunt (JS13), and in an exceptional situation, made tomb for the gr 'client, proteégée' (JS12) as well. From the data presented, it seems that women might have had a similar obligation towards their family household as men, depending probably on their status or social condition. They are found more often sharing the ownership of a tomb with other family members, such as mother and daughter (JS16, 11-12), niece and aunt (JS 13-14), brother and a sister (JS30), and a husband (JS24, 33). However, one notes that women did not make tombs for their sons or husbands.

Drawing conclusions from the funerary texts of Ḥegra is not totally safe because they represent only one perspective on society. And since it is anyway impossible to find out about the real past as it was, one would therefore be restricted to analysing and comparing aspects of these data with others, which can help in elucidating this case. For example, is it possible to understand the conjugal status of women by setting up certain hypothesis? To find out whether women owners of Ḥegran tombs were divorcees, widows, married or single, one would expect them to include or exclude certain members of the family. It is possible that this line of research can lead to some results. Firstly, if the woman was a divorcee, it is probable that her tomb would not include her ex-husband, but will include children and offspring. Secondly, if she were a widow,[154] she would probably include her husband, children and family. Thirdly, if she was not married or had never married, she would not include a husband, children or offspring, but might include other family members. Fourthly, if she had the status of a married woman, where she would probably sharing her tomb with him. It is improbable that a married woman would have a separate tomb with her children, while her husband sets up another tomb with other children.

If one examines these points, one finds firstly that no husband was included in any female tomb. This probably means that these tombs would have either belonged to divorcees or to single women. Not having any reference of including husbands in tombs shows that none of the female tomb owners of Ḥegra was a widow, except the single tomb stone found in Suwayda, made by a widow[155] for her *b'l*, 'husband' (CIS, II, 162). Having no tombs without offspring indicates that none of these tombs belonged to single women. Unless there were other familial and conjugal relations that are specific to them, the society is open to accept a wider range of possibilities. These possibilities attempt to explain the status of those women with children but without husbands.

The first possibility is that these women were divorcees, and being so, they were in charge of their children's welfare. This hypothesis, however, seems to present some problems, regarding the limited information about marriage laws among the Nabataeans, which are not enlightening about the possibility of divorce. Even though the story of the Nabataean king's daughter being repudiated and divorced by Herod II is recounted, it is not known whether that was permissible in Nabataean society. On the other hand, why would the children be the mother's responsibility, unless one is witnessing here another structure of familial relations, in which a matrilinear system operates? This could be made clearer through the second possibility, which suggests that there was a second or third wife.[156] Nonetheless, the problem of the affiliation of children and offspring remains to be faced either by the mother or the father.

A third possibility, regarding the fate of children and offspring, might suggest that these women were single mothers, either by deserting a husband or having another form of marriage arrangement that produces children without tying the woman to the husband, nor the children to their father. This type of relationship, in its turn, raises three main questions about custody of children, the female genealogical chains of affinity and the guardianship. The

[154] Jewish orphans always needed guardians, responsible for the child's well being. In the case of Babatha's orphan son Jesus, he had two guardians, a Jewish and a Nabataean and a woman supervisor (see Lewis 1978: 108; Cotton 1993: 96; Lewis 1994: 245).

[155] Another example of a probable widow from near Belenkli-Skelesi in Asia Minor, made a sarcophagus for herself, her husband, their children, daughters-in-law and grand-children(Parrot 1939: 114).

[156] Numismatic sources are informative about the kings as well as the queens. In the case of the last Nabataean kings, whose queens' names are known, one finds that two of them had two successive queens, Ḥāriṯah IV and Rab'el II. It is not clear whether these kings remarried after outliving their wives, or if they repudiated them. It is noted that the names of the first queen, Ḫuld in the case of Ḥāriṯah and Jamīlah in the case of Rab'el, cease to aspire once the second emerges. Although it seems surprising that the two queens died long before their husbands, Ḫuld died around 15 or 16 CE whereas Ḥāriṯah lived until 40 CE, and Jamīlah died circa 101 CE, whereas Rab'el died about 106 CE. It is unlikely that the kings repudiated their wives, for this was not an acceptable custom among the royalty and one should be surprised to find it otherwise.

tendency of males making tombs for other family members, especially that of husbands for their wives bears some significance about the level of responsibility embedded within the society. Although many women made tombs for male members of the family, including fathers, sons and brothers, the number of husband-for-wife tomb's as opposed to none wife-for-husband, suggests a patriarchal system.

It could be suggested in this respect that these children belonged to the mother and possibly adopted their maternal chains of affinity. Whatever possibility is chosen, women in all cases were also expected to be in charge of the household. This could expand sometimes to the woman's extended family and clients, in addition to the responsibility they were taking towards their children. The present conclusion, however, has a problem, for there are some limitations observed on female tombs regarding the legitimate hereditary line.

In most of the Ḥegran funerary inscriptions one finds that reference to offspring included in the tomb is worded in different categories: *lnpšh, lbnwhy, lbnth, lyldh, l'ḥrh, 'ṣdq b'ṣdq*, that is, 'for him/herself', 'for his/her sons', 'for his/her daughters', 'his/her children', 'his/her descendants', 'by legitimate heredity'.[157] These categories were not equally prevalent and some tombs would include or exclude some of them. It is not clear; however, whether this was a conscious act. Supposing it was, one would suggest the following interpretation.

A few categories had limitations in using some legal terms. Firstly, the reference to offspring in the female tombs did not contain the category 'by legitimate heredity'. Secondly, in the Jewish tomb (A8: JS 4) the formula 'descendants' (*'ḥrh*) is absent. Thirdly, in the Taymanite tombs, male and female (A3, B10), and the tomb of Sakīnah the Muzniyyah (C1), the 'descendants' (*'ḥrh*) formula is absent, as well as the wording for 'by legitimate heredity'. In these tombs the owners were not giving any reference as to making the tombs for their descendants, as in the Taymanite and Jewish tombs, nor to their legitimate heredity, as in the female tombs and in both Taymanite tombs (see al-Fassi 1997: 55).

From the first observation, it appears that since women did not possess the power to give legitimate inheritance to their descendants, it could be that female descendants were not regarded as having legitimate heredity per se. A situation suggests that women in general could not validate the legitimacy of their children, which was apparently established through the male's parentage only, the clearest feature of a patriarchal system. It is not possible, however, to dismiss the strong possibility that the single mothers of the Ḥegra female tombs were heads of their own households and that their children adopted the mother's genealogical line.[158] David Johnson finds that all children referred to in these tombs do not refer to any fathers, and must have followed a maternal genealogical chain of affinity (1987: 138). This result could contradict the previous suggestion that female tombs were owned by single mothers, either divorcees or second wives, whose children probably belonged to/and had adopted their mother's parentage. This finding cannot be understood in the presence of the limitations found on the legitimacy of their hereditary lines.

The term for legitimacy of heredity (*ṣdq*) is a common Semitic root found in many other languages sharing the same meaning. It was however, generally related to the legitimate status of kings and to the next heir to the throne (see Hoftijzer & Jongeling 1995 II: 962ff.). In Nabataean, it is more socially oriented.

If legitimacy is established by the male parentage, then the question that will arise is: Would the children of the Ḥegran single mothers be considered illegitimate? This might remain as an open question that could be discussed later. Yet the point that is worth noting is that these single mothers did not include in their tombs any sons, only daughters or other members. The offspring mentioned are all the offspring of their daughters. A remarkable finding, and it could explain the way these single mothers gained their custody, which was probably over their female children only, to whom and to whose offspring the mothers passed their inheritance, especially tombs. The absence of sons in the female tombs of Ḥegra coincides with the system known in pre-industrial societies where families care more for male offspring who are regarded as manpower and a source of wealth. Therefore, they might have been kept with their fathers.

One of the attempts to explain women's status was that provided by Daniel Ogden. He uses the category of 'bastardy' correlating between the high status of women in a society and the status given to bastards. It is tested by the principal question: whose child is it, the mother's or the father's? The status will be then measured by making the link between the recognition of maternal line rather than the paternal (1997: 225, 226). On the other hand, Gerda Lerner finds that the problem of women's status should be investigated within the level of women's control over their own sexuality and procreativity (1986: 7, 8). In tune with Lerner on sexual attitudes, Sergei Frantsouzoff considers matrilinearity; i.e. certain sexual liberty and economic independence, as markers for the high position that women occupied in southern Arabia, especially in Ḥaḍramawt and Qataban (forthcoming 19). Although the point of sexual liberty is an important staple for the discussion on bastardy

[157] For an elaborate discussion on the phrase *'ṣ dq b'ṣ dq* and its relation to Liḥyāntie, see Müller 1889: No. 16, 18 and Healey 1993b: 91-92.

[158] A question arises from the case of Jadalū d. of Bajarah from Ḍumayr who is called 'mother of Adramū', about whether this was a matrilinear line or only an echo of the tradition of calling women after their sons, which is known in Arabia since the pre-Islamic period (umm Adramū). It is not possible to resolve this since the remainder of the inscription refers to his father, 'Abd Mālik, the Strategos (CIS, II, 161).

and women status, I would leave it to a future independent study while concentrate here on the impact of matrilinearity in the Nabataean society.

Demonstrating bastardy within the Nabataean society would be hard, for although children of single mothers of Ḥegra tombs were denied the legitimacy on the basis of lack of legal heredity, it seems unlikely that these elite women's children were considered as illegitimate or that their mothers were outcasts, since they belonged to the upper-class stratum, headed by *strategoi* and *heparchoi*. Assuming that unmarried women with illicit children cannot belong to the upper class; or that bastards cannot belong to upper class society; or that upper class society does not recognise bastards; or simply, children born to unmarried women were considered legitimate and acceptable imposes an essentialist assumption on Ḥegran upper class women.[159] It is in fact possible to suggest that some of these women's children were bastards, demonstrating a possible sexual liberty that women might have had at the time. The possibility that children with matrilinear decent were illicit seems valid, except for the fact that women had only daughters in their tombs and bastardy is not limited to one sex.

From here one needs to discuss how matrilinear society operated and whether Nabataeans practised or recognised it.

1. Matrilinearity

Matrilinearity involves: firstly, tracing descent through the mother not the father. Secondly, associating descent with matrilocal residence, where the husband follows the place of the woman's family or tribe in what is also known as the 'postmarital residence'. Thirdly, the authority within the family will belong primarily to some male representative of the wife's kin (Maciver & Page 1961: 248), and fourthly, the inheritance takes place through the female line, i.e. her property (Stone 1976: 32). Matrilinearity can be considered to be a marker that demonstrates the rise or decline of women's status in a given society. Although it was attacked by many, as it is firmly rooted in the evolutionism of last century and in the theory of the matriarchal society of Bachofen in)1861(and L.H.Morgan (1851, 1877) (see Rosaldo & Lamphere 1974: 2; Dostal 1989: 47), matrilinearity and women's status can still be valid if combined with other markers and special social settings. It is important, however, to distinct matrilinearity from matriarchy. Anthropologists have dismissed the theory of the existence of a matriarchal society where women are the dominant sex, ruling over society, religion, have a matrilineal decent system and the major contributor to subsistence.

[159] See the example of noble and aristocratic women in Asia Minor in the first century BCE where the children born to unmarried common and noble women, were acceptable and given the name of their mothers (Stone 1976: 45).

It has been found that there is no such society available in reality, and that most and probably all contemporary societies, on whom much of this theory was based, are characterized by some degree of male dominance (Rosaldo & Lamphere 1974: 3).

According to Martin Wright's data and results, one cannot correlate woman's status and matrilinearity or matrilocality, for they are not significant on their own. Therefore, one needs to examine these systems with prudence. Merlin Stone, on the other hand, held the view that there is a cause and effect relationship between the veneration of the goddess and matrilinearity and the status of women (1976: 30-61, esp. 58-60). Although in the original form of matrilinearity, found in modern societies, men of the female kin are the controllers of property and in charge of their sister's family, the situation one is taking up in ancient society is removed from the current relationship. There is no proof for it; therefore, it is possible to consider matrilinearity, a system where children take their mother's lineage of parentage, as an indicator of women's control over their property. The fewer times we encounter property owners the more the society is developing towards patrilinear kinship (see the case of southern Arabia in Dostal 1989: 52). In the Nabataean case it can be said that an emphasis on economic independence and legal power, coupled with recognition of matrilinearity, can be significant in the Nabataean social context. One should not, however, forget the differences of class and their relation to the significance of matrilinearity, especially if it was to be associated with specific social strata.

To decide on the Nabataean system of descent, one should look at the different possibilities available to define societies in general, and then see which of them is more applicable to the Nabataean case. In this respect, the social system in general can be either:

1. Matrilinear.
2. Neither matrilinear nor patrilinear, but changing from one to the other.
3. Patrilinear, except in some cases such as:
    a. If the mother is prominent or is of a prominent family.
    b. If the patrilinear line is broken.

1. The first possibility is discarded because the genealogy lines provided by the Nabataean inscriptions display a clear majority of patrilinear parentage.

2. The second possibility is also excluded for there is not enough evidence for it, nor is it an easy system to use.

3. The third possibility, patrilinearity, is clearly the one used by Nabataean society. Since the majority of the genealogies given in Nabataean or even Greek inscriptions and papyri are patrilinear it is possible to agree that it was the prevailing system used by the Nabataeans. That does not, however, exclude the possibility of including other

types of systems within the principal line, because there are some matrilinear genealogies in a few cases that need to be put into context.

3a. In a patrilinear society, matrilinearity could be used in certain cases. Indeed, such as the Nabataean situation, and could explain the incidents of matrilinearity found within the royal line, or in some families in Ḥegra.

Putting Nabataean society in perspective, the first case of is found mainly among the royalty. Then it stretches from the royal house to the elite and whoever is in their class, such as the priestesses. Examples can be found within the Nabataean dynasty, probably in the exogamic marriages of its women, *ḥrtt br hgrw brt ḥrtt* (Ḥārithah s. of Hājar d. of Ḥārithah) (CIS, II, 354) and *qšm' br š'wdt brt mlkw br ḥrtt* (Qāsim s. of Sa'īdah d. of Mālik s. of Ḥārithah) (RES 1434). Other royal examples are to be found in the later Arabian history of the Laḫmīds of Ḥira: al-Muniḏir s. of Mā' al-Samā', who was his mother, and in Kinda, 'Amrw s. of Hind d. of 'Amrw s. of Ḥijr. Also available is the reference to the elite of Ḥegra who followed in the steps of the royalty, such as *'nmw br gzy't* (Ġānim s. of Juzay'ah) (JS 24: 36CE) *mḥmyt brt w'ylt* (Maḥmiyyah d. of Wā'ilah) (JS 14: 58CE), *'bd'bdt br mlykt* ('Abd'Obadah s. of Malīkah (JS 34: 71CE), *'mt brt kmwlt* ('Amah d. of Kamūlah) (JS 35: 74CE), and *tym'lhy br ḥmylt* (Taymāllāhī s. of Ḥamlah) (JS 27),[160] as well as the example of the Ḥegran priestess Kamkam, who holds a genealogy to her grand-mother, *kmkm brt w'lt brt ḥrmw*, or if one starts by her daughter, one would have three generations *klybt brt kmkm brt w'lt brt ḥrmw* (Kulaybah d. of Kamkam, d. of Wā'ilah, d. of Ḥarām) (JS 16: 1BCE- 1CE).

3b. The second possibility is broken patrilinear descent, which could explain the problem of succession after 'Obadah's death, that gave Sullay high expectations of the throne. This shows that the system where the heredity passes through the female line was not the general rule but was possible if an ambitious person was taking the opportunity and making advantage of it, and that was what Ḥāriṯah made sure would happen. A later example of such situation was found in the case of the Prophet Muḥammad's descendants. Although he died without a male descendant, his line continued through his daughter, Fātimah, and later through her sons, by which means the line returned to patrilinearity. In the Nabataean case, it is suggested that Ḥāriṯah gained his legitimacy to the throne through his mother, Hājar (Starcky1971: 151-159), then later the male line took precedence again, and the descent line became patrilinear.

According to the latter supposition, and in looking at the critical first year of Ḥāriṯah's reign, research finds that his choices to gain legitimacy of rule were to be advanced either through his wife, who could have been King 'Obadah's daughter, or through his mother, who was probably King Mālik's daughter. Both were *malikah* of the Nabataeans. In addition to the obvious importance of his wife, Ḥāriṯah's mother's role was interesting and I would argue that it was central, at least in the beginning, to Ḥāriṯah's ascent to the throne.

Ḥāriṯah's early coinage remarkably shows the bust of the queen, then of the king, in what I called earlier Type 1 of Ḥāriṯah's first year minting. The obverse shows the jugate bust of Ḥāriṯah and the queen, uniquely having the queen in the foreground, both diademed, with an eagle standing on the reverse, bearing an inscription referring to the king only, in his simple title, *ḥrtt mlk' mlk nbṭw*. In the first type, the queen is anonymous (Meshorer 1975: No. 47, 47a, plate XXVII), shows a remarkable and puzzling feature. Why is there such an emphasis on the queen on coins even before any queen's name appeared? The year 9/8 BCE was the first crucial year of Ḥāriṯah's reign, which witnessed the death of 'Obadah and the struggle for the throne between Ḥāriṯah and Sullay, the ambitious vizier. This queen is unlikely to be Queen Ḫuld, for no explanation can be given for such a portrayal, especially since Ḫuld appears later in the same year (probably the end of it) in the usual way behind the king, like the previous queen in 'Obadah's reign. Type I coin, made of two pieces, was the only type with these features, which carries special emphasis regarding this queen, who dominates the coin and takes precedence over the king. The only analogy found in the coinage of the 'Hellenistic' post-Achaemenid period is that of the Seleucid (originally Ptolemaic) queen, Cleopatra Thea, when she was co-ruling with her son, Antiochus VIII (126-121 BCE). On coins, she is shown as a senior partner in the foreground (SNG IV/III 1971: No. 5780-83) (plate XXVII).

It is probable; therefore, that Nabataean coin type 1 portrayed in fact, the queen mother with her son, i.e. Hājar and Ḥāriṯah. Hence, two questions remain. The first concerns the reason why the queen mother disappeared for twenty-seven years (she must have been in her sixties when she reappeared). The second is about the anonymity of the coin. One might not have adequate answers yet, but the disappearance of the queen mother could possibly be attributed to a struggle that emerged between her and her daughter-in-law. Ḫuld seems to have been a strong queen, who established her power to become an example for her successors. She was the first queen to be mentioned by name on coins and inscriptions. There is no reference to the queen mother, except that after the death or disappearance of Ḫuld, by the 16th year of Ḥāriṯah's rule. Šaqīlah I, Ḥāriṯah's sister, started to appear on coins instead of Ḫuld as one would expect. Two years afterwards, in his 18th year, an inscription is dedicated to Ḥāriṯah and Hājar, his mother, probably reconciliation from Šaqīlah's side for her own mother (for details see al-Fassi forthcoming/c).

As for the question of anonymity, it seems that the queen mother, Hājar, although she was powerful enough to be portrayed on coins in the foreground, type I, was not

[160] See *ḥršw brt s'wdt* (CIS, II, 786) from Wādī Mukattab in Sinai.

yet prepared to break the rule of anonymity, which did not necessarily mean that she was unknown among the Nabataeans. It is probable however, that her depiction on the coin in a dominating fashion was not imposed by herself, rather by King Ḥāriṯah who must have found it useful in his struggle for legitimacy, therefore, removing her from the foreground later by Ḫuld was not a great trouble. There is no other explanation of her importance than that she had a specific affinity with the dynasty, and it was through her that Ḥāriṯah had legitimised his claim to the Nabataean throne. On examining the inscription in the Wādī Mūsā, dating from 8 CE and referring to King Ḥāriṯah, Queen Hājar and King Mālik (Starcky 1971: 151-159), Starcky was led to give preference to a 'maternal line' view through which Ḥāriṯah was able to claim to power. Therefore, the maternal connection was essential in that period and seems to have continued to be so throughout later Nabataean history.[161] The importance accorded to Ḥāriṯah's mother probably led to some changes in Nabataean society that gave the space to royal women specifically to exercise more power; in particular, royal women were given or assumed the title *mlkt*, a status for which there is no equivalent among the royal men, although such a form of title was not new in Greater Syria and royal women were called by it (see the Syriac inscription about Queen Salmā found in Urfa (Edessa), in Drijvers 1972: no. 27). Thus it is probable that it became the rule that the mother of the legitimate Nabataean king be called *malikah*. Such a position of royal women seems to have been further enforced by Queen Ḫuld and her successors establishing a special status for royal women. The breach of anonymity, however, was exploited and further established by Queen Ḫuld as seen earlier (see also al-Fassi: forthcoming/ b).

To conclude, matrilinearity may be considered in the Nabataean mother queen's case as on the one hand, one of the main factors in the legitimising of Ḥāriṯah's reign, and on the other, as a marker in the direction of raising woman's status. From then onward, Nabataean queens appear in a positive presence on coins by showing their name. Their prominence was later expanded to include royalty members if the elite and possibly the average woman. The major arguments can be summed up as follows: firstly, matrilinearity was not necessarily a sign of women's high status. Secondly, this system was not necessarily prevalent for any single reason. There are reasons why a matrilinear system might be used or recognised within a patrilinear system that would take different answers according to the social and historical context and tradition.

The possibilities that would explain a matrilinear system according to the Arabian society are the following: 1. the exceptionality of the woman's blood lineage, such as belonging to a royal house or nobility; 2. being an influential, important, famous woman, such as a poet, healer, etc.; 3. belonging to an influential tribe that is more important than the husband's; 4. being an important woman in cult practices such as a priestess, who might not even marry; 5. belonging to an unknown father, or being an illegitimate child, a bastard. In all these cases, matrilinearity was a choice recognised where, either the woman is more important than her husband or her husband's clan by her exceptionality, or that the father is unknown for any reason. Taking the first and last explanatory possibilities suggested, and then this research will look at how matrilinearity cannot be considered always as a positive sign of women's status, for one cannot deny the difference in the status between a bastard and descent from a royal mother. As matrilinearity is a possible marker of a special status given to women, one needs to look at the other aspects where Nabataean women enjoyed certain recognition in relation also to matrilinearity.

III. The 'Sacred': Nabataeans and Priesthood

It is difficult to divorce politics from religion in ancient times, as well as today in some parts of the world. For a long time, possibly since the Neolithic age, the sovereign was a manifestation of the divine and his human incarnation (see al-Azmeh 1997: 11-34). This was the case both for kings and queens. The male sovereign would also be the master of war, of justice and the generator of unity and order. Since the time of early Sumerian records, one encounters the priest-ruler. Societies were first ruled by the 'pastor', the priest, known in Sumerian as *en* or *sanga*,[162] found also in southern Arabia in the form of *mukarrib* (Dostal 1989: 51, fn. 34) and *rašū 'm* (Al-Naim 2000: 114, 121). The next step for the priest-king was to deify himself. The dogma of the divine king progressed from a view of his being an intermediary between humans and the divinities, especially through the sacred marriage known among the Sumerians, where the king was incarnated in the image of the god Dumūzi in the sacred marriage with Innana-Ishtar, to being the son of god and goddess, and as husbands to the goddess Innana (Frymer-Kensky 1992: 58-59), then the god himself. The first king to call himself a god was the Akkadian Narāmsin, 'king of the universe and god of Agade' (Cerfaux & Tondirau 1957: 88). In Egypt, the Pharaoh was identified with Horus, through which the king became the son of Osiris. This concept was taken on by the later monarchies especially by the Macedonian Ptolemies, seeing its culmination in the time of Cleopatra VII (ibid. 81-82, 302-304). The king was either a manifestation of the god, or the vice-regent of gods such as Ahura Mazdāh, Yahweh and Marduk (Eddy 1961: vii),[163] or the divine himself (See Postgate 1992: 266ff.; al-Azmeh 1997: 19-34, esp. 24). The king's association with the divine would be

[161] The detailed thesis is found in my article to be published by Adumatu in July 2007 entitled 'Nabataean Queens: an analytical study'.

[162] *En* is one of the terms for a 'king' in some Sumerian cities. It originated from high priestly office. *sanga*, means originally 'chief accountant of the temple'. Both show the nature of the relationship between the ruler and the temple (Nemet-Nejat 1998: 217).

[163] See for example this Akkadian proverb: 'Man is the shadow of a god, and a slave is the shadow of a man; but the king is the mirror of a god' (Nemet-Nejat 1998: 217).

shown in the ceremonies applied to his funeral and tomb.[164] The level of deifying would depend on the power the ruler attained and the tradition within which he operated.

Priestesses emerged from a similar relation with rulers. The first queens or wives of a king known to be high priestesses were Lugalanda's wife Baranamtara of Lagash (ca. 2350 BCE), and Urukagina's wife Shag-Shag, also of the Early Dynastic Period. A daughter of a king was the famous Enḫeduanna, the daughter of Sargon of Akkad (ca. 2371-2316 BCE), who was the high priestess of the Moon-God Nanna of Ur and the temple of An, the supreme God of Heaven, at Uruk. Enḫeduanna was also the first poetess in history who left poetry and hymns to the goddess Inanna. She was followed by Enmenanna, Naram-Sin's daughter who held the same position of Enḫeduanna and called herself 'wife of Nanna'. The tradition of appointing princesses as high-priestesses continued throughout the Sumerian and Akkadian period (Batto 1974: 8, 30, n.2; Lerner 1986: 62-68; Frymer-Kensky 1992: 64-65); Nemet-Nejat 1998: 150). In ancient Egypt, a similar role was occupied by royal women. In the time of Ramesses II (1289-1224BCE) and later, they served as 'the so-called God's Wife of Amun, a role that combines the divine with the human in her person' (Hollis 1997: 224). Priestesses were categorised as belonging to the upper class in a society, either by their connection to royalty or the elite. Sacred marriage, as it seems, was not exclusive to the king or priestesses, we find that in southern Arabia Ma'in women were given in marriage to the God 'Aṯtar where he choses a woman in a certain day annually (RES 3306; Naim 2000: 710-713)

Priests and priestesses were expected to be guardians of the interests of the gods and goddesses, preservers of the temple, the supervisors of the gifts offered and the sacrifice presented, mediators between gods and worshippers, manifesting their oracles, supervising the fertility cult of sacred marriage especially in Sumer and Akkad, writing and reading the appropriate hymns and poems (Frymer-Kensky 1992: 64). It is not unlikely that the Nabataean king was also the high priest of Dushara, since Dushara is the dynastic god, 'God of (our) Lord', and that the queen was the high priestess of the mother goddess, Allāt-Isis (al-Fassi: forthcoming/ b).

Nabataean priests appear under different titles, which could either denote a hierarchy or simply different linguistic derivations. Among these are *khn* (*kāhin*), *kmr* (*kamar*),[165] *rb* (*rabb*) and *'pkl* (*'afkal*). The reference to several of these titles for one god or goddess shows a hierarchy rather than a mere linguistic difference. For Allāt, three priesthood titles are cited in two inscriptions from Ramm (see plate XXXII), which refer to a *khn 'ltw 'lht(')*, *kāhin* of Allāt the goddess (Savignac 1932: No. 2), and an *'pkl* (Savignac 1933: No. 2). A third, found in Ḥibran in Ḥawrān and dating from 47 CE, refers to a *kmr 'lt*, *kamar* of Allāt (CIS,II,170).

Al-'Uzzā priests were given the title *kāhin* and appear frequently in Sinai (CIS, II, 611) (see plate XXXIII). Savignac noted that the word *khn* is not familiar in Aramaic and suggested that this word was a borrowing from Arabic (1932: 592-93), whereas Teixidor regards it as more relevant to the Canaanite culture rather than Arabic (1995: 121). Her priests in pre-Islamic Arabia were from the tribe of banū Šaybān from Sulaym (Ibn Hišām I: 78; Ibn al-Kalbī 22). In the early Arabic Islamic sources, the *kāhin* and *sādin* were those who predict, tell secrets of the past and present and utter oracles of the exegesis of dreams with the aid of *jinn*, spirits, or underworld creatures. There were famous *kāhins* on the eve of Islam, such as Saṭīḥ and Šiqq (see Ibn Hišīm I: 30-33; James 1955: 92-93), as well as priestesses, *kāhināt* such as Sujāḥ and others. There is no information about Manāt's priests, although reference to her appears equally in male and in female tombs. In pre-Islamic Arabia, her priests also were men. It was known that the clan of 'Attāb s. of Mālik from the tribe of Ṭaqīf were her servants or sadanah (pl. of sādin) (Ibn al-Kalbī 16).

Afkal, originally the Akkadian *Apkallu*, means 'the wise' (Teixidor 1995: 121), and was also found in the Liḥyānite inscriptions (*Afkal* of Allāt (JS 277)). It is also found in many inscriptions from Sinai, in Tal al-Šuqāfiyyah, in Sīḥ Sidrah and other places for different deities (Littmann & Meredith 1954: No. 81; CIS, II, 526; 506, 526, 608, 766, 1236, 1748, 1885, 2491, 2665). Savignac suggested that *Afkal* was probably the highest religious authority, since the builders of the sanctuary at Ramm called themselves *ġlymw* 'the servants' of the *Afkal*, a term used normally in relation to the Lord, or the king (1933: 412). *kmr*, in the Official Aramaic *kmr'* (from Akkadian *kumritu*) for priest (Hoftijzer & Jongeling 1995 I: 516-517) appears twice in Nabataean. Once with Allāt in Ḥebran (CIS, II, 170) and the other time in the Temple of Winged Lions in Raqamū-Petra, which Hammond is arguing, belongs to Allāt (Hammond *et al* 1986: p.78, l. 2).[166]

The word for priestess is not attested so far in Nabataean, however, it is found in Liḥyānite as *'fklt* which could also be *'fkl lt* (JS 64L) where the *lām* is assimilated (al-Fassi 1993a: 264). Pre-Islamic priestesses were known in Arabia and a few references may be recorded briefly. Among these priestesses, *kāhināt*, there was Faṭimah al-Ḫaṯ'amiyyah in Makkah, Zarqā' al-Yamāmah in Najd, *kāhinat banī Sa'd*, Ṭurayfah, *kāhinah* of Yemen, Zabrā', between al-Šiḥr and Ḥaḍramawt, Salmā, the Hamdāniyyah al-Ḥimyariyyah and Ḥadas, from the north Arabian tribe of Ġanam (Ibn Hišām IV: 17; al-Suhailī 1:131-143; Zaydān 1967 III: 20).

[164] See for example the royal cemetery of Ur, including the king and queen, buried with human sacrifice of their court attendants who numbered over seventy men and women(Woolley 1934: 33ff., 63ff., 73ff.).

[165] Not found in Arabic.

[166] For other priestly titles see al-Fassi 1993a: 266-270; Teixidor 1995: 120-121; Healey 2001b: 163-165.

The priestess's role was not merely as a functionary of the rituals or of the oracle of a certain god or goddess, or to remove the spirits from a possessed (see the incantation text in Naveh 1979). Her role included what in modern classification would be listed under 'health and trade' or more generally, the 'public sector'. Discrimination between the public (and the secular) and the sacred have been challenged by anthropological and social studies (see for example Mann 1986 I: 126; Beard & Crawford 1989: 25-39). Here it is useful to point out some of the roles attributed to the temple and its functionaries that would clarify how the 'sacred' system functioned. Taking the different roles a priest or priestess used to play one should list all the following: being in charge of the different rituals, such as weddings, births, funerals, circumcision. It is possible that ancient priestesses had the secrets of using herbs; that they were expert healers. Their role might have extended to cover ceremonies of procreation in what is known in ancient Sumer as the 'sacred marriage', usually conducted between the goddess Innana-Ishtar (the love and fertility goddess or her representative, and the king, the representative of Dumuzi, Inanna's husband, which has been interpreted in later literature of Babylonia and Syria. as 'temple prostitution' (Frymer-Kensky 1992: 50-60).

Moreover, since the institution of the temple in most ancient societies, functioned as a bank (for example ancient Land of the Two Rivers, Mann 1986 I: 126; Driel 1999: 25) in today's terms, priests and priestesses would be expected to be involved in financial business. The temple used to collect tithes on silver, gold, offerings or provisions, as well as in silver or bronze coinage. The percentage is not clear in the inscription found on the inner wall of the Winged Lions Temple in Raqamū-Petra (Hammond *et al* 1986: 77-78). The allotting is to be given to the priest. Also included were fines collected on breaching tomb contract conditions, as found in Ḥegra. The inscription on the Kamkam tomb (JS 16) specifies clearly a sum of the fines to the priest. In addition to that, the temple was paid expiation. In the Winged Lions temple inscription there is a reference to a condition of payment in terms of acts of delinquency (Hammond *et al* 1986: 78, l.2). Even though the meaning is not clear enough, as the slab is broken half way, one would expect such functions to take place in the temple, or that such money would be paid in. Similarly, southern Arabia has left us an abundance of expiation inscriptions (see Frantsouzoff forthcoming; Al-Naim 2000: 106-111). The money that entered the treasury of the temple facilitated the investment deals that the priest/ess would have entered into, mainly investment in the caravan trade, as well as probably lending money to the state or individuals. Traces of the economic role are found in early Sumer and later, where the temple was the commercial centre, and undoubtedly, priests and priestesses would enter deals of buying, selling etc.

Furthermore, the temple was also used as an archive centre or a record house, as was noted twice in a papyrus and on tombs (Yadin 1963; 2002 doc 3; JS 36). Therefore, the temple with its crew of priests, priestesses, servants, slaves, worshippers, perhaps 'temple prostitutes', and perhaps travellers who are staying from aboard, was self-sufficient. The temple would function as a home for its priests/servants, as well as all the other roles it might have played. It encompasses the *ḥaram* or the sacred space that is protected by the sanctity of the temple's god or goddess. Its premises would usually include a resort of water either a well, cistern or a spring, as seen in Allāt's temple of Wādī Ramm (see plate XXXII). A *ḥaram* would be expected also to include a cemetery. It is expected also that the priesthood, similar to other professions, was hereditary within a family. Children were usually dedicated to the service of the god/dess. This is found in many traditions of Arabia, Babylonia, Egypt and Syria that priests and priestesses have special familial or marital arrangements that do not necessarily reflect the common custom. It includes celibacy or giving birth to children from unknown men. More can be demonstrated from the example below.

To sum up, any attempt, in the study of ancient societies, to separate the spheres of social life on the basis of imagining any line between the religious and the secular, or the sacred and the political/social, will not prove to be useful or informative, for it can easily lead to a belief that a real distinction existed.[167]

A. Kamkam the Priestess

The particular owner of tomb B19 in Ḥegra, Kamkam d. of Wā'ilah d. of Ḥarām, is of special interest here. Her tomb has interesting features that can help to clarify her identity (see plate IX). Kamkam's tomb is an early one dating from 1 BCE and in it she ordains a fine not to the king but to the priest, the *'afkal*. She does not name him or name the god/dess to whom he ministers. This is the only inscription that refers to a priest and ordains fines for him in addition to the fines for gods. It is expected that the fine that went to a deity went, in fact, to the temple. This case of specifying the priest with a special amount of fine shows, however, the important role that religion and the temple played in society at the end of the first century BCE. Kamkam did not specify a fine for the king. Interestingly though, the other contemporary tomb B6, which dates from 1 BCE as well, does not ordain any fines either for gods or kings (JS 8). It is possible that fines paid to the king were a later feature, copying an earlier allocation that used to go to the priest. Another possibility is that the priest occupied a higher and more prestigious position in Ḥegran society than the king or his representative, the governor, in that period, at the beginning of Nabataean rule over the city.

From another perspective relating to her special matrilinear genealogy, it seems possible that Kamkam was related to the type of temple where women were dedicated to the

[167] This section was part of a lecture given at the Anthropology Department, King's College in 1999. Special thanks is attributed to Prof. Madawi al-Rasheed, the head of the department's Seminar.

gods and might have sacred practices of procreation rituals. It is possible, therefore, to explain why she dedicated her fine to the priest *'pkl*[168] and not to the king, since her prime loyalty was to the gods and the temple's master. Avanzini has an opinion about women who appear in some South Arabian inscriptions with matrilinear genealogies. She wrote '*il me semble opportun de les* [polyandry and matrilinearity] *envisager comme des phénomènes propres à des femmes au statut spécial, probablement non-mariées, peut-être liées au culte*' (1991: 161). It seems probable; therefore, that Kamkam was a priestess, member of the second or third generation of priestesses dedicated to the temple. Hereditary professions are known in the ancient world, thus, having here a family of servants of the temple is not inconceivable, and that she belonged to a priesthood level below the *'pkl*.

The question remains: Whose temple was it? Kamkam, in addition to the fines, invoked special gods for curses. They included Manāt and her Qays, Allāt from 'Amnad, and Dushara's throne, in addition to Dushara proper, adding to them the god, Hubal as receiving fines. Kamkam's inscription provides the names of five gods and two specific epithets. That does not lead to a satisfactory conclusion as to which god/dess she was priestess, or which god/dess the Afkal was serving. That will stay an enigma until a temple is uncovered in Ḥegra and more inscriptions are found.

The exterior of her tomb is interesting also for it is differently designed, having bas-reliefs of an eagle centred on the arch of the door. Curiously enough, this feature is not found in any other tomb in Ḥegra. Although one can relate the eagle to a solar god who can be identified with Dushara (see Healey 1993a), yet, it is not enough to specify the principal god for whom Kamkam was a priestess. A final and simple suggestion could be that she was not a priestess of a specific god/dess, but rather for all the gods known in Ḥegra and northern Arabia, old and new. A dedication to all the gods appears for example in the female Taymanite tomb of Wašūḥ (JS 11-12). Having said that, suggesting the goddess Manāt, the principle goddess in the Ḥijāz, as the goddess of Kamkam is not unlikely to be.

IV. Conclusion

From this chapter, one can see that Nabataean women enjoyed a particular visibility within several domains. In the political, the queen, be it mother, wife or sister, has achieved and established a positive image that encouraged other women, although applicable mainly to the elite. It was not, however, a position that was accessible to any queen. It required a great deal of political skill and effort. The ability of some queens such as Ḫuld or Šaqīlah II to exercise sovereignty was no doubt due to their personal capacities and the way in which they have managed to dominate their circumstances (see more examples of consort queens in Ben-Barak 1987: 38-39). It is important to put the phenomenon of the Nabataean queens within the framework of the global world then. They represent many similarities with the other 'Hellenistic' 'Hellenistic' post-Achaemenid queens of the Ptolemies or Selucids. The situation of Zenobia is not much different from the regent queens of the above monarchies. The historical stage was friendly to women's participation in the public domain at that point as it seems, relatively at the least. This visibility flourished in legal as well as social aspects. Nabataean women entered transactions and disposed of their property without the need for a guardian, following the pattern of a general common law that governed the Nabataeans.

The above sections have shown the legal power that Nabataean women enjoyed and its significance. Although taking legal power as a marker for women's status has been criticised by Gerda Lerner, who does not find it significant, it has been argued that legal power can be significant once it is joined with other markers, a point that will be developed further in the coming chapter. It is, however, accepted that in any society, not all who qualify as 'persons' are equals. There are differences of gender, class, freedom, religion, age, etc. that played a role in differentiating and destabilising the common understanding of personhood. Certain legal practices, such as exercising different types of transactions, owning property and disposing of it, entering contracts without a guardian, inheriting and passing inheritance to offspring, demonstrate a capacity to acquire financial power and independence in a way that can be understood to empower elite women specifically, and enhance their status.

The case study of the Ḥegran women showed that the female tombs belonged to single mothers according to the social form that existed at the time. I argue that Nabataean women as wives, divorcees, one of many wives, or were unmarried, could take the recognised initiative of becoming the head of their own household. The tomb and the hierarchy expressed in a funerary text are a mirror of house structure, representative of the familial household. That includes a partial adaptation of a matrilinear system in terms of genealogy and economic authority in a household, which I would consider as a marker for the rise in women's status, especially in terms of women's economic autonomy.

The question that remains is how can the prominent nature of Nabataean women be explained? This will be the task of the next chapter.

[168] A partly similar situation is found in the Tal al-Šuqāfiyyah inscription, which is dated after the Ptolemaic king as well as the priest, *'pkl* (see Strugnell 1959: 31-32).

Chapter Five

Mapping Nabataea: Behind the Emergence of Woman

Previous chapters have demonstrated the special status that Nabataean women enjoyed, especially during the last couple of centuries of the kingdom's existence, that is, the first centuries BCE-CE. Previous sections have illustrated the political emergence of the queen, the legal power given to or obtained by women, and the role matrilinear genealogy played within society. This chapter is faced with the challenge of explaining how women's emergence came about. The question for concern here is why would the status of women progress at one time and deteriorate at another? This will be achieved by looking at the theory of the status of woman, assessing its application and suggesting possibilities to explain the specific Nabataean case.

I. Status

The status of women, if expressed vaguely, can lead to misinterpretation, especially when generalised in terms of society, class, wealth, etc., for as Ogden puts it, 'different women have different statuses in the same society (e.g. slave women, free women, queens); the same woman can have different status in different contexts in the same society (e.g. law versus religion); different individuals in a society (men or women) have different attitudes to women, both to women as a whole and as individuals; and social practices in general can have a very indirect relationship with their corresponding ideologies' (1997: 225). In general, it should be taken into consideration that the status of women is similar in all societies of the ancient world in terms of the ordinary role of women. It can be summed up as taking care of the household, rearing and raising children and giving a notably high respect to the mother. For such a role, a woman was always under the protection of the parental or marital house (Vercoutter 1965: 151-52). The following will look at the various ways to explain the status of women, so as to be able to pin down the form most representatives of Nabataean women.

The theory or theories of female status are many and sometimes contradictory in cross-cultural studies, sociology and women's studies (Whyte 1978: 31). The status of women is generally defined in terms of: '1. The degree to which females have authority and/or power in the domestic and/or public domains; and 2. The degree to which females are accorded deferential treatment and are respected and revered in the domestic and/or public domains', however, 'high female status in one domain precludes, or is antecedent to, high status in another domain' (Sanday 1974: 191). Though authority and deferential treatment are crucial in measuring female status, I wonder whether the legal status of women and its application can contribute to the definition of 'status'.

In this respect the theories answer two major questions, the 'how and when' and the 'why'. In the following, I shall explain these.

1. Firstly, the theories that answer the 'how' and 'when' question, or in other words when exactly and how did the status of women deteriorate? These in fact, are theories that deal with problems of 'origin' and describe historical developments. The leaders in this area are Harris and Ross (1987) and Gimbutas (1991). Most of these theories agree that women's status was different, or higher, prior to or in the early Neolithic period, that is, before the development of agriculture. This mode of production increased the burden of work for women, and at the same time there was an increase in population, which, in its turn, is correlated with female reproduction (see Harris and Ross 1987: 49-50; Gimbutas 1991: 324). According to Marija Gimbutas, the earliest civilisations of the world in China, Tibet, Egypt, the 'Near East' and Europe, were in all probability matristic i.e. 'Goddess civilisations', (accepting that agriculture was developed by women). It was also the Neolithic period, which witnessed or created the conditions for the matrilinear system to survive from Palaeolithic times. Gimbutas finds that women continued having matriclan systems during a period of high influence in farming, crafts, arts, and social functions (1991: 324). Gerda Lerner, on a similar line, dates the high status of women to the pre-writing period, according to her research on 'Mesopotamian' women (1986). This issue will not be expanded further as the point of concern here is not the origin of the problem, but rather the reason behind the continuing low status of women, if or when this occurs, and the reason behind the periodic emergence of a high status for women.

2. Secondly, theories that try to explain why the status of women would progress in one time and deteriorate in another. Among the views given, the major relevant reasoning is that connected to male absence, such as in the case of long periods of warfare or long-distance trade, in addition to other minor theories. The question

of concern here, however, is how women were empowered in one time and subordinated in another. This is the concern of the following section, which starts with a discussion of the long male absence.

II. Opportunity and Response

A. Male absence

Peggy R. Sanday, in a study derived mainly from modern societies according to anthropological methodology, formulated a hypothesis about male absence. She finds that the absence of men changes the balance of power between males and females. The predominant emphasis in her schema is on male absence, ecological factors, and changing demands on females. Any condition of prolonged male absence can result in females invading the subsistence sphere if social survival is to continue.[169] Certain ecological conditions can have the same effect. When females move into the subsistence sphere, her flow diagram in Figure 3[170] suggests three possibilities:

Women may occupy this sphere temporarily while males are absent; they may become the predominant labourers and remain in this sphere; or they may continue to occupy it in conjunction with males, and a condition of balanced division of labour may result. In the first case, the data of modern societies indicate that the public status of women does not change, whereas in the second case, the data indicate that women develop economic and political power. The evidence indicates that males develop an independent control sphere, with the result that women are treated as slave labour (Sanday 1974: 205-6). What remains is the third possibility of sharing responsibilities with women who stay in the public domain after the return of men. This seems to be one of the strongest factors in elevating the status of women, or at least, changing it.

The three cases occur in different societies according to their particularities that encourage and allow for one form rather than the other to formulate. From the three cases it appears that the empowerment of women only takes its ultimate form in the third case. Although latter form can explain female authority in some societies, it does not avoid the fact that such qualification cannot exist in an independent sphere, where women develop power on their own merit. One notes that for women's empowerment to operate, it needs to be free from male attendance. Or in other words, what blocks women from reaching authoritative positions in society is the male presence. The essence of women's empowerment only comes into existence in a negative situation, i.e. once it is not exposed to a male audience. In brief, her empowerment operates only in the absence of males. If that is the case, then there is something more problematic in the male-female relationship within society, which needs to be explored, however, it is beyond the scope of this study.

On the other hand, one can look at how women make use of the opportunity that male absence provides them, be it through war, trade, or death. The empowerment by death can be highlighted using the example of the power that widows gain from society, especially if they have male offspring. In this regard there are different illustrations in history. One can look at the third century CE to the case of Queen Zenobia of Palmyra who rebelled against the Romans and declared her city-state an empire (see Bowersock 1983: 123-137; Stoneman 1994). Another woman from the fourth century CE, Queen Mavia or Māwiyah was the widow of an Arab Sheikh who lead her people in southern Palestine to rebel against the Romans at the time of Valens (Bowersock 1980; Shahīd 1984: 138-202;) and in the mid-thirteenth century CE the empire of the Mongols was headed by the widow of the late Great Khān as regent (Morgan 1986: 40).

For the Nabataean case, research suggests that there are two principle causes for women's empowerment and elevation of status. These are, firstly, male absence in the form of involvement in full-time trade and secondly, the strong state that enforces law and order and secures the space for women to operate safely in the absence of their men. Each of these points will be explored individually below.

1. Trade

Long-distance trade can produce male absence in a given ancient society. Here long distance trade is defined by the length of time a caravan or journey takes. Difficult as it is to pin down, for ancient transport made every voyage a long one. But long-distance trade was specific in the ancient economy. It was only used for transporting and trading expensive and luxury goods. The land transport trade has been proven to be expensive, for it costs roughly sixty times as much as sea transport and ten times as much as transport by river except for the trade of luxury goods. Therefore, overland trade was exclusively concerned with trading and transporting luxury goods, which could be profitable even in limited volume which will equal high price (Hopkins 1983: xi, xx). The Nabataean caravan trade in frankincense and myrrh, an expensive luxury commodity (Pliny 12: 29-32) indicates that Nabataean trade was of the above type.[171]

[169] Male absence in some societies today takes the form of long periods of working a long-distance away, in what is known as the peasant immigration from the rural areas to the cities, and in other employment as when Arab, South Asian, and south-east Asian men work in the petroleum states.

[170] See Sanday's table for the theory of female status in the public domain, 1974: 196, fig.3.

[171] In the Ḥegra inscriptions, a reference was made to a brother who was away for long and whose place in the tomb was reserved for him whenever he returns (JS9).

The effects of long-distance trade on society were similar in some ways to long-range wars.[172] Women were left to take charge of their households during their husbands' absence, which can result in women destitute and the loss of land to creditors (see the case of Rome in Hopkins [1978] 1987: 30). On the other hand, women are forced to appear in the public stage to perform the tasks previously reserved for men and slaves. Most of their visibility, however, takes place among upper-class women who are usually more deprived of public appearance than rural women (Pomeroy 1984: 8-9). The peaceful nature, however, of this absence is one of its major differences from absence for war. Though male absence could be hazardous and anxiety-generating, nevertheless it was charged with hopes of welfare and economic increase, as well as creating needs and opportunity (Porten *et al* 1996: 76).

Although women, in this case, would be less stressed emotionally, they were faced with the additional demands of being in charge. On the other hand, men travelling with caravans conformed to an organised operation that could be planned for, and followed a rough time-table which corresponded with the harvest of frankincense and myrrh, at predictable times. These two aspects helped women in charge to be more efficient in management. Moreover, men would not be afraid that their place would have been taken on their return.

It would be useful to estimate the size of a caravan and its length of absence. This would help in understanding the impact that long-distance trade had on society, taking into consideration that the members of these caravans should be young and healthy men who could survive the difficulties of a long journey. Thereafter, the correlation would be made between the duration of caravans and the local subsistence needs, which encompass farming.

A caravan starting from Ḥegra to Šabwah in Ḥaḍramawt covers about 1285 miles in 52-66 days. 300 miles to Raqamū-Petra and another 125 to Ġazzah, gives a total of 69-88 days from Šabwah to the Mediterranean port (Strabo 16:4:19; Groom 1981: 213). If one takes Ḥegra to Šabwah as an example, the journey's duration was about two months. That means four months for a return journey, in addition to about a month of rest at each end, if no other problems delayed the caravan, such as unexpected weather. Thus, a caravaner would spend an average of five to six months in one journey a year, which is a part-time scheme of long-distance trade. At home women were left without their providers for half of the year. If the system changed into an intensified full-time long-distance trade, men would spend the whole year on the road and women would be expected to exercise more tasks and independence. This change has been proposed and argued by David Johnson (1987), who, in his study on Nabataean trade, comes to the conclusion that there was a relationship between the rise of Nabataean women's status and the shift in Nabataean trade from part-time to full-time. This happened by the first century CE, corresponding with changes happening in the economy of the region, at the end of the first century BCE and beginning of the first CE, with an increase in productivity and consumption (Hopkins 1983: xiv-xxi; Johnson 1987: 129-130). The increase in demand for the Arabian commodities (Groom 1981: 144) resulted in having a second harvest of frankincense (Pliny 12: 32). Johnson used an argument by Harris to suggest that long-distance trade is one of the activities that should lead to the increase of status for women, where they can develop a power base in the subsistence spheres. Johnson finds that the shift to full-time trade, and the increase of Nabataean sedentarisation by reliance on agriculture and abandonment of herding, culminated in Nabataean women's rise of status (1987: 129-130). Though Johnson's argument is useful and original, however, it can be elaborated.

Accepting that Nabataeans went in for full-time long-distance trade, that required men to be absent for almost all the year round, would raise the problem of explaining how the subsistence economy managed to carry on in the absence of men. And also requires finding out the extent of male participation in trade in proportion to the Nabataean population. A demographic study of the population requires scrutiny of three factors that determine the size and structure of all populations, these are mortality, and fertility and migration (see Parkin 1992: 72). One is aware that in a study of the current scale it would be difficult to realise these factors. What is possible to accomplish however, is a theoretical model that can be tested accordingly.

What is known about the Nabataean population comes from few classical sources. Diodorus, after Hieronymus, reported that by the fourth century BCE the Nabataeans were not more than ten thousand in number (Diodorus 19: 94) and in a later quotation Strabo, after Artemidorus, mentions how numerous the Nabataeans were (16: 4: 18). Other information comes from the military reports of losses or supports. They vary from 1000 to 50,000 soldiers, horsemen and infantry (Bowsher 1989: 19-20). A recent assessment suggests that the Nabataean army in the first century CE was about 10,000 (Parker 1986: 118; Bowsher 1989: 20). These figures can be vaguely significant to estimate the kingdom's population. One can try, however, to explore a hypothetical situation.[173] If one assumes that the inhabitants of Raqamū-Petra were about ten thousand by the end of the first century BCE, it is possible to assume that half the population, if not more, consisted of women. That leaves with five thousand men, from whom one can deduct another half who will constitute the elderly and children. That will leave about two and a

[172] See the examples of the queen of Mari, ḫibtu, empowered during her husband's war activities (ca. 1779/8-1745 BCE) (Batto 1974: 21), and the women of Sparta (see Moore's commentary on Xenophon's Poleiteia of the Spartans, 1975: 95-96). Muslim societies during *Islamic expansion* can also be a useful example to explore.

[173] See the discussion on estimated population hypotheses in Esse 1991: 132.

half thousand adult men who can be involved in the trade activity. Deducting from this number a few hundred for the administrative jobs etc. the expected number will be of about two thousand men leaving the city and their wives behind. Another similar number can be expected to join the caravan from the other major cities but smaller than Raqamū-Petra such as Ḥegra and Boṣra. This will bring the number of caravaners up to about four thousand men.

From another set of calculations it is possible to reach the number of camels involved in the frankincense caravan. Nigel Groom reaches an assumption that a camel-load of incense was 400 pounds (533 Roman pounds) (1981: 160). Then by multiplying the weight by the price Pliny gave to the pound of frankincense (varies between 6, 5 and 3 denarii per pound according to its quality) (12: 32: 65), it is found that the price fetched by a camel-load to equal between 2400 and 1200 denarii depending on the incense quality. To be able to work out the significance of these figures one needs to look at them in a comparative perspective. This can be done by using Biblical data. It is reported that the daily wage of an agriculture worker in Jerusalem in the first century CE was 1 denar (Mathew 20: 1-19; Healey *et al* 1997: 104), which equals to ¼ sela' of Ḥāriṯah (Healey *et al* 1997: 104). Considering that this wage rate is similar to the one in the Nabataean kingdom, and then a daily wage would be one quarter of a sela' or a *rb'* (Schmitt-Korte & Price 1994: 80), i.e. 91.25 sela' annually. This means that a single camel-load of luxury goods equals in Nabataean currency 600-300 sela', or the annual income of 6.5-3.2 people, supporting about 32.5-16 person (giving the lowest figure of 5 members in a family).

Out of some initial numbers given by Pliny (12: 32: 63-65), Groom again worked out the amount that Romans paid for frankincense estimated to be 9,900,000 denarii, 4,950,000 for myrrh, and 1,650,000 for other commodities (1981: 159).[174] Accordingly, the frankincense price when divided by the price of a camel-load of frankincense gives the figure of 4125 camels.[175] A caravan consisting of four thousand one hundred and twenty-five camels is assumed, in this regard, to carry about 1,650,000 pounds of frankincense and other goods, that equals to about 748 tons, which can, in its turn, be divided between the three major commodities involved in the caravan returning from southern Arabia: 448.8 tons for frankincense, 224.4 tons for myrrh and 7.480 tons for other commodities. Taking the number of camels as an average for a caravan, then a single caravan is found worth the annual wages of 27,123.2 agricultural labours. This is an indication of the frankincense size of trade, of which a major part returns to the Nabataeans in a single caravan journey.[176] The figures above should be then doubled to meet the bi-annual caravan scheme. An advantage that frankincense merchants had in their society financially, which was no doubt translated in a high standard of living for them and their families. This is the merchant elite whose women appear often in this book. They enjoyed the chance of enriching and also the ability to participate in their home and society affairs.

Although the number of loaded camels is not equal to the number of men involved in a caravan, it can be indicative of the general number of men. If there are over four thousand loaded camels, in addition to camels carrying food, water, tents etc. for the needs of travel, it would not be expected that the accompanying men to be less than half or two thirds the number of camels. Supporting the previous presumption of around four thousand men, in its turn the supposition that an average population of Raqamū-Petra would be around ten thousand will be strengthened. And Ḥegra maybe together with Boṣra will also count about then thousand. This calculation is based, however, on the assumption that the majority of the caravaners were Raqameans, Ḥegraeans and Boṣraeans.

What happens during men's absence, when they leave behind families of about four thousand people, divided between the urban cities of Raqamū-Petra, Ḥegra, Boṣra, etc? Assuming that all ancient economies relied principally on agriculture and on self-sufficiency for their subsistence (Hopkins 1983: xi), the Nabataeans needed to produce their own grain, wheat and barley, the staples of everyday life. Being a vulnerable and essential necessity, protection and maintenance must be provided for the sake of the community as a whole. One of the activities that affect harvest is war, whether for the victim or the attacker. In the first case, in raids, usually the enemy's harvest is the target. In the latter, as armies were not regular, most of the warriors were peasants, who had their own crops to harvest. Taking the example of war in Greece, most of the wars and raids usually took place after the harvest at

174 I am not using the calculation results of Groom in regard to the number of camels, for I believe he had an error counting the price of a pound of frankincense as 2.5 denarii, contrary to Pliny's price list that gives it the value of 6, 5 or 3 denarii per pound (Groom 1981: 160, 154-155).

175 Of course using this method of calculation one makes no allowances for the differential value in purchasing power. A far better method would be to follow economists of subsistence agriculture and work out purchasing power in terms of wheat equivalence (see Hopkins [1978] 1987: 98). The paucity of data does not allow this method to be used in the Nabataean case yet.

176 This can also be compared with an estimated minimum Nabataean economy. Doing that is based on the population number multiplied by the amount of grain consumption per year. The Nabataean population can be assumed to be about 520,000 people (the Nabataean surface in its maximum expansion measures about 520,000 km square. If that is divided by the average density number per square km, one can reach this figure. Taking the figure of 5 people per square km known during the Bronze Age [see Hassan 1981; Esse 1991]), however, the density should be much less than that taking into consideration the desert areas of the Nabataean surface. I would prefer, therefore, to choose the minimum number of one person per square km. As for the grain, that has been studied by Jones and Hopkins, and it has been found that the minimum annual consumption of grain is about 200kg, adding to that about 50kg of wasted grain and another 50 to be used as seeds for the next sowing, this will add up to 300 kg ([1978] 1987: 98ff.). Therefore, the size of the minimum Nabataean economy would be estimated at 156,000,000 kg of grain. What remains for a further study is the estimation of grain price in Nabataea or its neighbours.

home was completed, which used to be between May and June. Thus the best time for war for them was between June and July (Hanson 1998: 36-37). Likewise the long-distance trade activity which took men away from home would have a similar relationship with the time of harvest. Therefore, both the harvest of frankincense as well as the grain harvest at home should be taken into consideration and planned for. Since Nabataean traders were under the mercy of the frankincense harvest, they should plan to time, if possible, their own harvest before the journey. If they could not, then they would need to find someone to replace them to do the job.

In fact the cycle of the caravan journeys seems to harmonise relatively with the major farming dates (see table in plate VI). It is known that grain was cultivated in most of the Nabataean region. For example, in Raqamū-Petra wheat, barley, olives, vine and date seeds were found in the residential area of al-Zanṭūr (Karg 1996: 358). In al-Ḥumaymah wheat and barley were cultivated on a large scale (Oleson 1995: 718). These crops are still produced in these areas today (for Raqamū-Petra see Russell 1995: 696ff, and for Dedan see Nasif 1981: 174-175; 1995: 125 ff.). It is expected that the Nabataean caravan would start after the end of wheat harvest and corn sowing, which took place before summer and at the beginning of summer respectively in the area of Dedan and Ḥegra (Nasif 1995: 125), that is either in April and May, according to the calendar known in the south,[177] or May according to the northern calendar. It is worth noting that north Arabia had probably a slightly different calendar of seasons. Ibn Waḥšiyyah, who translated a major work on Nabataean[178] agriculture from Syriac in 291 H and dictated it in 318 H (10th century CE), noted how every people had their own definition of seasons (1993: 208). Therefore, this description of the cycle of a caravan in relation to harvests in the north and south would not be as exact as it might appear from first glance. Hence, one might suggest that at about the same time, from April to June, the harvest of frankincense would be carried out by incising trees and collecting the gum. By the end of June the frankincense would be ready. It would need, however, some time to dry up; therefore by September it would be in its best condition (Groom 1981: 146-147). Caravans that start in June would spend the wet monsoon period on the road and would reach Yemen by the end of July, or the beginning of August, the right time to have the gum ready and dry. Given a month of rest and trading, the caravan would start again on the return trip by the beginning of September and would arrive by the end of October, just at the time of wheat sowing and the corn harvest which would take the month of November. In southern Arabia the incisions for the autumn harvest would be made from November until the end of December or January. The northern Nabataean caravans would take the road again by December to reach the south by the end of January, when the autumn harvest was ready to collect (Nasif 1995: 125). They would spend another month there and would spend March and April on the road to reach Ḥegra and Raqamū-Petra around the time of the wheat harvest.

The above cycle seems too perfectly planned. Delays would often happen and unexpected weather changes would occur. Ancient travel was determined by the elements, which meant irregularity and uncertainty as well as hazard (Braudel[179] [1949] 1972 I: 360; Casson 1974: 65-94). That would mean, if there was a delay going south, that the crops were bought by other buyers or that the travellers got the left-overs. On the other hand, if there was a delay on the return trip, then that would mean someone else should take care of the crops and the remaining jobs. The job was not automatically done once the men returned from their long journey. Knowing how much care must be given to wheat cultivation, it is clear that substitute labour should be ready at home. For example, wheat was not to be sown on a random day in the month of November or December, but should be done in the right weather. It should not be sown on a cold windy day, or in a period without a moon. Also, it should be planted more than once over the first month in order to make sure the yield would not be under the mercy of different rainfalls and other climate changes, and should be harvested within one hundred days (see Ibn Waḥšiyyah 1993: 414-421). Therefore, sowing wheat in November or December would be harvested by March or April.

In the absence of men, women were expected to take over the responsibility. If the labour was hard, women would have taken part, or else they would be supervising the performance of slaves and boys. But who were the men involved in trade and who were their wives? Logically they must have been strong men who could endure the long travel, and those with a reasonable capital. Hence,

[177] According to the farmers of southern Arabia today, their four seasons roughly are: spring, from January to March, summer, from March to June, autumn, from July to September and winter from October to the end of December (Groom 1981: 146). Apparently, every people or town used to have their own seasonal calendar. Ibn Waḥšiyyah (10th century CE) gave the example of southern 'Iraq and Babylon. For al-'Abillah, Jooḥi, al-Maṣṣab and 'Abdasī, spring begins from the 10th February and lasts until 22nd May, summer from 23rd May until 22nd August, autumn is 12th October until 1st December and winter from 1st December until 10th February. As for Babylon, their spring lasts between 21st March and 11th June; summer lasts from there until 21st September from that date until 21st October is autumn; and finally, winter lasts until the beginning of spring, 21st March. Ibn Waḥšiyyah considered that the seasons do not differ dramatically between towns; however, the 'abillah of southern 'Iraq seasons correspond most closely with agriculture (1993: 208).

[178] It is not clear what the relationship between these Nabataeans and the Nabataeans of Raqamū-Petra was. According to the author's own introduction, he belonged to the Kasdāni Nabataeans, who were ancient Syrians. He gave some dates that date back thousands of years for his major sources and the principal writer of the book which he was translating (Ibn Waḥšiyyah 1993: 5-9). The major difference one notes is that his major area of concern as the seat of the Nabataeans was southern 'Iraq and Babylon, not southern Syria and Jordan.

[179] For the role of climate on ancient societies see, Braudel [1949] 1972 I: 260, 232-234. Although he is writing about the fifteenth century Mediterranean, it is not expected that weather elements and their effect on travel at that time differ much from ancient times.

they were either from the merchant elite stratum or seekers of adventure and opportunity who could profit and start a capital of their own. They were also the productive sector of society, leaving behind the weaker members of the community, the elders, functionaries of the state and the women who to the best of their ability took charge of the households, farms and other provision. It has also been argued that the Nabataeans created an advanced irrigation system in order that in the absence of males, the work would be manageable with the minimum of labour (Bowersock 1983: 60).

The relationship between the absence of men for trade reasons and the empowerment of women is noted on different levels. One of the interesting examples comes from the Old Assyrian period (*ca* 1920-1780 BCE) of the early second millennium BCE. The absence does not happen only in the form of long distance trade but also in long residence abroad. The personal trade correspondence from this period shows a remarkable mechanism of organising familial trade. The letters exchanged between men and women tell very interesting stories. Many women are found corresponding with their husbands about the affairs of their business, which was partly based on women manufacturing textiles in Aššur and trading them with Anatolia, where the Assyrian traders established important colonies, especially at Kaniš (present Kültepe). Lamassī, wife of Pūšu-ke-en is an example of these women (Veenhof 1972: 111-123). She was in charge of her household, managing its affairs and supervising, as well as participating in the production of wool cloth. Her letters were concerned with business issues, such as demands for wool, complaints about delay in sending silver etc. In addition, other documents refer to her as one of the receivers of gold, silver and precious shipments of ornaments. The accounts of Lamassī and other Old Assyrian women who lived in Aššur while their husbands lived in the cities of Asia Minor demonstrate the possibility of a relationship between women's empowerment as apparent in these documents and their husband's absence for a long period. Although neither the study of Veenhof (1972; 1977) nor of Larsen before him (1967) mention how long the Assyrian men usually stay in the Anatolian colonies, it is possible to suggest it was for some years, with short breaks[180]. Contemporary documents showed that trade that involved living abroad meant that men had to rely on their wives to take care of the house, children and staff; that they acted as their husbands' representatives and informants; and that they became involved in various commercial activities (Veenhof 1977: 113, Kuhrt 1998: 25-27). An attitude that seemed to become popular among merchant families in Old Assyrian times, and women proved to have succeeded not only in managing their familial affairs but also in participating in the business by manufacturing, transporting, paying taxes and collecting debts. Hence, they were exercising an extensive and high level of independent contractual practices that reflect legal power.

Another example was found in a society contemporaneous with the Nabataeans, the people of Elephantine. In Upper Egypt, women used to receive such letters from their husbands either on trade missions or in residence abroad (it is not clear which), in which they tell their wives of what happened to the merchandise they sent them in Memphis in Lower Egypt, and what they should do with what they have in Elephantine/Syene, including taking care of the children and the elderly (see Grelot 1972: No. 26, 28; Porten *et al* 1996: 74-77, B2, B1).[181] It is supposed that women's management and business at home involved the production of textiles, probably linen, for the reference to the garments that should be sent to Memphis opens up such possibility.

One can also look at the foreign wives of the Minaean traders. Apparently, since the Minaeans used to move about in their caravans and settle for sometime outside their land in southern Arabia, they have married from the local communities there. The 88 inscriptions of 'foreign wives, formerly known as the Hierodulen women' were collected between 1869 and1894 and comprehensively studied by Mlaker in 1943, then revised by al-Ghul in 1980 and by al-Said in 1995 and later in 2002 with the discovery of new inscriptions (57-58). It shows a long list of 86 women from 24 lands, towns and tribes, and with the new four texts published by al-Said the number of women rises to 90 (1995: 195-200; 2002:57-60, 62). They belonged to different places such as \azza, hgr, ddn, mṣr, qydr, yṯrb, lḥyn, yunm (Greece) and others, however, no reference is made to the Nabataeans, which suggests an earlier date for the inscriptions than the 4th Cent. BCE, however, al-Said in a thorough discussion dates the inscriptions to different dates in the span between the beginning of 4th and the 2nd Cent. BCE (2002: 62). These inscriptions were dedicated and placed in the temple of 'Aṯtar in Raṣāfum (Qarnaw)

[180] Remarkably, the letters do not express feelings of longing or demands for return from the women's side. The reason can possibly be either because the situation was routine and normal, or that there was other personal correspondence different from these family business letters.

[181] For example, letter B2 reads: 'Greetings, Temple of Banit in Syene. To my sister Tashai from your brother Makkibanit. I blessed you by Ptaḥ that he may show me your face in peace. Nabusha is well here. Do not worry about him. I am not making him leave Memphis. Greetings, Psami, Jakeh. Greetings, Nanaiḥem. And now behold, the amount of money that was in my hand I gave as wpd/rt to Banitsar son of Tabi sister of Nabusha, silver, 6 shekels an da zuz, silver zuz (to the ten). And now, send (word) to Tabi that she dispatch to you wool from part of the silver, 1 sh(ekel's worth). and now, if you be given a lamb and its wool, send (word) to me; and if you be given the wool owed by Makki, send (word) to me. And if you not be given (anything), send (word) to me and I shall complain against them here. And now, I bought olive oil and a tunic for Jakeh, and also for you, 1 pretty vessel, and also perfumed oil for the Temple of Banit. But [I] have not yet found a man (with whom) to dispatch them to you. And now, dispatch castor oil, 5 handfuls. And do give grain to Waḥpre; and let him buy beams and leave (them) in his house. Do not stand before him; every beam which he will find he should buy. And if the shepherd (or: Reia) gives you wool, send (word) to me. Greetings, Teṭosiri; take care of her. For your welfare I sent this letter. (External Address) To (*sealing*) Tashai from Makkibanit son of Psami. (To) Syene (*cord*) (to be) delivered' (Porten *et al* 1996: B2).

in Main, in what al-Ghul interpreted as documenting the marriage contracts of these women to the Minaean traders who settled abroad (ibid. 2002: 54). Although there is no direct information about the Minaean men leaving their wives behind to manage their business, it is very likely that that was the case with them, since these men need to travel back and forth with the Minaean caravans at least once a year to guarantee quality and deals. Although Nabataeans were not known to have colonies abroad similar to the Minaeans, there is evidence that there was one in Qaryat ḏū Kahl (Qaryat al-Faw) in southern Arabia, north of Najrān. Some Nabataean inscriptions and pottery were found in good quantity there (al-Ansari 2005: 521), however, the full result of the site has not been published yet. Such a place would be expected to be the post in which some merchants settled to direct their affairs from the closest point to the southern states and centres for the production of frankincense and myrrh, though Qaryat ḏū Kahl itself known to have had some cultivation of frankincense (ibid. 515-516) .

In these cases, the men are found and expected to share the attitude of relying on their wives to manage the home business while they are away. Despite the fact that they would have their male siblings or other kinsmen staying back home, the reliance on wives and the duties given to them were different and remarkably more important. Probably the element of trust was more applicable within the man's own household, or their women happened to be of special training and able to bear responsibility. Given this comparison, whether the reliance on women, especially wives, to manage the business of absent men was common to all societies from Nile to Oxus, or whether it was particular to merchant communities which developed a common tradition of business education that involved women as well as men, especially the examples of the Assyrian and the Elephantine are significant in showing how women were involved in family affairs and how they were also in charge in their husbands' absence, not only in managing the household but also in managing the business. The comparison supports also the relationship that was made between male absence, especially for long trading travels, and the empowerment of women and their independence.

One cannot, however, claim that the mere absence of men allowed the opportunity for women's empowerment. I believe that, if it had not been for the strong state that secured law and order, empowerment would not have been possible.

B. State Enforcement of Law and Order

The impact of a strong state on the stability of society and economy does not need much proving, for this is what states are for. My argument is related to a specific sector of society, to women. I argue that the strong state had an essential positive impact on women's empowerment that was reflected in the aspects of Nabataean women's life discussed earlier. In the following, I would explain how the strong state had such an impact on women's status by looking at the elements that determine the strength of a state in relation to women. These elements are: size, peace, law and order, defence, irrigation systems, coinage etc. Having the concept of the ideal role of a strong state underlined, then questions about what social effect a strong state has on society and on women in particular will be raised.

The size of states used to be a vital factor in a state's strength and has been demonstrated by many studies (see Taagepera 1978; Treadgold 1997) which draw on the relationship between size, population, resources and power. Treadgold takes the example of Byzantium. He finds that the state's power and strength increases every time it expands its frontiers (1997:8-9; 2001: 4).

Taking the example of the Roman Empire, Keith Hopkins in his model of the ancient economy, proposes that there was an increase in non-agricultural productivity in the Mediterranean in the first two centuries CE, and suggests that there were three stimuli that affected productivity in handiwork and commerce. One of them was *peace*. He finds that the Roman peace which prevailed in the area for over two centuries had freed the inhabitants of the Roman world from major military disturbances, piracy or brigands. This without exaggeration should have had an impact on the economy (1983: xvii-xix), but who established peace and how did it operate? In the case of the Romans it was, among other factors, the strong state, which neutralised wars and allowed uninterrupted stable life to prevail, regulated taxes and state's income. The role of the state in economy has been demonstrated in John K. Davies's model of ancient economy, where he draws attention to the importance of the state component in the entities that comprise the model, that is by providing, among other things, security and legal protection for persons, property and family, which have a reciprocate relationship with taxes etc. (1998: 250). Or, in other words, the state and its political power constitutes one of the social means through which human societies develop towards civilisation, in 'multiple, overlapping, intersecting networks of power' (Mann 1986 I: 523-24).

In the case of Nabataea, the state gained its strength and reliability through an overlap of power structures that enforced these qualities. The state's strength with the economic and political expansion and growth occurring in the Nabataean state, allowed it to play an important role as one of the few semi-independent states surviving the Romans and Parthians, or at least, the only state which had special relations with the Romans, and probably similarly with the Parthians. The Nabataean Raqamū-Petra was the only capital, which neither the Roman nor any other troops reached (Paltiel 1991: 26). They had a great sense of political and diplomatic balance that allowed their state to avoid annexation for a century and a half after the whole region to their east and west was captured by the Romans. In the context of international relations between competing empires, the Parthians in the east and the Romans in the north and west, the Nabataeans managed to play the role of a buffer state that allowed them to remain autonomous, though not as autonomous as the southern Arabian kingdoms. The success of the Nabataeans in maintaining their independence was not only due to their diplomatic skill and geopolitical circumstances but also it had a cultural dimension in that the attempt to articulate a distinct Nabataean identity which was not reducible to either Roman or Parthian influences helped them consolidate their independence. Ultimately, the independence of the Nabataean state rested on its ability to become a container of a Nabataean *ethnie*. The weakness of the Nabataean *ethnie* showed itself in the way in which the Nabataeans failed to sustain themselves (for a similar case of the Assyrians, see Yoffee 1988: 56-58).

They realised the importance for their economy of the lucrative frankincense trade, which was always essential and dated back to the first formation of the Nabataean state. By the fourth century BCE it was mentioned as an area of economy under their control, as reported by Hieronymus.[182] They also realised how much stability, security and safety is needed for caravans to operate. Strabo in the first century CE wrote that the 'camel traders travel back and forth from Raqamū-Petra to this place [Leuke Kome, in the land of the Nabataeans] in safety and ease' (16: 4: 23).

A strong state was further enhanced in Nabataea under the rulership of Ḥāriṯah IV (9BCE-40CE), whose long reign and strong seizure of power established law and order around the country. The many fortified towers and garrisons in the principal towns and along the caravan routes on land and at the ports (Parker 1986 & 1987: 297-98; Graf [1994] 1997: V/267) suggest a strong hold to secure the kingdom's interests, especially on the frontiers with desert areas. Nomadic activities here need further discussion.

The relationship between the state and the nomads[183] becomes problematic and unstable during the later periods of Roman and Byzantine rule (see MacAdam 1986; Parker 1986; 1987; Graf 1989). It is found, however, that the Nabataeans did not have such a hostile relationship. Apart from the incident of Damasi's revolt against the Nabataeans (Winnett 1973: 54-57), there is no other incident of opposition, which is due either to lack of evidence or to the fact that there was no such opposition except within the urban domains from where Damasi emerged. I would support the second possibility and would argue that the Nabataeans did not have an antagonistic relationship towards the nomads. As seen earlier, the nomads formed part of the Nabataean *ethnie* or social composition and that the tribal structure of the urban Nabataeans showed strong links with their nomadic branches. Some of the clans were settlers, whereas others lived in the desert, though were absorbed into the settled community (Macdonald 1991: 116). Therefore, Nabataeans were not a foreign ruling entity, nor alien to the social structure within the Nabataean frontiers and their periphery. Moreover, some of the settled clans belonged to the elite, principally of the merchant class. In brief, there is no need to believe that either nomads or peasants were static in their social structure. Contrary to some assumptions in sociological, anthropological or historical studies, social systems and organisational boundaries do not exist; they are in continuous construction, open and fragile. Therefore, no human population was confined within a single system, but rather interacted in response to the aspects of power (see Eisenstadt 1988: 236-237).

It is possible to see examples of interactive relationship and economic influence in the tribe Rawḥ-Quṣayy in the town of Ṣalḫad in Ḥawrān. Members of this tribe were also the servants and the priests of the goddess Allāt. Inscriptions show a clan of known nomadic origin as partly settled in the town and becoming part of the town's elite. The clan dedicated on its own an entire temple to the mother of the gods that was renovated over the span of a century (CIS,II,170; 182; Milik 1958 : ins 1).[184] Needless to say, priests were among the elite stratum of ancient societies, and for a tribe to build a temple in a city showed an attachment to an urbanised centre on the one hand, and an economic strength that continued throughout a century, on the other.

There is no reason to doubt that the Nabataeans recruited nomads among their military forces too. While the view that nomads were particularly skilled in ancient warfare has been recently shown to be exaggerated (to the extent that the nature of nomadic society did not allow it to sustain military operation for any length of time and the logistic abilities of nomads vis-à-vis agrarian beurocratic state was limited) it is the case that nomads still have some military utility especially in low intensity warfare (see the discussion on the nomad fighting system in Bronson 1988: 203-207). Ḥegra (Bowsher 1986: 23-25) and Dūmah (Muaikel & al-Theeb 1996: 48) were two of the most heavily militarised Nabataean towns. A supposition evidenced from the number of inscriptions with military titles these two towns have produced as well as what can be seen today of their fortifications.[185] Ḥegra, however, seems to have been where the higher ranks resided,[186] whereas Dūmah was smaller in comparison and was where officials of lower ranks with their troops resided (see al-Fassi 1993b). I would argue that most of the epigraphic remains in Dūmah, especially

[182] 'For not a few of them are accustomed to bring down to the sea frankincense and myrrh and the most valuable kinds of spices, which they procure from those who convey them from what is called Arabia Eudaemon' (Diodorus 19: 94).

[183] What I mean by nomads here are the groups of the Nabataean population that live in the deserts of Arabia and are in continuous contact with the urbanised towns.

[184] See Imaging Nabataea, chapter 2.

[185] See plate xxii for al-Ṣaʻīdī castle in wādī al-Sirḥān.

[186] See for example the tomb that the prefect (Heparchus) Tarṣū s. of Taym form himself and his wife ʻAydah d. of ʻAbd ʻAbdnūn and their children (JS 38: 63/4CE) (see plate xii).

the monumental ones, should belong to families that are associated with the Nabataean army and garrison (see al-Theeb 1992; al-Muaikel & al-Theeb 1996: ins 5, 6, 7, 14, 16, 17, 20, 21, 22). If one also considers keeping and registering long genealogies as a mark of nomadism, then one would take the inscription found with the longest genealogy recorded among the Nabataeans, dating from 27 CE (Winnett & Reed 1970: no.16; Healey 1993b: 246; al-Muaikel & al-Theeb 1996: no. 34) (see plate XXI) as belonging to a Nabataean from a nomadic origin, probably occupying a military position in a garrison stationed around the oasis of Dūmah. As for Ḥawrān nomadic tribes, there is evidence that they were more involved with the Nabataean army, which was discussed earlier.[187]

In short, Nabataean defence strategy[188] and construction work, although it was directed to protect the frontiers of the desert as well as the caravan routes, was not directed against the nomads. Instead, peace was achieved by co-operation with the nomadic tribes, who conformed to the Nabataean state's rules and laws and became part of the Nabataean social texture and *ethnie*.[189]

Furthermore, the state's strength and authority can also be demonstrated by the Nabataean exceptional sophisticated water preservation and irrigation systems (Bowersock 1983: 60, 64). These had an important impact on the economy and the growth of cities and settlements, resulting in self-sufficiency in food.[190] Another aspect that was supportive of a strong economy and state was the coinage. It became a political tool towards establishing an image of an independent Nabataea, especially under the reign of Ḥāriṯah IV, who established a strong monetary system that seems to have replaced most of the previous barter system, in the same time he 'nationalised' it by dropping the Greek version of the coins of his predecessors and struck his coins in Nabataean with Nabataean epithet. The Nabataean coinage was mainly directed for local trading within the Nabataean realm. It was heavily struck, annually, in different weights, both in silver and bronze, but rarely in copper (Schmitt-Korte & Price 1994: 111, 78-109). If such abundance in using Nabataean coinage does not demonstrate an economic control, it is sufficient to show a political stability and strength.

Peace through law and order had its impact on the economy, and similarly had an impact on society. The crucial point in the Nabataean case is that when the state exercises its capacity to protect its community and secure its inhabitants, what it does in fact, is destabilise the gender relationship by pulling the rug from under the feet of men and similar individual power-bases. In other words, the state, on the one hand, does not leave much of the protection role for a family or community to the male kin, and, on the other, it makes the kin and male members relax from their fear and concern about the safety of their females. The result is that male members in society benefit from the strong state by leaving their women and children behind for long periods without fear about their welfare or safety. As the role of the state is substituted for many of the traditional political, social and economic roles that were played by the tribe, individuals or other types of polities, either coercively or voluntarily, it enforces taxes. In return, the community benefits from the new arrangement. From one side, men do not have any more the burden of permanent responsibility, alert all the time, on call for protection on demand. On the other, women do not have much fear, or, if they have, they do not depend entirely or solely on their male kin. They have another refuge, another resort that they can depend on: the state's institutions. Certainly, the degree of dependence will rest on the level of trust, reliability, acceptance and strength of the state.[191]

The transfer of tribe's role to the state, at least partially, gave women more freedom of movement and control over their own property. This was an important factor that made Nabataean women develop their legal power through inheritance and bestowing inheritance, both of which show them as owners of property with the right to dispose of it. Having a legal system enforced by state law gives women liberty from relying on the law of custom, which is governed by the elderly, usually male members of the tribe or the family. Even if the law of custom was in force, it seems that under a state law one can have the option of implementing either. The state's law and protection would, however, be more effectively implemented when men are not around and the state plays the legal role that maintains family welfare during male absence. In these circumstances, there was a yield to women in domestic and public spheres. An example can be demonstrated from society's recognition of single women, be it divorcees or second wives or others, as we have seen in Ḥegra. Those women, discussed in chapter four, became the heads of their own households. Though these principally included their female offspring, they comprised other family members as well as fathers, aunts etc. The financial independence and authority within a certain sphere could not have been possible had men been around all year, or had they been the providers upon whom women depended solely, or if they had been living in an unsafe environment. The combination of these circumstances, which prevailed in a certain period, allowed Ḥegran women to expand their familial authority to the extent of founding their own independent monumental tombs.

[187] See chapter three, the discussion on tribes.

[188] See Ammianus' comment on the country of the Nabataei, it is 'a land producing a rich variety of wares and studded with strong castles and fortresses, which the watchful care of the early inhabitants reared in suitable and readily defended defiles to check the inroads of neighbouring tribes' (xiv: 8: 13).

[189] See Identity and *ethnie* in the chapter on Imaging Nabataea.

[190] For Nabataean irrigation and hydraulic system see al-Muheisen 1990, 1993 and Oleson 1995.

[191] Compare, for example, Islam restoring law and order in the Peninsula in the first century of Hijrah/7th CE, or the Gengis Khān Mongols' establishment of law and order in the 13th century in Central Asia (Morgan 1998).

Having a strong state that maintains law and order through its legal and social institutions is one of the major causal factors, coupled with a specific economic activity that requires a male absence from society, long-distance trade, to explain the empowerment that Nabataean women enjoyed by the end of the first century BCE and the first CE.

III. Conclusion

This chapter has searched an adequate reason to explain how women would enjoy a high status in Nabataean society. It has highlighted how difficult it is to generalise a theory of status to all sectors of society, whose differences can be defined by age, status, freedom etc. It is too complicated to be able to draw a line from where high status begins or a low status ends. I am aware that the Nabataean women discussed were the elite women in particular, and more specifically urban women of cities such as Raqamū-Petra, Ḥegra and with a lesser degree, Boṣra, with a few exceptions. High status is the stratum of society in which women can exercise power and authority in domestic and public domains, which includes questions on sexuality, politics, legal representation and social impact.

Chapter five has also looked at the factors that were behind the scene, which may explain the position of Nabataean women. Research suggests that Nabataean women's empowerment was caused by two major factors: male absence in long-distance trade, and the strong Nabataean state that enforced law and order. The productive sector of society was involved in long-distance trade, which became intensified by the end of the first century BCE and was developed to a full-time trade that necessitated absence most of the year. At the same time, the established strong state saw its zenith at the time we are concerned with, the reign of King Ḥāriṯah IV, lover of his people, who, except for a battle he fought with Herod, as far as it is known, did not have major wars or disturbances. A stable state that collects its taxes and defends its people enforces law and order by different means, militarily and legally, and by institutions that keep law and order. Institutions, such as courts and public councils were what facilitated women's public involvement. In the absence of men, women had the opportunity to develop power in their households as well as their own community. Away from the authority of their clans and tribes, women found in the state the alternative means of protection.

Conclusion

Interpreting Female Nabataea

It is difficult to know where one will end a journey or indeed exactly how that journey might be concluded. My beginning was looking at the social structure of ancient Arabia. As my journey progressed my attention was drawn to women in particular. At the end of *this* journey, although I have satisfied some of my curiosity and intellectual interest, I find that I have only scratched the surface of such a huge area of research.

However, one thing was certain; I did not want to write a repetitive work, which could be achieved by merely collecting materials and collating quotations. Though the topic of women's history has been a burning issue in the last few decades, pre-Islamic women were not included in it, whether it is for lack of interest or lack of material, I cannot say. Probably both reasons apply. This was how a challenge started to formulate itself. In the beginning I saw it as easy. There are limited inscriptions, coins and archaeological studies and a thesis on women's role could be drawn from there. The problem was that the more I got involved in my subject, the more I found it hard to justify writing history in this way. Reflecting again, I could not make sense of it. The picture in fact was getting more and more blurred. The ambition of reconstructing the past and women's life became a myth. I reached a point where I found it was impossible to carry on in this direction. There was no way that anyone could claim to reconstruct the past as it really was. From there on I started my second stage of research in the epistemology of writing ancient history, its limits and horizons. I could not get away from engaging in the problems of the ancient history of the Nabataean region as part of the 'Oriental', 'Near East' and 'Hellenistic' traditions. I had to participate in the debate and find a position for this study and for the period of history and region with which I am concerned. In doing so, and since the subject is to do with gender, there also was a necessity to decide where to position work on Nabataean women within the feminist debate on women's history.

The main objective was to avoid writing merely descriptive research. A lot of thinking was invested in the reasons behind the descriptions of Nabataean women available in the material. Formulating the questions was very challenging. The question of why Nabataean women were so visible in the first centuries BCE-CE, not earlier or later, was crucial and stimulating, alongside the question of how this happened, and what facilitated it.

To try and answer these questions I needed to establish certain grounds. Firstly, the notion of 'Nabataean' needed exploring in order to lay out the social frame in which Nabataean women operated. What was reached from there was an understanding of Nabataean identity, which seems to have been established and maintained by the state in the first place. This placed the Nabataean *ethnie* into an aristocratic entity. I also needed to find out how much Nabataean women were visible, especially in the domains where data is available, such as the social and the legal spheres. Though the information was limited, it was significant.

Principally, research suggests and can claim that patriarchy was not inherent to Nabataean society or to the Nile to Oxus, and that Nabataeans were no more or less patriarchal than their contemporaries. They were, in fact, less patriarchal than, for example Jewish, Greek and Roman societies. In other words, patriarchy as a system which is historically constructed in a particular time, place and social context, was not embedded in their social structure.

Nabataean society, however distinctive, was not exceptional in an eccentric way. It was, I found, trying to maintain its own identity in the midst of strong currents and influences from many directions. Therefore, there was the possibility to reach the question of why Nabataean women were different and visible? How did they rise in status? It is true that a lot of what I am doing is imagining cases and situations. These imagining situations needed, however, prudent experiment, to avoid complete fiction.

Gradually, I noticed the fact and importance of the absence of men and its affect on women's status. The impact could be seen with the Nabataean intensifying their trade activity from once to twice a year, which meant the absence of men for most of the year. I was also able to demonstrate how the numbers in manpower involved in a single caravan had a significant effect on the cities' provision of subsistence products such as grain. It was shown how male absence must have been covered by women working in their place or managing hired workers and slaves to guarantee production.

In this respect, it was possible to demonstrate that the high revenue brought by the frankincense trade to major Nabataean towns such as Ḥegra, Raqamū-Petra, Boṣra, etc., allowed their families to live a life of a very high standard. This encouraged some women to have their own business and households.

The visibility and empowerment would not, however, have been possible if it was not for the strong state. Showing the strength of the Nabataean state at that period was not problematic. The task was to demonstrate how this factor facilitated the process of empowerment of women. The way to do it, was by drawing comparisons between the state and the patriarch or male kin in a family or a tribe. It has been argued that the absence of men allowed the state, represented in its institutions, to replace the male kin position in the responsibilities of protection, and guarantee of provisions.

In other words, women were provided with a secure environment in which to mobilise and express their autonomy. After this was manifested, first in the image of the queen, the elite women followed and took their chances of empowerment.

The findings of the present study suggest the possibility of applying this 'model' to the status of women in similar contexts of ancient polities which are involved in caravan trade, such as Palmyra, Ḥaṭra and Makkah. The possibility of such an extension must await another study.

Epilogue

A Tale of Two Cities: Second Part: Raqamū [192]

Raqamū, the city to marvel at, is neither rainbow-coloured nor peacock heavenly-dyed; she is something remarkable and unimaginable even in a dream. She is a hidden diamond donned in silk garments and damask, happy to flirt with the sun on the one hand and on the other the birth and ripeness.

No matter how long We have lived in Raqamū, We still feel amazed and filled with wonder by her beauty. We are not sure if this wonder is an eternal passion or a spiritual attraction. There is no doubt that both of them live in the soul. It is true that Raqamū, has had a long life but in Our eyes her beauty lies in her daily renewal so that for Us she is as a luxuriant young girl. Even though We look at her with the eyes of the compassionate goddess who is incarnated in Our blood, this does not mean that We are biased towards her attributes and favouring her unjustifiably. Indeed Our royal position does not allow Us to exaggerate or pretend. These feelings are those of any Raqami towards her or his city, which is the source of her or his pride and dignity. No doubt, however, long life has its role to play in beauty, after all one has had longer to attain certain perfection. For instance, by the time one reaches one's forties, one has seen and experienced many trials and tribulations. By this time, taste and cultivation have also been refined. We were keen at the time of Mālik, Our brother and partner, to enhance Our city, to decorate it with temples and colonnades, to refurbish what has been demolished and straighten its flaws, to found temples and baths, erect statues and columns and set up fountains. This refinement added to the earlier work of Raqamis. The splendid alley, Sīq, with its paved, niched-ornamented passage, shows their faithful efforts.

From Our palace that stands on the left of the colonnaded street over the hill, Our balcony overlooks Allāt's temple, which has been built on the other side of the street with its beautifully carved lion-headed columns.[193] *To the left, stands majestically the temple of Ba'al Šamīn in its marble and alabaster with its statues and arches. Situated to the right of the palace, it is not possible to see the theatre carved-in-rock.*[194] *From here, it is only common to hear the audiences cheering or mourning, according to what is presented, comedy or tragedy. The stories of Dumuzi and 'Ištar, or the Isis and Osiris are frequently to be played out with some modification to apply it on Allat-al-'Uzza and Dušara. In front of the palace, spreads out the beautiful gardens and pools that have beautified Raqamū since the time of Our father Ḥāriṯah the Great. They have been a delight to watch and to wonder about them in the afternoons. To the south of the palace, the elegant villas are spread all over the hill as far as the eye can see. None of them out does the other in its perfection with its faultless architecture, engraved doors or frescoed walls. Far to the south-east and south-west, one can see the facades of tombs on the mountains of Umm al-Bayyārah and al-Maḏbaḥ,*[195] *sculptured and carved in a masterly way by expert artists. The carving and works of art are still growing on the faces of all the mountains that Our Raqamū encompasses. What We cannot see from the palace of Raqamū's wonders too is the Khaznah or Allāt-Isis temple. This marvel of art and architecture is the first thing one can see when entering Raqamū through the Sīq*[196] *and entering the eastern gate. It is the greatest of all temples, which does not look like anything the eye has seen. They call it the Treasury of the Queen,*[197] *because of the big jar on its pointed top, a seven hundred-cubits high monument. It is a unique hewn monument that was founded during the time of 'Obadah and was completed at the time of Our father, Ḥāriṯah the Great, Lover of his People. The exceptional quality of Our artists, architects and sculptors, from 'Aftaḥ to Ḥūrū, is unrivalled in any city in the world today. They say that Ḥegra, where the company of 'Abd 'Obadah has expanded, includes many facades that imitate the art of Raqamū. It is, however, not possible that they could surpass the spectacle of the Khaznah or Deir. We hope that one day We can travel to all the corners of Our kingdom, from Boṣra to Dedan and from Dūmah to Ġazzah, if we live longer.*

Undoubtedly, We are living in a new phase of challenge that Our city and country are confronting. This time, however,

[192] These are pages from the diaries of Queen Šaqīlah's first years as Queen-Regent.

[193] See plate XXVI for an overview of the palace (?) and temple.

[194] See same plate.

[195] See plate xxvii.

[196] See plate xxiv.

[197] See plate xxiii.

We have to face it alone, without Mālik. He passed away a year and a few months ago and left Us on Our own to manage the affairs of this country in the name of Rab'el, who is still a nine-year old child. It is true that 'Unays, the wise Aḫu, is helping Us in every matter, but the latter has also grown older and is near to death. In fact, he has started to prepare his tomb, which he chose to be on the top of Ḫubṯā Mountain[198] *and overlooks the theatre, next to the tombs of the rest of the important people of the city.*

Ruling has its own demands and commitments. On top of this is the preparation of the annual report, which should be presented before the Raqamis and the other cities' representatives. This report needs the revision and precision of accountants and auditors responsible for collecting taxes from the caravan trade, agriculture, industry, lands, etc. Thereafter, they need to allot money to each sector. There are too many demands. Firstly, there is the temple and its tithes, which should arrive on time. Then there are the development projects, both designed to cope with the increase in population and construction, and provided to the maintenance of water canals, reservoirs, dams, etc. Some of the money should also be allocated to enforce the patrol and observation units on the caravan routes, paying the palace expenditure, as well as striking this year's coins. We decided, after consulting the experts in the palace, to introduce two new fractions of the silver coins, a half and a quarter, to facilitate the trading transactions. These coins bear Rab'el's name and Our name, as his mother.

We have waited for so long to have a son on the throne. At times of despair, We thought this would never happen. Although We trust the wisdom of Jamīlah, Our eldest daughter, and Hājar's and Sa'īdah's, there has to be a male on the throne. After more than twenty years of marriage, the gods had mercy and responded to Our prayers, incantations and the burning of hundreds of talents of frankincense. We first had Rab'el, then, two years later, We had Qāsim.

Even having a son on the throne was not enough to give a strong state. Being a minor did not help the king to keep the loyalty of all the Nabataeans. We found that We bore the burden of keeping the kingdom from going astray. Any simple act can be misinterpreted these days as a sign of weakness. That is why immediately after Mālik's death the kingdom suffered from the uprising of Damasi the Ḥegran, who belongs to the noble and traditionally loyal family of Damasifus. He conspired with the major tribes of Arabia, Ḍaif, Muḥārib and Māsikah to march against Raqamū for unravelled reasons. Damasi thought the house of Nabatū had grown weak by having Us as a queen regent and a young king on the throne, underestimating Our power and authority and underestimating the purity and sacredness of the blood that runs in Our veins. It did not take Us, thanks to Allāt and Dushara, more than a few months to recover order in the southern frontiers. Although We had Our troops disciplining the rebels, We demonstrated to them at the same time how a strong monarch treats her opponents, by showing them mercy and granting them pardon. We gave Our orders for Damasi to reside back in Ḥegra providing that he shows his respect to the throne and regrets what he had done. Our interest in the south, however, should find an alternative; Ḥegra should no longer be Our only bet. We should lessen Our dependence on it's revenue in order for a similar situation not to occur again. This is a decision to be dealt with as soon as We can. Thereafter, We had the Romans to worry about.

Recently, We received a second letter from the Emperor Titus asking for more help in the siege of Jerusalem. Our brother Mālik didn't have the time before he dies to send him the troops he needed. So we had to carry out the request and deal with it. It is true that Our relationship with Judaea was not good, especially after the many disturbances that touch Our western borders, but We are not at war with them at the moment. But, refusing the Roman request will make them find an excuse to attack Raqamū. We have the Parthians, whom We can always invite to help Us, but We prefer not to throw away Our sons in wars We are not prepared for. There is always a price that should be paid for such help. This is added to the fact that any war will not be for our interest. It will negatively affect the traffic of caravans, its safety and smooth flow, on which a great part of Our economy depends.

If We want to keep Nabataea's autonomy, We need to handle this problem carefully. After discussing the matter with the Queen's Brother, 'Unays, We decided to respond to the Roman demand and send them the requested troop. What We did not take into account was the continuous groups of Jerusalem Jews who were pouring over to the kingdom's borders and reaching Raqamū, trying to find themselves a refuge after the brutal destruction that Jerusalem experienced. We had to provide shelter and support to them, for the sake of long neighbourliness and the old marriage alliances between the two royal houses. We accepted to settle part of them around the Dead Sea, another in Naqab cities and a third in Ḥegra and Taymā. Some of them preferred to continue their march to southern Arabia, where they have some ancient contacts. As for Raqamū, it was not possible to contribute much, for it was already crowded by its own population, whose gardens, markets, and villas expanded outside the walls in the east towards al-Jī, and in the west towards Baiḍā[199] *and Ṣabra. Thanks to Dushara, Allāt and al-'Uzzā, however, We were able to control the situation at this moment and Our hope is that it will not get worse.*

There is no doubt that Our success in suppressing the rebellious attempts in the kingdom and Our regaining of power has made many commercial partners trust our system and become interested in affirming their relationships with us. These days, just a few months after

[198] See plate xxv.

[199] See plate xxvii.

the first of Our ruling years, We are preparing to receive three delegations, from Tadmor, Hajar and Ḥaṭra. They are interested to establish new agreements of cooperation and alliances similar to those We had with the kingdoms of southern Arabia, such as Qaryat Ḏū Kahl, Saba' and Yaṯrib. These diplomatic visits prove that the prosperous period of Ḥāriṯah and Mālik is still active. Even if We have lost part of Ḥawrān in Our brother's time, We have, however, recovered the loss by expanding Our power in Naqab, Sinai and the Red Sea.

In addition to these official flows of groups, there were the caravan flows, by which the news of Our districts, and the news of their men and women are carried. A lot of the communication and transportation between the Nabataean cities became much easier these days and more women are able now to travel and come to Raqamū. Many of the women of the noble families in Ḥegra, Dūmah and Boṣra come to Raqamū to show their loyalty and respects, such as 'Amah d. of Kamūlah and Haynah d. of 'Abd 'Obadah. The latter was Damasi's niece, who came with a few members of her family to receive Our blessings and to show their regret for the act of their kin and their gratitude for Our forgiveness. We granted them Our benedictions.

We noticed how articulate the Ḥegran women were and that they made an impression. Many of them became influential, even outside their own town, as merchants, business-women, owners of real estate, etc. More women have been following their model and are seen more often in Raqamū. It is a step that We have been encouraging and blessing throughout Our reign. In Our turn We were following the steps of Our mother Šaqīlah and all Our ancestor mothers.

All the signs show that the coming years will bring a heavier burden on Our shoulders until Rab'el reaches maturity and is able to take charge of the kingdom's affairs. We shall probably marry him soon to Jamīlah, for We can then rely on her and her inherited strong will and determination to carry the huge responsibilities of governance.
(and... to be continued).

Bibliography

The Holy Qur'ān

The Old Testament

AbdulAlim, M 1987, 'Herodōt yatahaddaṯ 'an al-'Arab wa bilādihim', *Ages* 2/1: 7-24.

Abu Duruk, H 1986, *Muqaddimah 'an āṯār Taymā'*. al-Idārah al-'āmmah lil-'āṯār wa-l-matāḥif, Riyadh.

Abu Taleb, M 1984, 'Nabayati, Nebayot, Nabayat and Nabaṭu: The Linguistic Problem revisited', *Dirasat* 11/4: 3-11.

Adelson, R 1995, *London and the Invention of the Middle East, Money, Power, and War 1902-1922*, Yale University Press, New Haven, London.

Ahmed, L 1992, *Women & Gender in Islam*, Yale University Press, New Haven, London.

'Ajloony, A 2003, *Ḥaḍārat al-anbāṭ min ḫilāl nuqūšihihim*, Mašrū' bayt al-anbāṭ lilta'līf wa al-našr, Petra, Jordan.

al-Abduljabbar, A.A 1995, 'The Rise of the Nabataeans. Sociopolitical Developments in 4th and 3rd Century BC Nabataea'. (Unpublished Ph.D. Thesis), UMI no. 9614525, Indiana University, Indiana.

al-Andalusī, I.S [d. 685 H] 1982, *Našwat al-ṭarab fī tārīḫ jāhiliyyat al-'Arab*, (ed. N.Abd al-Rahmān), Maktabat al-'aqṣā, Amman, 2 vols.

al-Anṣārī, A 1977, *Bayn al-tārīḫ wa al-āṯār*, ? Jeddah.

al-Ansari, A.A 1966, 'A Critical and Comparative Study of Lihyanite Personal Names', (Unpublished Ph.D. Thesis), 1966, University of Leeds, Leeds.

al-Ansari, A.A 1970, 'The Chronology of Lihyan', *Bulletin of the Faculty of Arts, University of Riyadh*, 1: 53-60.

al-Ansari, A.A 2005, al-mamālik al-'arabiyah min al-niṣf al-ṯānī min al-'alf al-ṯānī qabl al-mīlād 'ilā ẓuhūr al-'islām, in *al-Kitāb al-marji' fī tārīḫ al-'ummah al-'arabiyyah, Vol. I, al-juḏūr wa al-bidāyāt*, al-munaẓẓamah al-'arabiyyah lil-tarbiyah wa al-ṯaqāfah wa al-'ulūm, Tunis, 513-527.

al-Ansari, A.A., Ghazal, A.H., & King, G 1984, *Mawāqi' 'Aṯariyyah wa ṣuwar min Ḥaḍārat al-'Arab fī al-Mamlakah al-'Arabiyyah al-Su'ūdiyyah, al-'Ula (Dedan), al-Ḥijr (Madā'in Ṣāliḥ)*, King Saud University, Riyadh.

al-Azmeh, A 1997, *Muslim Kingship, Power and the Sacred in Muslim, Christian, and Pagan Polities*, I.B. Tauris Publishers, London, New York.

Albright, W.F 1953, 'Dedan', *Geschichte und altes Testament*, pp. 1-12.

Alcock, S.E 1993, 'Surveying the Peripheries of the Hellenistic World', *Centre and Periphery in the Hellenistic World*, (Studies in Hellenistic Civilisation), (eds P. Bilde, T. Engberg-Pedersen, L. Hannestad & J. Zahle), Aarhus University Press, Aarhus, pp.162-175.

al-Fassi, H.A 1993a, *al-Ḥayāt al-ijtimā'iyyah fī šamāl ġarb al-jazīrah al-'arabiyah fī al-fatrah mā bayn al-qarn al-sādis qabl al-mīlād wā al-qarn al-ṯāni al-mīlādī*, Rutūš, Riyadh.

al-Fassi, H.A 1993b, 'al-Waẓā'if al-ḥukūmiyyah wa al-'askariyyah fī mamlakat al-'Anbāṭ', *Ages* 8/2: 311-320.

al-Fassi, H.A 1995, 'al-'Anāṣir al-sukkāniyyah al-wāfidah 'alā sukkān šamāl ġarb al-Jazīrah al-'Arabiyah min muntaṣaf al-qarn al-sādis qabl al-mīlād wḥattā al-qarn al-ṯānī li-lmīlād', *Dirāsāt tārīhiyaḫ* II, King Saud University, Riyadh, pp.1-42.

al-Fassi, H.A 1997, 'The Taymanite Tombs of Mada'in Ṣāliḥ (Hegra)', *PSAS* 27: 49-57.

al-Fassi, H.A, Forthcoming/a, 'The Funerary Prohibitions of the Nabataean inscriptions of Hegra (Mada'in Ṣālih)', *Festschrift to Prof. A.T. al-Anṣārī*, Riyadh.

al-Fassi, H.A, Forthcoming/b, 'The Nabataean Queen: an analytical study', *Adumatu* 2007.

al-Fassi, H.A, Forthcoming/c, 'Visibility and Power: An Assessment of Nabataean Women's Status', *OIB-Publication Project, Proceedings of ECOSOC Conference (BTS 114)*, Eds Kropp/Maraqten/Sader, Cambridge University Press, Cambridge, 2007.

al-Hamdānī, Ḥ (d. 345H) 1394/1974, *Ṣifat jazīrat al-'arab*, (ed. M.A. al-'Akwa' al-Ḥiwālī), Riyadh.

'Alī, J 1970-1980. *al-Mufaṣṣal fī Tārīḫ al-'arab qabla al-'Islām*, Beirut, Baghdad. 10 vols.

Ali, N 1999, 'Community and Individual Identity of the Kashmiri Community: A Case Study of Luton', (Unpublished Ph.D. Thesis), University of Luton, Luton.

al-Iṣbahānī, A.F [d. 356H), *Kitāb al-'aġānī*, Dār al-fikr, ? 23 vols.

al-Khathami, M.S 1999, 'The Kingdom of Liḥyān-History, Society, and Civilization in Pre-Islamic Arabia', (Unpublished Ph.D. Thesis), University of Manchester, Manchester.

al-Khraysheh, F 1995, 'New Safaitic Inscriptions from Jordan', *Syria* 72: 401-414.

al-Maqrīzī, A (d. 845H/ 15th C. CE), 1324H, *al-Ḫiṭaṭ al-maqrīziyah*, Maṭba'at al-Nīl, Cairo, 4 vols.

al-Muaikel, Kh. & al-Theeb, S 1996, *al-Āṯāṯr al-Nabaṭiyyah min manṭiqat al-Jawf*, ?, Riyadh.

al-Muheisen, Z 1990, 'Maître de l'eau et agriculture en Nabatène: l'exemple de Pétra', *Aram* 2/1: 205-220.

al-Muheisen, Z 1993, 'Tiqaniyyat at-tawzī'āt al-mā'iyyah 'ind al-'Anbāṭ', *Dirāsāt 'aṯariyyah wa-tārīḫiyyah*, Maṭbū'āt jam'iyat al-'āṯār bi-al-'Iskandariyyah, Munāsabat al-'īd al-mi'awī li-l-jam'iyyah, pp. 23-46.

al-Murayḫī, M 1999, 'Naqš Raqūš bil-Ḥijr (Madā'in-Ṣāliḥ): ru'yah jadīdah' *Dual majlis al-ta'awun lidual al-Ḫalīj al-ʻarabiyyah ʻabr al-ʻuṣūr, 1st scientific meeting*, UAE: Dubai, pp. 31-72.

al-Naim, N.A.A 2000, *al-Tašrīʻāt fī janūb ġarb al-jazīrah al-ʻArabiyyah ḥattā nihāyat dawlat Ḥimyar*, Maṭbūʻāt maktabat al-malik Fahd al-waṭaniyah, Riyadh.

al-Naseef al-Dosari, A.S 1998, 'Military Organization in Early Islam (AH 1-40/ 622-661)', (Unpublished Ph.D. Thesis), University of Manchester, Manchester.

al-Otaibi, F.M 2005, 'Rome and Nabataea: Post-Colonialism and the Writing of History', (Unpublished Ph.D. Thesis), University of Manchester, Manchester.

al-Qalqašandī, A [d. 821H] n.d. *Nihāyat al-'arab fī ma'rifat 'ansāb-al-ʻarab*, dār al-kutub al-ʻilmiyyah, Beirut.

al-Rasheed, M 1991, *Politics in an Arabian Oasis*, The Rashidi Tribal Dynasty, I.B.Tauris & Co Ltd Publishers, London, New York.

al-Rosan, M.M 1987, *al-Qabā'il al-ṯamūdiyyah wa al-ṣafawiyyah- dirāsah muqāranah*, Jāmiʻat al-malik Suʻūd, Riyadh.

al-Said, S 2002, 'Zawjāt al-maʻīniyīn al-'ajnabiyāt fī ḍaw' nuṣūṣ jadīdah', *Adumatu* 5: 53-72.

al-Saud, A.S 1997, *Central Arabia during the early Hellenistic period*, King Fahd National Library Pulications, Riyadh.

al-Suhaylī, A [d. 581 H] 1967, *al-Rawḍ al-'anif fī šarḥ al-sīrah al-nabawiyyah*, ed. A.al-Wakeel, Dār al-kutub al-ḥadīṯah, Cairo.

al-Ṭabarī, [d.310H/ 932CE] 1987, *The History of al-Ṭabarī (Tā'rīkh al-rusul wa-al-mulūk).* (tr. W. Montgomery Watt & M.V. McDonald), State University of New York Press, Albany, Vol. VII.

al-Ṭabarī, M [d.310H/ 932CE] n.d. *Tārīḫ al-'umam wa-al-mulūk*. Dār al-kutub al-ʻilmiyyah, Beirut, 5Vols.

al-Theeb, S 1992, 'Nuqūš Nabaṭiyyah jadīdah min qārat al-mazād, skāka al-Jawf, al-Mamlakah al-ʻArabiyyah al-Suʻūdiyyah', *Ages* 7/2: 215-254

al-Theeb, S 1993, *Aramaic and Nabataean Inscriptions from North-West Saudi Arabia*, maktabat al-malik Fahd al-waṭaniyyah, Riyadh.

al-Theeb, S 1994, *Dirāsah taḥlīlyyah li-l-nuqūš al-ārāmiyyah al-qadīmah fī Taymā al-Mamlakah al-ʻArabiyyah al-Suʻūdiyyah*, ?, Riyadh.

al-Theeb, S 1997, 'The Native Land of the Nabataeans', *NAS* 4: 233-242.

al-Theeb, S 1998, *Nuqūš al-Ḥijr al-Nabaṭiyyah*, Maṭbūʻāt maktabat al-malik Fahd al-waṭaniyyah, Riyadh.

Altheim, F. & Stiehl, R 1968, *Die Araber in der Alten Welt*, V/1, Walter de Gruyter & Co, Berlin, 2 vols.

al-Yaʻqūbī, A [d. 275H] 1980, *Tārīḫ al-yaʻqūbī*, dār bayrūt li-lṭibāʻah wā-an-našr, Beirut.

Ammianus, Marcelinus [d. end of 4th Cent. CE] 1937, *Res Gestae*, (ed. T. Page), LCL, London, 3 vols.

Antiquities Sites of al-Ula and Madain Saleh. ?. Department of Antiquities & Museums. Riyadh.

Arrian [d. 2nd cent. CE], 1976, *Anabasis Alexandri*, (tr. P.A. Brunt), LCL, London.

Asad, T 1993, *Genealogies of Religion, Discipline and Reasons of Power in Christianity and Islam*, Johns Hopkins University Press, Baltimore, London.

Austin, R.W.J 1983, 'Islam and the Feminine', *Islam in the Modern World*, (eds D. MacEoin & A. al-Shahi), Croom Helm, London, Canberra, pp. 36-48.

Avanzini, A 1991, 'Linguistic Data and Historical Reconstructions between Semitic and Epigraphic South Arabian', *SS*, Otto Harrassowitz, Wiesbaden, 108-118.

Bagnall, R.S 1997, 'The People of the Roman Fayum', *Portraits and Masks, Burial Customs in Roman Egypt*, (ed. M.L. Bierbrier), The Trustees of the British Museum, The British Museum Press: pp.7-15

Baldwin, G 1982, *Nabataean Cultural Influences upon Israel until 106 AD*, (Unpublished Ph.D. Thesis), Southwestern Baptist Theological Seminary, Fort Worth, Texas.

Bartlett, J.R 1990, 'From Edomites to Nabataeans: The Problem of Continuity', *Aram* 2: 25-34.

Batto, B.F 1974, *Studies on Women at Mari*, The Johns Hopkins University Press, Baltimore & London.

Beard, M. & Crawford, M 1989, *Rome in the Late Republic, Problems and Interpretations*, Duckworth, London.

Beauvoir, Simone De [1949] 1988, *The Second Sex*, (tr. H.M. Parshley), Picador Classics-Pan Books, London.

Beck, L 1995, 'Tribe', *The Oxford Encyclopedia of the Modern Islamic World*, (ed. J.L.Esposito), Oxford University Press, New York, Oxford, 4: 230-234.

Beeston, A.F.L., Ghul, M.A., Müller, W.W., & Ryckmans, J 1982, *Sabaic Dictionary, Dictionnaire Sabaéen, al-Muʻjam al-Saba'ī*, Éditions Peeters, Louvain-la-Neuve, Librairie du Liban, Beirut.

Ben-Barak, Z 1987, 'The Queen Consort and the Struggle for Sucession to the Throne', *La Femme dans le Proche-Orient Antique*, (ed. J.-M. Durand), Éditions Recherche sur les Civilisations, Paris, pp.33-40.

Ben-Zvi, I 1961, 'Les Origines de l'Etablissement des Tribus d'Israël en Arabie', *Le Muséon* 74: 143-190.

Bernal, M [1987] 1991, *Black Athena, The Afroasiatic Roots of Classical Civilisation*, Vintage, London.

Bignasca, A., N. Desse-Berset, R. Fellmann Brogli, R. Glutz, S. Karg, D. Keller, B. Kolb, Ch. Kramar, M. Peter, S.G. Schmid, Ch. Schneider, R.A. Stucky, J. Studer & I. Zanoni (eds), 1996, *Petra, Ez Zantur I*, (Terra Archaeologica II, Monographien der Schweizerisch-Liechtensteinischen Stiftung für Archäologische Forschungen im Ausland), Verlag Philipp von Zabern, Maïnz.

Blanc, P.-M, Dentzer, Jean-Marie, et Ph.Tondon 2002, 'Le Quartier Est, La Phase Nabatéenne, dans: Le Développement Urbain de Bosrta de l'époque Nabatéenne à l'époque Byzantine: Bilan des recherches Françaises 1981-2002', *Syria* 79: 75-154.

Bosworth, A.B 1996, *Alexander and the East, the Tragedy of Triumph*, Clarendon Press, Oxford.

Boucharlat, R 1989, 'Documents arabes provenant des sites "hellenistiques" de la Penisule d'Oman', *L'Arabie Préislamique et son Environement Historique et Culturel*, (ed. T.Fahd), E.J.Brill, Leiden, pp 109-126.

Bowersock, G.W 1978, 'The Greek-Nabataean Bilingual Inscription at Ruwwafa, Saudi Arabia', *Le Monde Grec, Hommage à Claire Préaux*, Université de Bruxelles, Bruxelles, pp. 513-522.

Bowersock, G.W 1980, 'Mavia, Queen of the Saracens', *Studien zur Antiken Sozialgeschichte, Festschrift Friedrick Vittinghoff*, Köln, Wien, pp. 477-95.

Bowersock, G.W 1983, *Roman Arabia*, Harvard University Press, Cambridge, Massachusetts, London.

Bowsher, J.M.C 1986, 'The Frontier Post of Medain Saleh', *The Defence of the Roman and Byzantine East*, (eds Ph. Freman & D. Kennedy), (British Institute of Archaeology at Ankara, Monograph No. 8), BAR International Series 297, Oxford, pp. 23-29.

Bowsher, J.M.C 1989, 'The Nabataean Army', *The Eastern Frontier of the Roman Empire*, (eds D.H. French & C.S. Lightfoot), (British Institute of Archaeology at Ankara, Mongraph No. 11), BAR International Series 553(i), Oxford, I: 19-30.

Bowsher, J.M.C 1990, 'Early Nabataean Coinage', *Aram* 2: 221-228

Braudel, F [1949] 1972, *The Mediterranean and the Mediterranean World in the Age of Philip II*, Tr. S.Reynolds, Collins, London, 2 Vols.

Bremen, Riet van 1996, *The Limits of Participation: women and civic life in the Greek East in the Hellenistic and Roman periods*, Dutch monographs on ancient history and archaeology ; v. 15. J.C. Gieben, Amsterdam.

Brinkman, J.A., Civil, M., Gelb, I.J., Oppenheim, A.L. & Reiner, E 1964-1992, *The Assyrian Dictionary*, (The Oriental Institue of the University of Chicago), Chicago, USA, & J.J.Augustin Verlagsbuchhandlung, Glückstadt, Germany, 17 vols.

Bronson, B 1988, 'The Role of Barbariansin the Fall of States', *The collapse of Ancient States and Civilizations*, (eds N. Yoffee & G.L. Cowgill), The University of Arizona Press, Tucson, pp. 196-218.

Broome, E.C 1973, 'Nabaiti, Nebaioth and the Nabataeans: The Linguistic Problem', *JSS* 18/1: 1-16.

Brosius, M 1995, *Women in Ancient Persia* (559-331 BC), Clarendon Press, Oxford.

Browning, I 1989, *Petra*, Catto & Windus, London.

Cantineau, J [1930] 1979, *Le Nabatéen*, Otto Zeller, Osnabrück, 2vols.

Carena, O 1989, *History of the Near Eastern Historiography and its Problems: 1852-1985, Part One: 1852-1945*, (Alter Orient und Altes Testament, Veröffentilichungen zur Kultur und Geschichte des Alten Orients und des Alten Testaments), (eds K.Bergerhof, M.Dietrich, O.Loretz). Verlag Butzon & Bercker Kevelaer, Neukirchener Verlag Neukirchen-Vluyn, Germany.

Cary, M. & Scullard, H.H 1975, *A History of Rome, down to the reign of Constantine*, 3rd edn. Butler & Tanner, Rome, London.

Caskel, W 1950, *Das Altarabische Königreich liḥjān*, Scherpe-Verlag, Krefeld.

Caskel, W 1954, 'The Beduinization of Arabia', *Studies in Islamic Cultural History*, (ed. G.E. von Grunebaum), American Anthropological Association Memoires LXXVI, Menasha, pp. 36-46 (original article in German in ZDMG 1953: 29-36).

Cassimatis, H 1985, 'Imagerie et Femme', *La Femme dans le Monde Méditerranéen I, Antiquité*, CNRS, Maison de l'Orient No 10, Lyon, pp. 19-28.

Casson, L 1974, *Travel in the Ancient World*, George Allen & Unwin Ltd, London.

Cerfaux, L. & Tondriau, J 1957, *Le culte des souverains dans la civilisation greco-romaine*, Series Bibliothèque de théologie, sér. 3 , v. 5, Desclée & Cie, Tournai.

Chahin, M 1987, *The Kingdom of Armenia*, Croom Helm, London, New York, Sydney.

Colledge, M.A. R 1967, *The Parthians*, Series Ancient peoples and places, v.59, Thames & Hudson, London.

Collier, J.F 1974, 'Women in Politics', in *Woman Culture & Society*, eds Rosaldo, Michelle Z, and Lamphere Louise, Stanford University Press, Stanford, California, pp.89-95.

Cooke, G.A 1903, *A Text-Book of North-Semitic Inscriptions, Moabite, Hebrew, Phoenician, Aramaic, Nabataean, Palmyrene, Jewish*, The Clarendon Press, Oxford.

Corpus Inscriptionum Semiticarum, II: Pars II, Tomus 1, F. 2-3, 1902-1907, Reipublicae Typographeo, Paris.

Corpus Inscriptionum Semiticarum, Inscriptiones Ḥimyariticas et Sabaeas Continens: IV, 1889, Reipublicae Typographeo, Paris.

Cotton, H 1993, 'The Guardianship of Jesus son of Babatha: Roman and local law in the Province of Arabia', *JRS* 83: 94-108.

Cotton, H 2001, 'Ein Gedi between the Two Revolts', *SCI* 20: 139-154

Cotton, H. 2002, 'Women and Law in the Documents from the Judaean Desert', *Le Rôle et le Statut de la Femme en Egypte Hellénistique, Romaine et Byzantine*, Actes du Colloque International, Bruxelles-Leuven 27-29 Nov 1997, eds Henri Melaerts & Leon Mooren, Peeters, Paris, Leuven, Sterling, Va., pp 123- 147.

Cuissini, E 1995, 'Transfer of Property at Palmyra', *Aram* 7: 233-250.

Cumont, F 1926, *Fouilles de Doura-Europos* (1922-1923), Librairies Orientaliste Paul Geuthner, Paris, 2 Vols (Texte, Atlas).

Dalman, G 1912, *Neue Petra-Forschungen und der Heilige Felsen von Jerusalem*, J.C.Hinrichsche Buchhandlung, Leipzig.

Davies, J.K 1998, 'Ancient economies: models and mudles', *Trade, Traders and The Ancient City*, (eds H. Parkins & C. Smith), Routledge, London, New York, pp. 225-256.

Dentzer, J.-M 1981, 'Les Fouilles de Sī', Phase Hellénistique en Syrie du Sud', *CRAIBL*: 78-102.

Dijkstra, K 1995, *Life and loyalty : a study in the socio-religious culture of Syria and Mesopotamia in the Graeco-Roman period based on epigraphical evidence*, Series Religions in the Graeco-Roman world ; v.128, E.J. Brill, Leiden.

Dio Cassius [d. 235CE], *Roman History*, (tr. E.Cary), 1968, William Heinemann Ltd., Harvard University Press, London, Cambridge, Massachusetts, 9 Vols.

Diodorus, C. Siculus [d.circa 21 BCE], 1954, *The Library of History*, tr. Russel M. Geer, Harvard University Press, Heinemann, London; Cambridge, Mass., 12 Vols.

Dostal, W 1989, 'The transition from Cognatic to Unilinear Descent Systems in South Arabia', *Kinship, Social Change, and Evolution*, Proceedings of a Symposium held in Honour of Walter Dostal, (eds A. Gingrich, S. Haas, S. Haas & G. Paleczek), (Vienna Contributions to Ethnology and Anthropology, Vol. 5), Verlag Ferdinand Berger & Söhne, Horn-Vienna, pp. 47-62.

Driel, G. Van 1999, 'Capital Formation and Investment in an Institutional Context in Ancient Mesopotamia', *Trade and Finance in Ancient Mesopotamia, Mos Studies 1*, (ed. J.G. Dercksen), Nederlands Historisch-Archaelogisch Institut te Instanbul, Nederlands Instituut voor het Nabije Oosten, Leiden, pp. 25-42.

Drijvers, H.J.W 1972, *Old-Syriac (Edessean) Inscriptions*, Brill, Leiden.

Dunlop, D.M 1954, *History of the Jewish Khazars*, Princeton University Press, Princeton, New Jersey.

Eadie, J 1985, 'Artifacts of Annexation: Trajan's Grand Strategy and Arabia', *The Craft of the Ancient Historian, Essays in Honor of Chester G. Starr*, (eds J.W. Eadie & J. Ober), University Press of America, Lanham, New York, London, pp.407-424.

Eddy, S.K 1961, *The King is Dead, Studies in the Near Eastern Resistance to Hellenism 334-31 BC*, University of Nebraska Press, Lincoln.

Ehrhardt, N. 1983, *Milet und seine Kolonien: Vergleichende Untersuchung der kultischen und politischen Einrichtungen*, Europäische Hochschulschriften, Reihe III, Geschichte und ihre Hilfswissenschaften, Bd. 206. P. Lang, Frankfurt am Main, New York.

Eisenstadt, S 1988, 'Beyond Collapse', *The collapse of Ancient States and Civilizations*, (eds N. Yoffee & G.L. Cowgill), The University of Arizona Press, Tucson, pp. 236-243.

Elsadda, H., Ramadan, S. and Abu Bakr, U. (eds) 1998, *Zaman annisā' wa al-dākirah al-badīlah*, Multaqā al-mar'ah wa al-ḏākirah, Cairo.

Eph'al, I 1984, *The Ancient Arabs, Nomads on the borders of the Fertile Crescent 9th-5th centuries B.C.*, The Magness Press, the Hebrew University, Jerusalem.

Eskoubi, Kh.M 1999, *Dirāsah taḥlīliyah muqaranah linuquš min manṭiqat Rum janūb ġarb tayma'*, wakālat al-āṯār wa-l matāḥif, Riyadh.

Esse, D.L 1991, *Subsistence, Trade and Social Change in Early Bronze Age Palestine*, (Studies in Ancient Oriental Civilization No. 50), The Oriental Isntitue of the University of Chicago, Chicoago, Illinois.

Farès-Drappeau, S 2005, *Dédan et Liḥyān, Histoire des Arabes aux confines des pouvoirs perse et hellénistique (IVe-IIes. Avant l'ère chrétienne)*, Travaux de La Maison de L'Orient et de la Méditerranée, Lyon.

Feldman, Louis H 1986, *How much Hellenism in Jewish Palestine?*, Hebrew Union College Annual 52.

Fowden, G 1993, *Empire to Commonwealth, consequences of monotheism in late antiquity*, Princeton University Press, Princeton.

Frankfort, H [1954] 1970, 'The Ancient Near East', *Orientalism and History*, (ed. D.Sinor), Indiana University Press, Bloomington, London, pp. 1-15.

Frantsouzoff, S forthcoming, La femme en Arabie du Sud antique.

Frey, P.J.-B 1952, *Corpus Inscriptionum Iudaicarum*, Vol. II, Asie-Afrique, Città del Vaticano, Pontificio Istituto di Archeologia Cristiana, Roma.

Frymer-Kensky, T 1992, *In The Wake of The Goddesses, Women, Culture, and the Biblical transformation of Pagan Myth*, The Free Press, New York.

Ġabban, A. [1990]1993, 'al-'ābār al-sulṭāniyah bi-wādī al-Zurayb bi-l-Wajh', *Šamāl ġarb al-mamlakah al-'arabiyyah al-Su'ūdiyyah, buḥūṯ fī al-tārīh wa al-'āṯār*, Riyadh, pp.13-60.

Gadd, C.J 1958, 'The Harran Inscriptions of Nabonidus', *AS* 8: 36-91.

Gardner, J.F 1986, *Women in Roman Law & Society*, Croom Helm, London.

Gatier, P.L. & Salles, J.F 1988, 'Aux Frontières Méridionales du Domaine Nabatéen', *L'Arabie et ses Mers Bordières*, (ed. J.F.Salles), GS Maison de L'Orient, Lyon, pp. 173-190.

Gawlikowski, M 1982, 'The Sacred Space in Ancient Arab Religions', *Studies in the History and Archaeology of Jordan SHAJ I*, Amman, pp. 301-303.

Gimbutas, M 1991, *The Civilization of the Goddess, The World of Old Europe*, ed. Joan Marler, HarperSanFrancisco, San Francisco, California.

Glueck, N 1965, *Deities and Dolphins*, Ferrar, Straus & Giroux, New York.

Graf, D.F 1983, 'Dedanite and Minaean (south Arabian) Inscriptions from the Ḥisma', *ADAJ* 27: 555-569.

Graf, D.F 1989, 'Rome and the Saracens: Reassessing the nomadic Menace', *L'Arabie Préislamique et son Environement Historique et Culturel*, (ed. T.Fahd), E.J.Brill, Leiden, pp. 341-400.

Graf, D.F 1990a, 'Arabia during Achaemenid Times', *Achaemenid History IV, Centre and Periphery,*

(Proceedings of the Groningen 1986 Achaemenid History Workshop), (eds H. Sancisi-Weedenburg & A. Kuhrt), Nederlands Instituut Voor Het Nabjie, Oosten, Leiden, pp. 131-148.

Graf, D.F 1990b, 'The Origin of the Nabataeans', *Aram* 2: 45-75.

Graf, D.F 1990c, 'Qura 'Arabiyya & Provincia Arabia', *Géographie Historique au Proche-Orient (Syrie, Phénicie, Arabie, grecques, romaines, byzantines)*, (eds P-L. Gatier, B.Helly & J.-P.Rey-Coquais), Centre National de la Recherche Scientifique, Centre de Recherches Archéologiques, Editions du CNRS, Paris, pp. 171-211.

Graf, D.F [1994] 1997, 'The Nabataean Army and the *cohortes ulpiae petraeorum*', *Rome and the Arabian Frontier: from the Nabataeans to the Saracens*, (Originally published in *The Roman and Byzantine Army in the East*, ed. E. Dabrowa, Uniwersytet Jagiellónski, Kraków), Ashgate, Variorum collected studies, UK, USA, pp. 265-311.

Graf, D.F 2000, 'Aramaic on the periphery of the Achaemenid realm', *Archäologische Mitteilungen aus Iran und Turan* 32: 75-92

Graf, D.F 2003, 'Language and Lifestyle as Boundary Markers: The North Arabian Epigraphic Evidence', *MA* 16: 27-56

Graf, D.F 2004, 'Nabataean Identity and Ethnicity: The Epigraphic Perspective', *SHAJ* VIII: 145-154.

Greenfield, J.C 1991, 'Kullu nafsin bimā kasabat rahīnā, the Use of rhn in Aramaic and Arabic', *Arabicus Felix: Luminous Britannicus, Essays in Honour of A.F.L. Beeston on his Eightieth Birthday*, (ed. A. Jones), (Oxford Oriental Institute Monographs; 11), Ithaca Press Reading, Oxford, pp. 221-227.

Grelot, P 1972, *Documents Araméens d'Égypte*, Les Éditions du Cerf, Paris.

Groom, N 1981, *Frankincense and Myrrh, a study of the Arabian incense trade*, Longman, Librairie du Liban, London, New York, Beirut.

Grushevoi, A.G 1985, 'The tribe 'Ubaishat in Safaitic, Nabataean and Greek inscriptions', *Berytus* 33: 51-54.

Haldon, J 1984/85, ' 'Jargon' vs. 'the Facts'? Byzantine History-Writing and Contemporary Debates', *BMGS* 9: 95-132

Hall, S 1992, 'The West and the Rest: discourse and Power', *Formations of Modernity*, (eds S. Hall & B. Giben), Polity Press, Blackwell, Open University, Cambridge, Oxford, pp. 276-318.

Hammond, Ph 1973, *The Nabataeans – Their History, Culture and Archaeology*, (Studies in Mediterranean Archaeology, Vol. 37), Gothenburg, Sweden.

Hammond, Ph 1981. 'Ein nabatäisches Weiherelief aus Petra', *Die Nabatäer: Enträge einer Ausstellung im Rheinischen Landesmuseum Bonn* (ed. G. Hellenkermper Salies), Rheinland-Verlag, Cologne (BJ 180 [1980]): 137-141.

Hammond, Ph 1990, 'The Goddess of the 'Temple of the Winged Lions' at Petra (Jordan)', *Petra and the Caravan cities*, (ed. F. Zayadine), Department of Antiquities, Amman, pp. 115-30.

Hammond, Ph., D.J. Johnson & R.N. Jones 1986, 'A Religio-Legal Nabataean Inscription from the Atargatis / Al-'Uzza Temple at Petra', *BASOR* 263: 77-80.

Hanson, V.D 1998, *Warfare and Agriculture in Classical Greece*, (revised edition), University of California Press, London.

Harding, G.L 1952, *Some Thamudic Inscriptions from the Hashimite Kingdom of the Jordan*, (with the collaboration of E. Littmann), E.J. Brill, Leiden.

Harding, G.L 1971, *An Index and Concordance of Pre-Islamic Arabian Names and Inscriptions*, University of Toronto Press, Toronto, Buffalo.

Harris, M. & Ross, E.B 1987, *Death, Sex, and Fertility, population regulation in preindustrial and developing societies*, Columbia University Press, New York.

Hāšim, L 1996. 'Dirāsah li-majmū'at al-nuqūd al-Nabaṭiyyah al-bronziyyah fī mathaf al-Salṭ', (Unpublished MA Dissertation), Jordan University, Amman.

Healey, J.F 1989a, 'A Nabataean Sundial from Madā'in Ṣāliḥ', *Syria* 66: 331-336.

Healey, J.F 1989b, 'Were the Nabataeans Arabs?' *Aram* 1/1: 38-44.

Healey, J.F 1993a, 'Sources for the study of Nabataean Law', *NAS* 1: 203-214.

Healey, J.F 1993b, *The Nabataean Tomb Inscriptions of Mada'in Salih*, (JSS Supp. 1), Oxford.

Healey, J.F 1996, 'Dushara as Sun-God', *I Primi Sessanta anni di Scuola*, (Studi Dedicati dagli amici a Sergio Noja Noseda, nel suo 65 Compleanno), Fondazione Ferni Noja Noseda Studi Arabo Islamici, 7: 37-53.

Healey, J.F 2001a, ''Romans always Conquer' Some Evidence of Ethnic Identity on Rome's Eastern Frontier', *Archaeology of the Roman Empire, A tribute to the life and works of Professor Barri Jones*, ed. N.J. Higham, BAR International Series 940, Oxford, 167-171.

Healey, J.F 2001b, *The Religion of the Nabataeans: A Conspectus*, Brill, Leiden, Boston, Köln.

Healey, J.F 2005, 'New Evidence of the Aramaic Legal Tradition: from Elephantine to Edessa' *Studia Semitica: JSS Jubilee Volume (JSS Supplement 16)*, eds P. S. Alexander, G. J. Brooke, A. Christmann, J. F. Healey & P. C. Sadgrove, Oxford University Press, Oxford, pp. 115-127.

Healey, J.F., & Smith, G.R 1989, 'Jaussen-Savignac 17-The Earliest Dated Arabic Document', *Atlal* 12: 77-84, pl. 46, Arabic 101-110.

Healey, J.F., Schmitt-Korte, K., & Wenning, R 1997, '*Scripta Nabataea* und *Sela Aretas*, Epigraphische Zeugnisse und Münzwesen der Nabatäer', *Petra, Antike Felsstadt zwischen arabischer Tradition und griecheischer Norm*, (eds T.Weber & R. Wenning), (Sonderhefte der Antiken Welt, Zaberns Bildbände zur Archäologie), Werlag Philipp von Zabern, Mainz am Rhein, pp. 99-104.

Heather, P [1996] 1997, *The Goths*, Blackwell Publishers, Oxford.

Herodotus, [d. circa 425 BCE] 1981, *Historia*, (tr. A.D. Godley), LCL, London, 4 vols.

Hill, B 1999, *Imperial Women in Byzantium 1025-1204, Power, Patronage and Ideology*, Women and Men in History, Longman, Essex.

Hill, G.F 1922, *Catalogue of the Greek Coins of Arabia, Mesopotamia and Persia (Nabataea, Arabia Provincia, S. Arabia, Mesopotamia, Babylonia, Assyria, Persia, Alexandrine Empire of the East, Persis, Elymais, Characene)*, The Trustees of the British Museum, London.

Hodgson, M.G.S [1958] 1974, *The Venture of Islam, conscience and history in a world civlization*, Vol I: *The Classical Age of Islam*, The University of Chicago Press, Chicago, London.

Hoftijzer, J. & Jongeling, K 1995, *Dictionary of the North-West Semitic Inscriptions*, (Handbuch der Orientalistik, Bd. 21/1), Leiden, New York, 2 vols.

Hollis, S.T 1997, 'Queens and Goddesses in Ancient Egypt', *Women and Goddess Traditions in Antiquity and Today*, (ed. K.L. King), Fortress Press, Minneapolis, pp. 210-238.

Homès-Fredericq, D 1963, *Hatra et ses Sculptures Parthes, Etude Stylistique et Iconographique*, Nederlands Historisch-Archaeologisch Instituut in het Nabije Oosten, Istanbul.

Hopkins, K [1978] 1987, *Conquerors and Slaves*, (Sociological Studies in Roman History, Vol 1), Cambridge University Press, Cambridge, London, New York, New Rochelle, Melbourne, Sydney.

Hopkins, K 1978, 'Rules of Evidence, Review of Fergus Millar's *The Emperor in the Roman World* (31 B.C.-A.D. 337)', *JRS* 68: 178-186.

Hopkins, K 1983, 'Introduction', *Trade in the Ancient Economy*, (eds P. Garnsey, K. Hopkins & C.R. Whittaker), Chatto & Windus, The Hogath Press, London, pp. ix-xxv.

Hopkins, K 1999, *A World Full of Gods: the strange triumph of Christianity*, Plume-Penguin, USA, London, New-Zealand, Australia.

Ibn al-Kalbī, H [d. 204 H] 1924, *Kitāb al-Aṣnām*, (ed. A.Zaki Pasha), al-Dār al-qawmiyyah li-l-ṭibā'ah wā al-našr, Cairo.

Ibn Ḥazm, A [d. 456 H] 1982, *Jamharat 'ansāb al-'Arab*,(ed. A.M. Harūn) (5th edn.), Dār al-ma'ārif, Cairo.

Ibn Hišām [d. 213 H] 1996, *al-Sīrah al-Nabawiyyah*, (eds J. Thabit, M. Mahmud & S. Ibrahim), Dār al-ḥadīṯ, Cairo, 5 Vols.

Ibn Khaldūn, A [d. 808 H] ? . *Muqaddimat ibn Haldūn*, Kitāb al-Ša'b, Cairo.

Ibn Manẓūr [d. 711 H] ?, *Lisān al-'Arab, Dār al-ma'ārif*, Cairo, 6vols.

Ibn Waḥšiyyah, A. al-Kasdānī [4th century H/ 10th century CE] 1993, *al-Filāḥah al-Nabaṭiyyah*, (ed. T.Fahd), Vol.I, al-Ma'had al-'ilmī al-Faransi li-l-dirāsāt al-'Arabiyyah bi-Dimašq, Damascus.

Ilan, T 2001, 'Witnesses in the Judaean Desert Documents: Proposopographical Observations', *Scripta Classica Israelica* 20: 169-178.

Inglebert, H 1997, 'Pars Oceani Orientalis, Les Conceptions de L'Orient dans les āuvre Géographiques de L'Antiquité tardive (300-550)', *Des Sumériens aux Romains d'Orient, La Perception Géographique du Monde, Antiquités Sémitiques II*, J.Maisonneuve, Paris, pp177-198.

Ingraham, M., Johnson, Th., Rihani, B. & I.Shatla 1981, 'Preliminary Report on a Reconnaissance Survey of the Northwestern Province (with a note on a brief survey of the Northern Province)', *Atlal* 5: 59-83, pl. 64-97.

Invernizzi, A 1993, 'Seleucia on the Tigris: Centre and Periphery in Seleucid Asia', *Centre and Periphery in the Hellenistic World*, (eds P. Bilde, T. Engeberg-Pedersen, L. Hannestad, J. Zahle & K. Randsborg), (Studies in Hellenistic Civilisation), (eds P. Bilde, T. Engberg-Pedersen, L. Hannestad & J. Zahle), Aarhus University Press, Aarhus, pp. 230-250.

Isaac, B 1992, 'The Babatha Archive: A Review Article', *IEJ* 42: 62-75.

James, E.O 1955, *The Nature and Function of Priesthood*, Thames & Hudson, London.

Jameson, S 1968, 'Chronology of the campaigns of Aelius Gallus & C. Petronius', *JRS* 58: 71-84.

Jastrow, M 1921, 'Veiling in Ancient Assyria', *RA* 14: 209-38

Jaussen, A. & Savignac. R 1909-1911, *Mission Archéologique en Arabie I, II*, Librairie Orientaliste Paul Geuthner, Paris.

Jeremias, A 19321, ' Der Schleier von Sumer bis Heute', *Der Alte Orient* 31/1: 7-70, pl. i-viii. J.C. Hinrichs'sche Buchhandlung, Leipzig.

Johnson, D. J 1987, 'Nabataean Trade: Intensification and Culture Change', (Unpublished Ph.D. Thesis), The University of Utah, Utah.

Jones, S 1997, *The Archaeology of Ethnicity, Constructing identities in the past and present*, Routledge, London, New York.

Josephus [d. 93 CE] 1943, *Jewish Antiquities*, (Tr. R.Marcus), Harvard University Press, London, Cambridge, Massachusetts, 9 vols.

Josephus [d. 93CE] 1927, *The Jewish War*, (tr. H.St. J.Thackeray), William Heinemann, London, G.P. Putnam's Sons, New York, 3 Books.

Karg, S 1996, 'Pflanzenrest aus den Nabatäischen und spätrömischen Schichten', *Petra. Ez Zantur I*, (eds A. Bignasca, N. Desse-Berset, R. Fellmann Brogli, R. Glutz, S. Karg, D. Keller, B. Kolb, Ch. Kramar, M. Peter, S.G. Schmid, Ch. Schneider, R.A. Stucky, J. Studer & I. Zanoni), (Terra Archaeologica II, Monographien der Schweizerisch-Liechtensteinischen Stiftung für Archäologische Forschungen im Ausland), Verlag Philipp von Zabern, Maïnz, pp. 355-358.

Kawami, T.S 1987, *Monumental Art of the Parthian Period in Iran*, (Acta Iranica 26. 3ème série, Textes et Mémoires Vol XIII), E.J.Brill, Leiden.

Khairy, N 1981, 'A New Dedicatory Nabataean Inscription from Wadi Musa, (With additional note by J.T.Milik)', *PEQ* 113: 19-26.

Khairy, N 1986, 'Three Unique Objects from Petra', *PEQ* 118: 101-108.

Khairy, N 1990, *The 1981 Petra Excavations*, Vol. 1, Otto Harrassowitz, Wiesbaden.

Khalifeh, I.A 2000, 'Review of S. al-Saud's Central Arabia during the early Hellenistic period', *Adumatu* 1: 66-73.

Kirwan, L.P 1984, 'Where to Search for the Ancient Port of Leuke Kome', *SHA* II, King Saud University Press, Riyadh, pp. 55-61.

Knauf, E.A 1985, *Ismael Untersuchungen zur Geschichte Palastinäs und Nordarabiens im 1 Jahrtaunend v.Chr*, Otto Harrassowitz, Wiesbaden.

Knauf, E.A 1989, 'Nabataean Origins', *Arabian Studies in Honour of Mahmoud Ghul: Symposium at Yarmouk University December 8-11, 1984*, (ed. M.M. Ibrahim), Otto Harrassowitz, Wiesbaden, pp. 56-61.

Kornemann, E. Von 1925, 'Neuerscheinungen, Zur Geschvisterehe im Altertum', *Klio* 19: 355- 361.

Koshelenko, G.A. & Pilipko, V.N 1994, 'Parthia', *History of Civilizations of Central Asia*, Vol II, *The development of sedentary and nomadic civilzations: 700 B.C. to A.D. 250*, (ed. J.Harmatta), (co-eds B.N. Puri & G.F. Etemadi), UNESCO Publishing, France, pp. 131-150.

Kuhrt, A 1995, *The Ancient Near East c.3000-330* BC, Routledge, London, New York , 2 vols.

Kuhrt, A 1998, 'The Old Assyrian merchants', *Trade, Traders and The Ancient City*, (eds H. Parkins & C. Smith), Routledge, London, New York, pp.16-30.

Kuhrt, A. & Sherwin-White, S 1994, 'The Transition from Achaemenid to Seleucid Rule in Babylonia: Revolution or Evolution?', *Achaemenid History VIII Continuity and Change, Proceedings of the last Acheamenid history workshop April 6-8 1990-Ann Arbor, Michigan*, (eds H. Sancisi-Weerdenburg, A. Khurt & M. Cool Root), Nederlands Instituut Voor het Nabije Oosten, Leiden, pp311-327

La Bianca, O.S 1985, 'The return of the Nomad: an Analysis of the Process of Nomadization in Jordan', *ADAJ* 29: 251-4.

Lacerenza, G 1988-89, 'Il Dio Dusares a Puteoli', *Puteoli, Studi di Storia Antica*, (ed. G.Camodeca), XII-XIII: 119-149.

Lacerenza, G 1994, 'Due nuove iscrizioni del tempio di Dusares dell'antica Puteoli', *Annali* 54/ 1: 15-17.

Lane, E.W 1968, *Arabic-English Lexicon*, Librairie du Liban, Beirut.

Langdon, S 1927, 'The "Shalamians" of Arabia', *JRAS*: 529-533.

Larsen, M.T 1967, *Old Assyrian Caravan Procedures*, Nederlands Historisch-archaeologisch Institut in Het Nabije Oosten, Istnabul.

Larsen, M.T 1987, 'Orientalism and the Ancient Near East', *Culture & History CH* 2: 96-115.

Larsen, M.T 1989, 'Orientalism and Near Eastern archaeology', *Domination and & Resistance*, (eds D. Miller, M. Rowlands & C. Tilley), Unwin Hyman, London, Boston, Sydney, Wellington, pp. 229-239.

Lattimore, O [1947] 1962, 'Inner Asian Frontiers: Chinese and Russian Margins of Expansion', *Studies in Frontier History, Collected Papers 1928-1958*, Oxford University Press, London, New York, Toronto, pp. 134-159.

Lemaire, A 1974, 'Un Nouveau Roi Arabe de Qedar dans l'Inscription de l'Autel à Encens de Lakish', *RB* 81: 63-72.

Lerner, G 1979-1981, *The Majority Finds its Past, Placing Women in History*, Oxford University Press, Oxford, New York, Toronto, Melbourne.

Lerner, G 1986, *The Creation of Patriarchy*, Oxford University Press, Oxford.

Levi Della Vida, G 1938, 'Una Bilingue Greco-Nabatea a Coo', *Clara Rhodos* 9, (ed. C. Rhodos), pp. 139-147.

Lewis, N 1978, 'Two Greek Documents from Provincia Arabia', *ICS* III: 100-114.

Lewis, N 1994, 'The Babatha Archive: A Response', *IEJ* 44: 243-246.

Linnekin, J [1990] 1993, *Sacred Queens and Women of Consequence, Rank, Gender, and Colonialism in the Hawaiian Islands*, The University of Michigan Press, Ann Arbor.

Littmann, E 1914, *Nabataean Inscriptions*, (Semitic Inscriptions, Sec. A), (Publications of the Princeton University Archaeological Expeditions to Syria in 1904-5 and 1909), Brill, Leiden.

Littmann, E. & Meredith, D 1953, 'Nabataean Inscriptions from Egypt I', *BSOAS* 15: 1-28.

Littmann, E. & Meredith, D 1954, 'Nabataean Inscriptions from Egypt II', *BSOAS* 16: 211- 46.

Liverani, M 1973, 'Memorandum on the Approach to Historographic Texts', *Orientalia* NS 42: 178-194.

Luckenbill, D.D 1926-7, *Ancient Records of Assyria and Babylonia*, Chicago, 2 vols.

Lyttelton, M 1990, 'Aspects of the Iconography of the Sculptural Decoration of the Khasneh at Petra', *Petra and the Caravan Cities*, (ed. F. Zayadine), Department of Antiquities, Amman, pp. 19-29.

Lyttelton, M. B. & Blagg, T.F.C 1990, 'Sculpture from the temenos of Qasr El-Bint at Petra', *Aram* 2: 267-286.

MacAdam, H.I 1986, *Studies in the History of the Roman Province of Arabia, The Northern Sector*, (BAR International Series 295), Oxford.

Maccabées, 1st & 2nd book (tr. by S. Tedesche, Introduction and Commentary by S.Zeitlin), 1950, 1954, 3rd book (tr. & commentary by M.Hadas),1953, Harper & Brothers, New York, 3 books.

Macdonald, M., M. Al Mu'azzin, & Nehmé L 1996, 'Les Inscriptions Safaïtiques de Syrie, cent quarante ans après leur découverte', *Comptes rendus de l'Académie des Inscriptions et Belles-Lettres CRAIBL*, pp. 435-494.

Macdonald, M.C.A 1980, 'Safaitic Inscriptions in the Amman Museum and other Collections II', *ADAJ* 24: 185-208.

Macdonald, M.C.A 1991, 'Was the Nabataean Kingdom a 'Bedouin State'?' *ZDPV* 107: 102-119.

Macdonald, M.C.A 1992, 'North Arabian epigraphic notes-I', *AAE* 3: 23-43.

Macdonald, M.C.A 1993, 'Nomads and the Ḥawrān in the Late Hellenistic and Roman Periods: A Reassessment of the Epigraphic Evidence', *Syria* 70/3: 303-413.

Macdonald, M.C.A 1995a, 'Ṣafaitic', *EI* 8: 760-762.

Macdonald, M.C.A 1995b, 'Quelques réflections sur les Saracènes, l'inscription de Rawwāfa et l'armée romaine', *Présence arabe dans le Croissant fertile avant l'Hégire*, (ed. H. Lozachmeur), Editions Recherche sur les Civilisations, Paris, pp. 93-101.

Macdonald, M.C.A 1998, 'Some Reflections on Epigraphy and Ethnicity in the Roman Near East', *MA* 11: 177-190.

Macdonald, M.C.A. & King, G.M.H 1999, 'Thamudic', *EI* X 10: 436-438.

Maciver, R.M. & Page, C.H 1961, *Society, An Introductory Analysis*, Macmillan & Co, London.

Mailser, B 1949, 'HaRekam and HaHegar', *Tabriz* xx: 316-319 (in Hebrew).

Mann, M 1986, *The Sources of Social Power, Vol I: A history of power from the beginning to A.D. 1760*, Paperback Library, Cambridge.

Manniche, L 1987, *Sexual Life in Ancient Egypt*, KPI, London, New York.

McClees, H 1920, *A Study of Women in Attic Inscriptions*, Columbia University Press, New York.

McGraw Donner, F 1981, *The Early Islamic Conquests*, Princeton University Press, Princeton, New Jersey.

McKenzie, J 1990, *The Architecture of Petra*, (British Acaemy Monographs in Archaeology 1), Oxford University Press, Oxford.

Mendelsohn, I 1949, *Slavery in the Ancient Near East*, Oxford University Press, New York.

Meshorer, Y 1975, *Nabataean Coins*, (Qedem), Institute of Archaeology, Jerusalem.

Meza, A.I 1993, 'An Egyptian Statuette in Petra', *ADAJ* 37: 427-431.

Meza, A.I 1996, 'The Egyptian Statuette in Petra and the Isis Cult Connection', *ADAJ* 40: 167-176.

Milik, J.T 1958, 'Nouvelles Inscriptions Nabatéennes', *Syria* 35: 227-251.

Milik, J.T 1971, 'Inscriptions Grecques et Nabatéennes de Rawwafah, Preliminary Survey in N.W. Arabia, 1968', (*Parr et al*), BIA 10: 54-60.

Milik, J.T 1976, 'Une Inscription Bilingue Nabatéenne et Greque à Petra', *ADAJ* 21: 143-152.

Milik, J.T 1980, 'La Tribu des Bani 'Amrat en Jordanie de L'Époque Grècque et Romaine', *ADAJ* 24: 41-54.

Milik, J.T 1981, 'Additional note to A New Dedicatory Nabataean Inscription from Wadi Musa', *PEQ* 113: 25-26.

Milik, J.T 1982, 'Origines des Nabatéens', *SHAJ* I: 261-265.

Milik, J.T. & Starcky, J 1970, 'Nabataean, Pamyrene, and Hebrew Inscriptions', *Ancient Records from North Arabia*, (Winnett, F.V. & Reed, W.L.), University of Toronto Press, Toronto, pp. 141-164.

Milik, J.T. & Starcky, J 1975, 'Inscriptions recémment decouvertes à Pétra', *ADAJ* 20: 111- 130, Pl. xxxvii-xlvii.

Mirkin, H 1984, 'The Passive Female, the Theory of Patriarchy', *AS* 25/ 2: 39-57.

Momigliano, A 1990, *The Classical Foundations of Modern Historiography*, University of California Press, Berkeley, Los Angeles, Oxford.

Moore, J.M 1975, *Aristotle and Xenophon on Democracy and Oligarchy*, Chatto & Windus, London.

Morgan, D 1986, *The Mongols, Series The Peoples of Europe*, Blackwell, Oxford.

Morris, I 1992, *Death-Ritual and Social Structure in Classical antiquity, Key themes in Ancient History*, Cambridge University Press, Cambridge.

Muffs, Y 1969, *Studies in the Aramaic Legal Papyri from Elephantine*, E.J. Brill, Leiden.

Müller, D.H 1889, *Epigraphische Denkmäler aus Arabien* (Nach Abklastschen und Copieen des Herrn Professor Dr. Julius Euting in Strassburg) (DSAWW 37), Wien.

Munif, A [1984] 1994, *Cities of Salt*, (Tr. P.Theroux), Vintage, London.

Munslow, A [1997] 1998, *Deconstructing History*, Routledge, London, New York.

Murray, M.A. & Ellis, J. C 1940, *A Street in Petra, British School of Archaeology in Egypt*, London.

Nasif, A.A 1981, Al-'Ulā, *An Historical and Archaeological Survey with Special Reference to its Irrigation System*, King Saud University, Riyadh.

Nasif, A.A 1995, *al-'Ulā, dirāsah fī al-turāṯ al-ḥaḍārī wa-l-'ijtimā'ī*, ?, Riyadh.

Naveh, J 1979, 'A Nabatean Incantation Text', *IEJ* 29: 111-9.

Negev, A 1961, 'Nabataean Inscriptions from 'Abdat (Oboda), I', *IEJ* 11: 127-138.

Negev, A 1974, 'A Nabataean Statuette from Jordan', *PEQ* 106: 77-78, pl. xii-xiv.

Negev, A 1976, 'The Nabatean Necropolis at Egra', *RB* 83: 203-236.

Nehmé, L 2003, 'Les Inscriptions des Chambres funéraires Nabatéennes et la question de l'anonymat des tombes', *Arabian archaeology and epigraphy AAE* 14: 203-258.

Nehmé, L. & F. Villeneuve 1999, 'Petra, Métropole de L'Arabie Antique', Seuil, Paris.

Nemet-Nejat, K.R 1998, *Daily Life in Ancient Mesopotamia*, Greenwood Press, Westport, Connecticut, London.

Noja, S 1979, 'Testimonianze Epigrafiche di Giudei nell'Arabia Settentrionale', *BO* 122, 21 Anno: 283-317.

Nöldeke, Th 1892, 'Some Characteristics of the Semitic Race', pp. 1-20.

Nuṣḥī, I 1976, *Tārīh Miṣr fī 'aṣr al-Baṭālimah*, 4th edn, Maktabat al-'anglo al-Maṣriyyah, Cairo, 4vols.

Ogden, D 1997, 'Wọmen and Bastardy in Ancient Greece and the Hellenistic World', *The Greek World*, (ed. A. Powell), Routledge, London and New York, pp.219-244.

Oleson, J.P 1995, 'The Origins and Design of Nabataean water-supply systems', *SHAJ* V: 707-719.

Oppenheim, A.L 1964, *Ancient Mesopotamia, Portrait of a Dead Civilisation*, The University of Chicago Press, London, Chicago.

Oren, E.D 1982, 'Excavations at Qasrawet in North-Western Sinai, Preliminary Report', *IEJ* 32: 203-211.

Paltiel, E 1991, *Vassals and Rebels in the Roman Empire, Julio-Claudian Policies in Judaea and the Kingdoms of the East*, (Latomus Vol. 212. Révue d'études Latines), Bruxelles.

Parker, S.T 1986, 'Romans and Saracens: A History of the Arabian Frontier', (Dissertation Series 6, ASOR), Winona Lake, USA.

Parker, S.T 1987, 'History of the Roman Frontier East of the Dead Sea', *The Roman Frontier in Central Jordan, Interim Report on the Limes Arabicus Project, 1980-1985*, (BAR International Series 340(i), Oxford, pp. 739-824.

Parkin, T.G 1992, *Demography and Roman Society*, The John Hopkins University Press, Baltimore, London.

Parlasca, I 1990, 'Terrakotten aus Petra, ein Neues kapitel Nabatäischer Archäologie', *Petra and the Caravan Cities*, (ed. F. Zayadine), Department of Antiquities, Amman, pp.87-106.

Parlasca, K 1998, 'Bemerkungen zum Isiskult in Petra, Nach Petra und ins Königreich der Nabatäer', *Notizen von Reisengefahrten, für Manfred Lindner zum 80 Geburtstag*, (eds U. Hubner, E.A. Knauf & Wenning, R.), Philo, Bodenheim, pp. 64-70.

Parpola, S 1970, *Neo-Assyrian Toponyms*, Programming and computer printing by Kimmo Koskenniemi, *Alter Orient und Altes Testament*, (eds K. Bergerhof, M. Dietrich & O. Loretz), Verlag Butzon & Bercker Kevelaer, Neukirchener Verlag des Erziehungsvereins, Neukirchen-Vluyn.

Parr, P.J 1960, 'Nabataean Sculpture from Khirbet-Brak', *ADAJ* 4-5: 134-136, pl. xv,xvi.

Parr, P.J 1962, 'A Nabataean Sanctuary near Petra; A Preliminary Notice', *ADAJ* 6-7: 21-23 pl. viii-xi.

Parr, P.J 1967-68, 'Recent Discoveries in the Sanctuary of the Qasr Bint Far'un at Petra', *ADAJ* 12-13: 5-19.

Parr, P.J 1990, 'A Commentary on the Terracotta Figurines from the British Excavations at Petra, 1958-64', *Petra and the Caravan Cities*, (ed. F. Zayadine), Department of Antiquities, Amman, pp. 77-86.

Parr, P.J 1996, 'Further Reflections on Late Second Millennium Settlement in North West Arabia', *Retrieving the Past, Essays on Archaeological Research and Methodology in Honor of Gus W. Van Beek*, (ed. J.D. Seger), The Cobb Institute of Archaeology, Mississippi State University, Eisenbrauns, Winona Lake, Indiana, pp. 213-218.

Parr, P.J., Harding, G.L. & Dayton, J.E 1970, 'Preliminary Survey in N.W. Arabia, 1968', *BIA* 8, 9: 193-242.

Parr, P.J., Harding, G.L. & Dayton, J.E 1972, 'Preliminary Survey in N.W. Arabia, 1968', (with contributions by A.F.L. Beeston & J.T. Milik), *BIA* 10: 23-62.

Parrot, A 1939, *Malédictions et violations de tombes*, Librairie Orientaliste Paul Geuthner, Paris.

Parsons, J.C 1994, 'Mothers, Daughters, Marriage, Power: Some Plantagenet Evidence, 1150-1500', *Medieval Queenship* (ed. Alan Sutton), Stroud, Gloucestershire, pp. 63-78.

Perikhanian, A 1983, 'Iranian Society and Law', *The Cambridge History of Iran, The Seleucid, Parthian and Sasanian Periods*, (ed. E. Yarshater), Cambridge University Press, Cambridge, London, New York, New Rochelle, Melbourne, Sydney, Vol 3 (2): 627-680.

Periplus of The Erythraean Sea, (ed. & tr. W.H. Schoff), 1974 [1912], Oriental Books Reprint Corporations, New Delhi.

Peters, F.E 1977, 'The Nabataeans in the Hawran', *JAOS* 97/3: 263-77.

Pigulevskja, N.V [1964] 1985, *al-'Arab 'alā ḥudūd Bīzanṭah wā-Iran min al-qarn al-rābi' īlā al-qarn al-sādis al-mīlādī*, (tr.from Russian S.O. Hāšim), al-Majlis al-waṭanī li-'ṯaqāfah wa-l-funūn wa-l-adab, Kuwait.

Pitard, W.T 1994, 'Arameans', *People of the Old Testament World*, (eds A.J. Hoerth, G.L. Mattingly & E.M. Yamauchi. fr. A.R. Millard), The Lutterworth Press, Baker, Cambridge, Baker Books, Michigan, pp. 207-30.

Pliny [d. *ca* 79 CE] 1969, *Naturalis Historia*, (tr. H.Rackham, ed. E.H. Warmington), LCL, London, 10 vols.

Pomeroy, S.B [1975] 1994, *Goddesses, Whores, Wives & Slaves*, Women in Classical Antiquity, Pimlico, London.

Pomeroy, S.B 1984, *Women in Hellenistic Egypt from Alexander to Cleopatra*, Schocken Books, New York.

Porten, B. with J.J. Farber, C.J. Martin, G. Vittmannl, L.S.B. MacCoull & Clackson, S 1996, *The Elephantine Papyri in English, Three millennia of cross-cultural continuity and change*, E.J. Brill, Leiden, New York & Köln.

Postgate, J.N 1992, *Early Mesopotamia, Society and Economy at the Dawn of History*, Routledge, London, New York.

Potts, D. T 1992, *The Arabian Gulf in Antiquity: From Alexander the Great to the Coming of Islam* Vol II, Clarendon Press, Oxford.

Renfrew, C 1987, *Archaeology and Language, the Puzzle of Indo-European Origins*, Jonathan Cape, London.

Répértoire d'Epigraphie Sémitique, 1900-1935, Imprimerie Nationale, Paris, 6 Tomes.

Richardson, P 1996, *Herod, King of the Jews and Friend of the Romans*, University of South Carolina Press, Columbia, South Carolina.

Roche, M.-J 1996, 'Remarques sur les Nabatéens en Méditerrannée', *Semitica* 45: 73-99.

Rosaldo, M. Z. & Lamphere, L(eds) 1974, 'Introduction', *Women, Culture & Society*, Stanford UP, Stanford, California, pp. 1-15.

Roth, M. T 1997, *Law Collections from Mesopotamia and Asia Minor*, (P. Michalowski), (Society of Biblical Literature, Writings from the Ancient World Series Vol. 6), Scholars Press, Atlanta, Georgia.

Rothenberg, B 1970, 'An Archaeological Survey of South Sinai', *PEQ* 102: 4-29.

Russell, K.W 1995, 'Traditional Bedouin agriculture at Petra: Ethnoarchaeological insights into the evolution of food production', *SHAJ* V: 693-705.

Sachau, E 1884, 'Eine Nabatäische Inschrift aus Ḍmêr', ZDMG 38: 535-543.

Sadurska, A. & Bounni, A 1994, *Les Sculptures Funéraires de Palmyre*, (Rivista Di Archaeologia, dir. G. Traversari. Supplementi 13), Giorgio Bretschneider Editore, Roma.

Safar, F. & Mustafa, M.A 1970, *al-Ḥaḍar madinat al-Šams*, Baghdad.

Said, E [1987] 1995, *Orientalism*, Penguin Books, London.

Said, E 1994, *Culture and Imperialism*, Vintage, London.

Saller, R.P. & Shaw, B.D 1984, 'Tombstones and Roman Family Relations in the Principate: Civilians, Soldiers and Slaves', *JRS* 74: 124-156.

Samson, J 1985 *Nefertiti and Cleopatra, Queen-Monarchs of Ancient Egypt*, The Rubicon Press, London.

Sancisi-Weerdenburg, H 1987, 'Decadence in the Empire of Decadence in the Sources? From source to synthesis: Ctesias', *Achaemenid History I, Sources, Structures and Synthesis*, (ed. H. Sancisi-Weerdenburg), Nederlands Instituut voor het nabije Oosten, Leiden, pp. 33-46.

Sanday, P.R 1973, 'Toward a Theory of the Status of Women', *American Anthropologist* 75/4: 1682-1700.

Sanday, P.R 1974, 'Female Status in the Public Domain', *Women, Culture, & Society*, (eds M.Z. Rosaldo & L. Lamphere), Stanford University Press, Stanford, California, pp. 189-206.

Sartre, M 1982, *Trois Études sur l'Arabie Romaine et Byzantine*, Collection Latomus, Latomus, Bruxelles.

Sartre, M 1985, *Bostra, des Origines à l'Islam*, Librairie Orientale Paul Geuthner, Paris.

Savignac, R 1932, 'Note de Voyage-Le Sanctuaire d'Allat à Iram', *RB* 41: 581- 597.

Savignac, R 1933, 'Le Sanctuaire d'Allat à Iram (1)', *RB* 42: 405-422.

Savignac, R 1937, 'Le Dieu Nabatéen de La'aban et son Temple', *RB* 46: 401- 416.

Sayed, A.A 1981, 'Ṣilāt al-'Anbāṭ bi-Miṣr', *Majallat kulliyyat al-'ādāb wa al-'ulūm al-'insāniyyah*, (King AbdulAziz University in Jeddah), 1: 42-63.

Sayyid, B.S 1997, *A Fundamental Fear, Eurocentrism and the emergence of Islamism*, Zed Books, London, New York.

Scagliarini, F 1995, 'La Chronologie dédanite et liḥyanite: mise au point', *Présence arabe dans le Croissant fertile avant l'Hégire*, (ed. H. Lozachmeur), Éditions Recherche sur les Civilisations, Paris, pp. 119-132.

Schaeffer, H 1915, *The Social Legislation of the Primitive Semites*, New Haven, London.

Scheidel, W 1996, *Measuring Sex, Age and Death in the Roman Empire, Explorations in ancient demography*, (JRA supp. 21) (eds P. Foss & J.H. Humphrey), Ann Arbor, Michigan.

Schmitt-Korte, K 1990, 'Nabataean Coinage – Part II, New Coin Types and Variants', *NC* 150: 105-34.

Schmitt-Korte, K. & Cowell, M 1989, 'Nabataean Coinage-Part I, The Silver Content Measured by X-Ray Fluorescence Analysis', *NC* 149: 33-58.

Schmitt-Korte, K. & Price, M 1994, 'Nabataean Coinage-Part III, The Nabataean Monetary System', *NC* 154: 67-131, pl. 10-12.

Seyrig, H 1941, 'Postes Romaines sur la route de Médine', *Syria* 22: 218-223.

Shahīd, I 1984, 'The Reign of Valens', *Byzantium and the Arabs in the Fourth Century*, Dumbarton Oaks Research Library and Collection, Washington, D.C. pp. 138-202.

Sherwin-White, S 1978, *Ancient Cos, Vandenhoeck & Ruprecht*, Göttingen.

Sherwin-White, S. & Kuhrt, A 1993, *From Samarkand to Sardis*, Duckworth, London.

Sidebotham, S.E 1991, 'Ports of the Red Sea and the Arabia-India Trade', *Rome and India, The Ancient Sea Trade*, (edsV. Begley & R.D. De Puma), The University of Wisconsin Press, USA, pp. 12-38.

Smith, A.D 1987, *The Ethnic Origins of Nations*, Basil Blackwell, Oxford, New York.

Smith, W.R 1903, *Kinship and Marriage in Early Arabia*, AMS Press, London.

Southgate, B 1996, *History: What & Why? Ancient, Modern, and Postmodern Perspectives*, Routledge, London, New York.

Sprenger, A 1875, *Die alte Geographie Arabiens als Grundlage der Entwicklungsgeschichte des Semitismus*, Bern.

Starcky, J 1954, 'Un Contrat Nabatéenne sur papyrus', *RB* 61: 161-181.

Starcky, J 1955, 'The Nabataeans: A Historical Sketch', *BA* 18: 84-106.

Starcky, J 1965, 'Nouvelle Épitaphe Nabatéenne donnant le Nom Sémitique de Pétra', *RB* 72: 95-97, pl. v-vi.

Starcky, J 1966, 'Pétra et les Nabatéennes', *Supplement au Dictionnaire de la Bible*, Paris, VII: col. 900-1017.

Starcky, J 1971, 'Une Inscription Nabatéenne de l'An 18 d'Arétas IV', *Hommages André Dupont-Sommer, Librairie d'Amérique et d'Orient*, Paris, pp. 150-59.

Starcky, J. & Strugnell, J' 1966, 'Pétra: Deux Nouvelles Inscriptions Nabatéennes', *RB* 73: 236-247.

Stiehl, R 1970, 'A New Nabataean Inscription', *Beiträge zur alten Geschichte in deren Nachleben, Festschrift of F. Altheim*, Berlin, pp. 87-90.

Stone, M 1976, *When God was a Woman*, Harvest Book, Harcourt Brace & Company, San Diego, New York, London.

Stoneman, R 1994, *Palmyra and its Empire, Zenobia's Revolt against Rome*, The University of Michigan Press, Ann Arbor.

Strabo [d. 24 CE] 1989, *Geography*, (tr. H.L. Jones), LCL, London, 8 vols.

Strugnell, J 1959, 'The Nabataean Goddess 'Al-Kutba and her Sanctuaries', *BASOR* 156: 29-36.

Sullivan, R.D 1990, *Near Eastern Royalty and Rome, 100-30 BC*, University of Toronto Press, Toronto, Buffalo, London.

Sylloge Nummorum Graecorum, 1971, IV/III: Syria-Nabataea, The British Academy, London.

Sylloge Nummorum Graecorum, 1972, VI/I: The Greek and Hellenistic Coins, The British Academy, London.

Taagepera, R 1978, 'Size and Duration of Empires: Systematics of Size', *SSR* 7: 108-127.

Taköcs, S.A 1995, *Isis and Sarapis in the Roman World*, E.J. Brill, Leiden, New York, Köln.

Tarn, W.W 1929, 'Ptolemy II and Arabia', *JRA* 15: 9-25.

Tarn, W.W 1952, *Hellenistic Civilisation*, (3rd ed), Edward Arnold & Co. London.

Tarrier, D 1990, 'Baalshamin dans le monde Nabatène: À Propos de découvertes récentes', *Aram* 2: 197-203.

Taussig, H 1997, 'Wisdom/Sophia, Hellenistic Queens, and Women's lives', *Women and Goddess Traditions, in Antiquity and Today*, (ed. K.L King), In *Studies in Antiquity and Christianity*, Fortress Press, Minneapolis, pp. 264-280.

Teixidor, J 1995, 'Le Campement; Ville des Nabatéens', *Semitica* 43-44: 111-121.

Thurston, B.B 1989, *The Widows, A Women's Ministry in the Early Church*, Fortress Press, Minneapolis.

Treadgold, W 2001, *A Concise History of Byzantium*, Palgrave, New York, China.

Treadgold, W 1997, *A History of the Byzantine State*, Stanford University Press, Stanford, California.

Van den Branden, A 1950, *Les Inscriptions Thamoudéens*, (Bibliothèque du Muséon, Université de Louvain, Vol. 25), Louvain-Heverlé .

Van den Branden, A 1957, 'La Chronologie de Dédan et de Liḥyān', *BO* 14/1: 13-16.

Van den Branden, A 1966, *Histoire de Thamoud*, 2e edit., Publications de la l'Université Libanaise, Beirut.

Vaux, R. de 1935, 'Sur le Voile des Femmes dans l'Orient Ancien', *RB* 44: 397-412.

Veenhof, K.R 1972, *Aspects of Old Assyrian Trade and its Terminology*, E.J. Brill, Leiden.

Veenhof, K.R 1977, 'Some Social Effects of Old Assyrian Trade', *Trade in the Ancient Near East*, British School of Archaeology in Iraq, London, pp. 109-118.

Vercoutter, J 1965, 'La Femme en Égypte Ancienne', *Histoire Mondiale de La Femme, Préhistoire et Antiquité*, (ed. P.Grimal), Nouvelle Librairie de France, Paris.

Wegner, J.R 1988, *Chattel or Person? The status of women in the Mishnah*, Oxford University Press, New York, Oxford.

Wenning, R 1987, *Die Nabatäer Denkmäler und Geschichte*, Freiburg, Schweiz.

Wenning, R 1994, 'Eine neuerstellte Liste der nabatäischen Dynastie', *Boreas* 16: 25-38.

West, C 1989, 'Black Culture and Postmodernism', *Remaking History*, (Discussions in Contemporary Culture, Dia Art foundation No. 4), (eds B. Kruger & P. Mariani), Bay Press, Seattle, pp. 87-96.

Whitelam, K.W 1996, *The Invention of Ancient Israel: the silencing of Palestinian history*, Routledge, London, New York.

Winnett, F.V 1937, *A Study of the Lihyanite and Thamudic Inscriptions*, Toronto.

Winnett, F.V 1939, 'The Place of the Minaeans in the History of Pre-Islamic Arabia', *BASOR* 73: 3-9.

Winnett, F.V 1973, 'The Revolt of Damasī: Safaitic and Nabataean Evidence', *BASOR* 211: 54-57.

Winnett, F.V. & Reed, W.L 1970, *Ancient Records from North Arabia*, (With contributions by J.T. Milik & J. Starcky), University of Toronto Press, Toronto.

Woodhouse, W.J 1920a, 'Slavery (Greek)', *ERE* 11: 612-618.

Woodhouse, W.J 1920b, 'Slavery (Roman)', *ERE* 11: 621-631.

Woolley, C.L 1934, *Ur Excavations Vol II, The Royal Cemetery, Text*, (Publications of the joint Expedition of the British Museum and of the Museum of the University of Pennsylvania to Mesopotamia), Published for The Trustees of the two Museums by the aid of a grant from the Carnegie corporation of New York, UK.

Wright, G.R.H 1962, 'The Khazne at Petra: A review', *ADAJ* 6-7: 24-57.

Wright, G.R.H 1969, 'Strabo on Funerary Customs at Petra', *PEQ* 101: 113-116.

Yadin, Y 1962, 'Expedition D-The Cave of the Letters', *IEJ* 19: 227-257.

Yadin, Y 1963, 'The Nabataean Kingdom, Provincia Arabia, Petra and En-Geddi in the Documents from Naḥal Ḥever', *JEOL* 17: 227-241.

Yadin, Y., Greenfield, J.C., Yardeni, A. and B.A.Levine, additional contributions by H.M. Cotton & Naveh J 2002, *The Documents from the Bar Kokhba Period in the Cave of Letters, Hebrew, Aramaic and Nabatean-Aramaic Papyri*, Israel Exploration Society, Institute of Archaeology, Hebrew University, Shrine of the Book, Israel Museum.

Yaḥia, L 1978, *Dirāsāt fī-l-ʻaṣr al-hillinistī*, Dār al-nahḍa l-ʻarabiyah, Beirut.

Yardeni, A 2000, *Textbook of Aramaic, Hebrew and Nabataean Documentary Texts from the Judaean Desert and related material*, The Ben-Zion Dinur Center for Research in Jewish History, Jerusalem.

Yardeni, A 2001, 'The decipherment and Restoration of Legal Texts from the Judaean Desert: A Reexamination of Papyrus Starcky (P.Yadin 36)', *SCI* 20: 121-137.

Yoffee, N 1988, 'The Collapse of Ancient Mesopotamian States and Civilization', *The collapse of Ancient States and Civilizations*, (eds N. Yoffee & G.L. Cowgill), The University of Arizona Press, Tucson, pp. 44-68.

Zayadine, F 1970, 'Une Tombe Nabatéenne près de Dhatrās (Jordanie)', *Syria* 47: 117-134, pl. x.

Zayadine, F 1974, 'Excavations at Petra', *ADAJ* 19: 135-156.

Zayadine, F 1981, 'L'iconographie d'al-'Uzza - Aphrodite', *Mythologie Gréco-romanie, Mythologies Péripheriques, Études d'iconographie*, (Colloques Internationaux du CNRS n. 593), (eds L. Kahil & C. Augé), CNRS, Paris, pp. 113- 118.

Zayadine, F 1982, 'Recent Excavations at Petra (1979-81)', *ADAJ* 26: 365-93.

Zayadine, F 1984, 'Al-'Uzza Aphrodite', *LIMC*, Artemis Verlag, Zürich und München, II/1:167-69; II/2: 1169-70.

Zayadine, F 1990, 'The Pantheon of the Nabataean inscriptions in Egypt and the Sinai', *Aram* 2: 151-174

Zayadine, F 1991, 'Sculpture in Ancient Jordan', *Treasures from an ancient land, The Art of Jordan* (ed. P.Bienkowski), National Museums and Galleries on Meresyside, UK, pp.31-61.

Zayadine, F 1999, 'Pétra, le Sīq, une voie processionnelle, Jordanie, Sociétés, Rites et Religions', *Dossiers D'Archéologie* 244: 46-53.

Zaydān, J [1902-06] 1967, *Tārīḫ al-tamaddun al-Islāmī*, Dār maktabat al-ḥayāt, Beirut, 2 vols.

Plate I

Aral Sea
Black Sea
Caspian Sea
Oxus River
Samarqand
Athens
Antioch
Edessa
Manbij/Hierapolis
Hatra
Dura Europos
Palmyra
Berytus
Sydon
Damascus
Tyr
Xtesephon
Selucia
Persia
Babylon
Alexandria
Gazzah
Hira
Ur
Raqamu-Petra
Dumah
Memphis
Hegra
Dedan
Persian Gulf
Hajar
Egypt
Yaṯrib
Elephantine
Red Sea
Uyūn
Nile River
Qaryat dhu Kahl
Najran
Maraoe
Shabwah
Arabian Sea
Marib
Axum

Map of Nile to Oxus. © author

Plate II

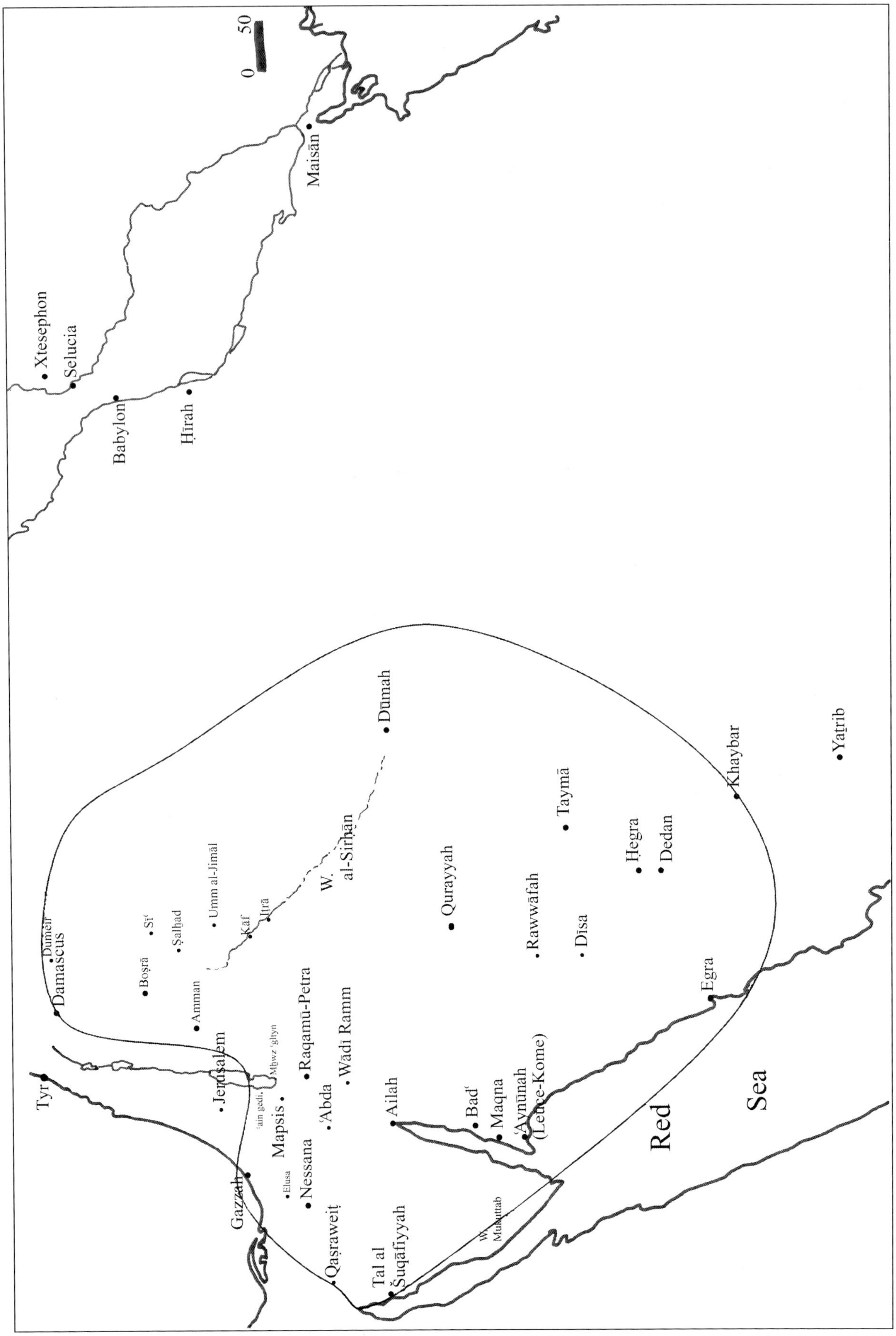

Map of Nabataea at maximum expansion. © Author

Plate III

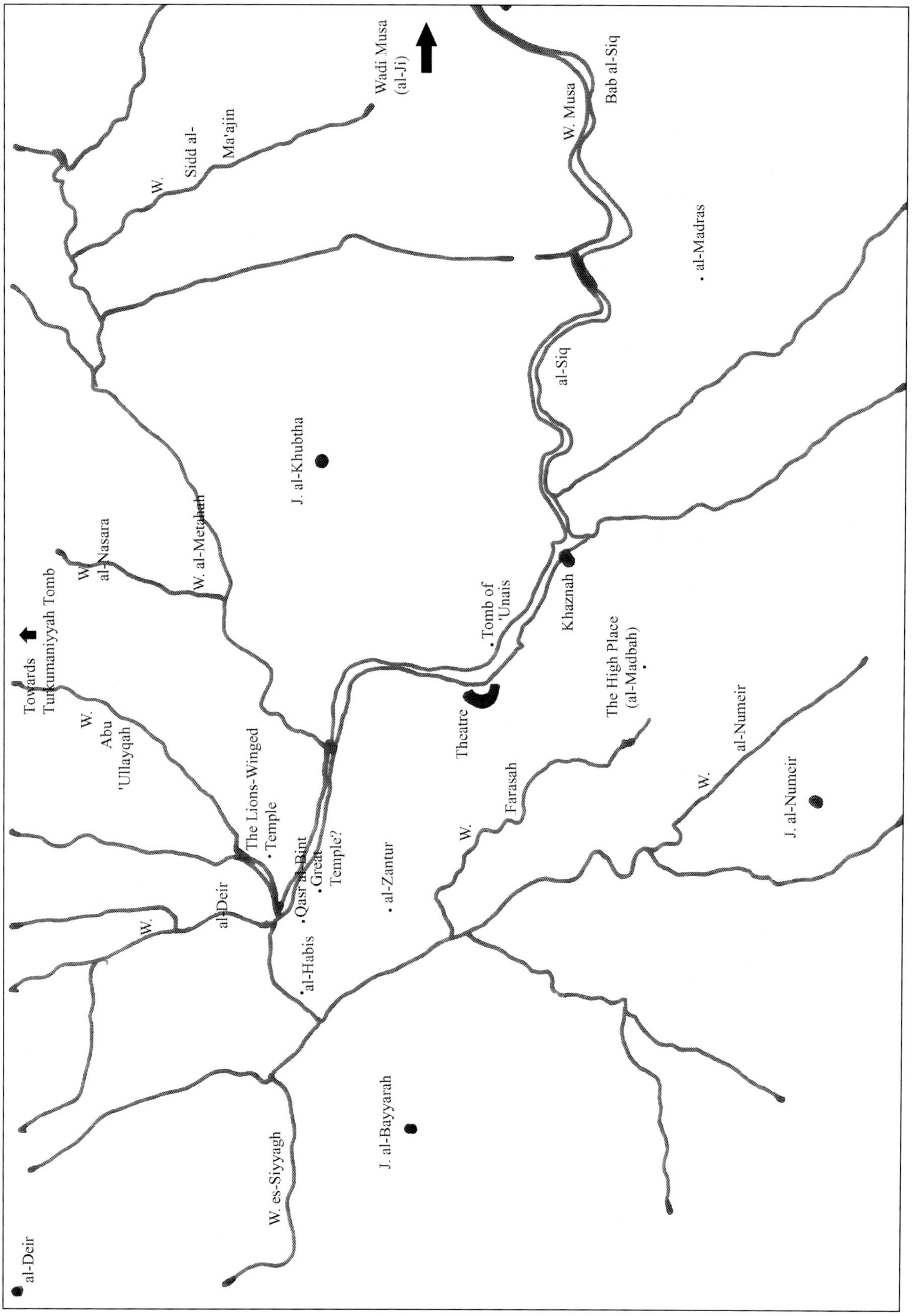

Raqamu-Petra (based on Nehmé 1998)

PLATE IV

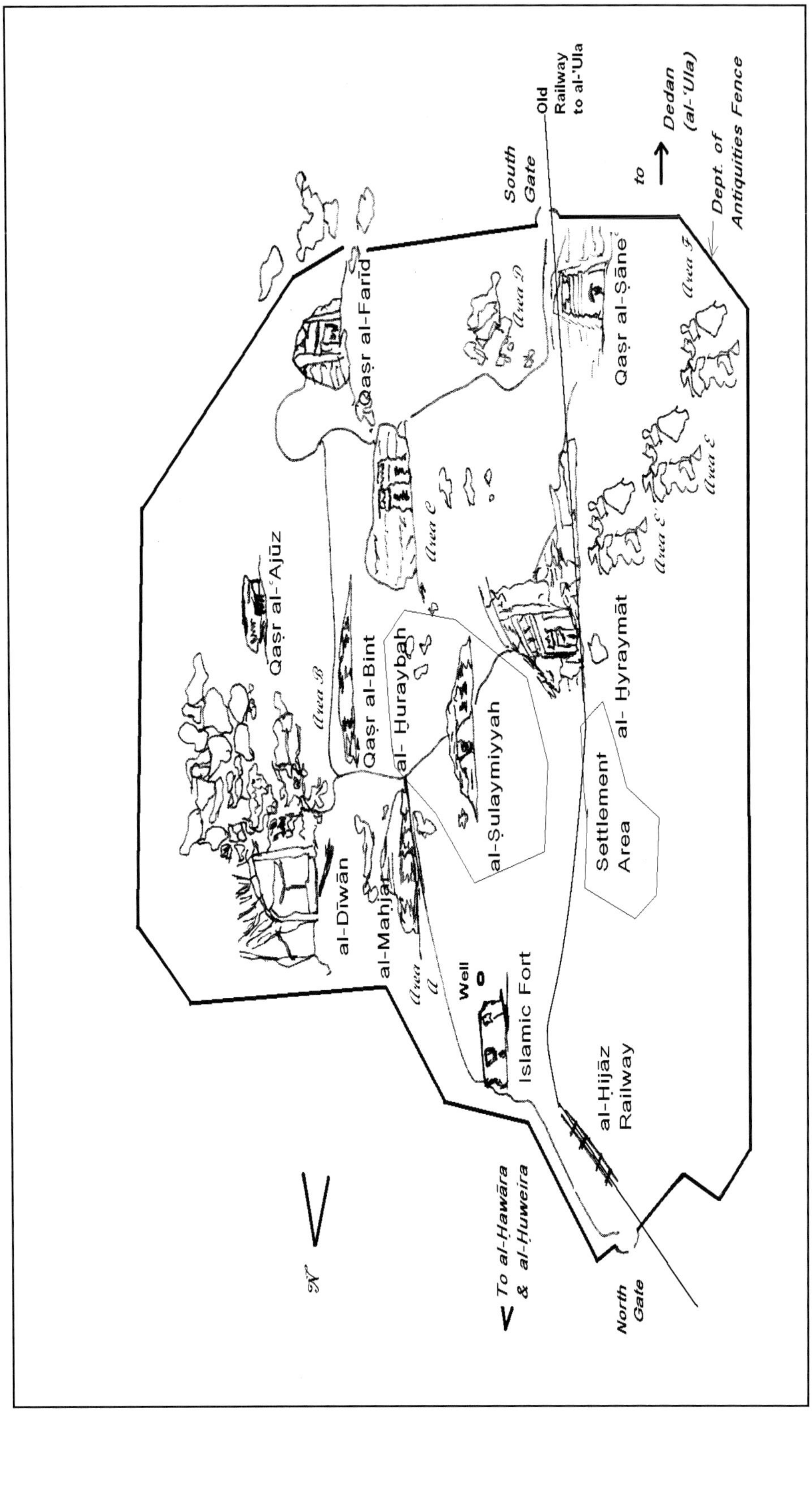

MAP OF ḤEGRA (MADĀ'IN ṢALIḤ) MAP MODIFIED BY AUTHOR AFTER *ANTIQUITIES SITES*.

PLATE V

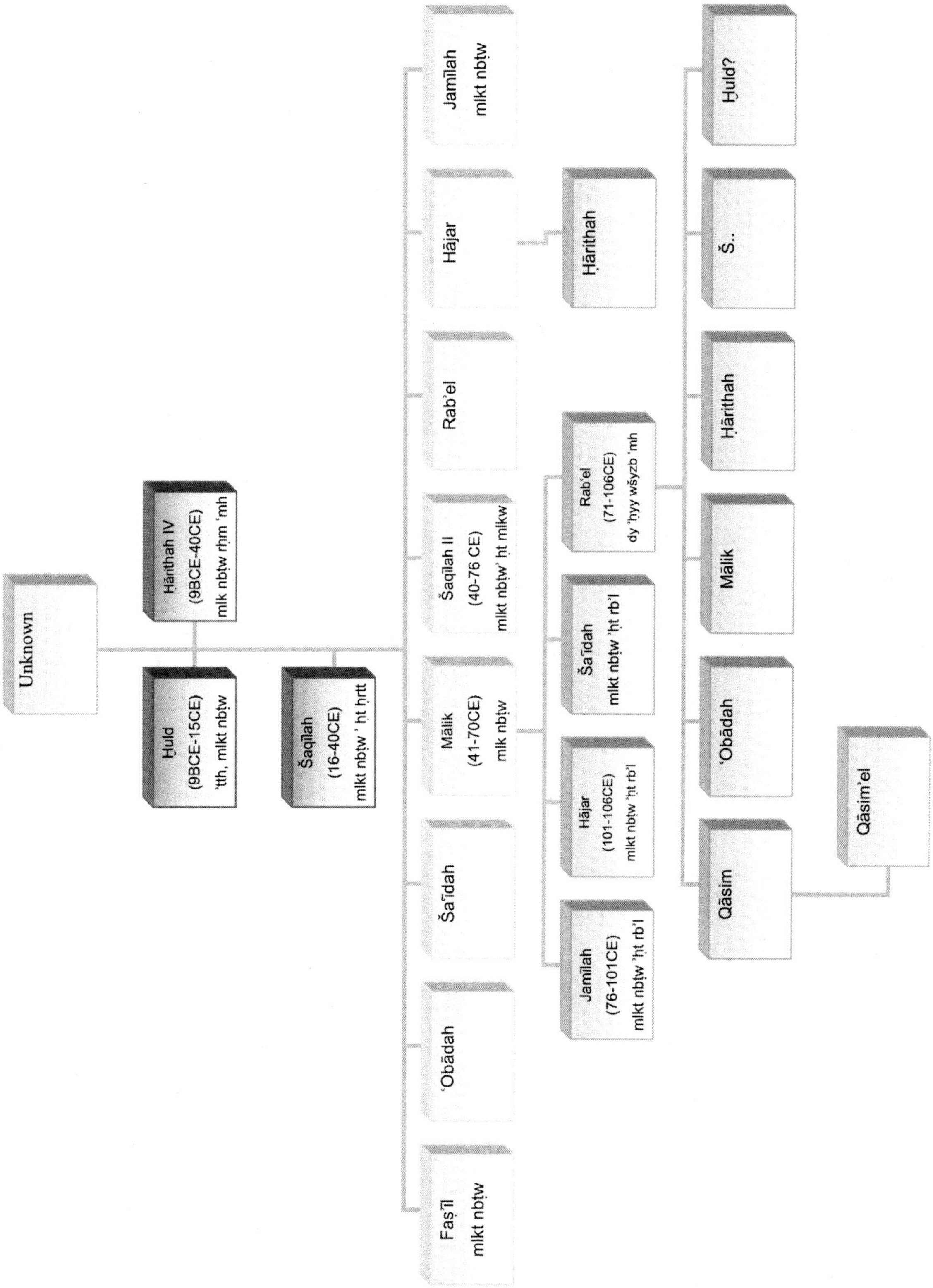

NABATAEAN GENEALOGICAL ROYAL TREE (STARTING FROM KING ḤARITHAH IV) © DRAWN BY AUTHOR

PLATE VI

Timetable of Harvest and Caravans

Travelling between North and Southern Arabia

Months	Frankincense H. (SA)	Corn H. (NA)	Wheat & Barley H. (NA)	N. Caravans
January				arrive to S
February	ready for export		harvest	return to N
March			harvest	
April	incision and harvest			arrive to N
May	incision and harvest			
June	incision and harvest	sowing		start for S
July	monsoon			
August	monsoon			arrive to S
September	ready for export			return to N
October				
November	incision and harvest	harvest	sowing	arrive to N
December	incision and harvest		sowing	start for S

* Journey to south takes about two months and a half. Therefore, the departure and arrival of caravans vary in the month.

Assembled by the author.

Plate VII

Ḥegra (Madā'in Ṣaliḫ) the Atālib mountains from the west. © author

Ḥegra (Madā'in Ṣaliḥ) view from the south. © author

PLATE VIII

TOMBS C9, C10, ḤEGRA (MADĀ'IN ṢALIH). © AUTHOR

BLOCK OF AL-KHURAYBAH, ḤEGRA (MADĀ'IN ṢALIH). © AUTHOR

Plate IX

Tomb of Kamkam, "the Priestess" (B19: JS 16) (Privately from Prof. Healey)

Tomb of Šabb and Nubayqah (E6: JS 33) © author

Plate X

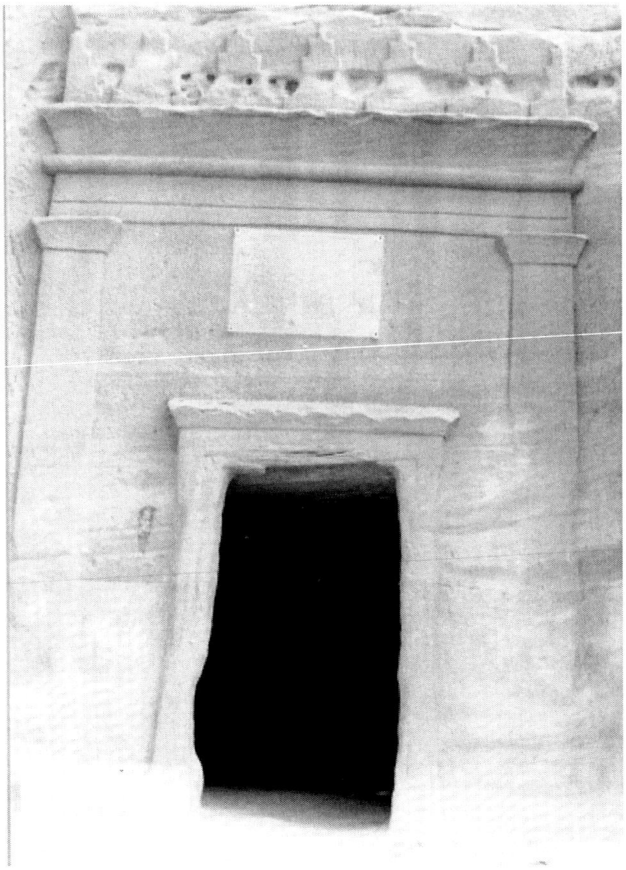

Tomb of Wašūḥ d. of Bajrah the Taymanite (B10: JS 11-12)
© author

Tomb of Haynah d. of Wahab (C14: JS 26)
© author

Plate XI

Tomb of Hājar d. Ḥafi & Maḥmiyyah d. Wā'ilah (after JS 1: fig. 151-152)

Qaṣr al-'Ajūz with the C Block at the back (after Healey 1993: plate viii)

Plate XII

Ḥegra (Madā'in Ṣalih), tombs F4: JS 38 of the Prefect Tarṣu of Taym, 63 CE (after rain). © author

Plate XIII

Tomb E18: JS 36 of Ḫalaf s. of Qasantan 31 CE (reference to the Temple of Qayšah) Ḥegra (Madā'in Ṣaliḥ)
© author

Ground Burial, Ḥegra (Madā'in Ṣaliḥ)
© author

Plate XIV

al-'Ula-Dedan Mountains © author

Plate XV

al-'Ikma Inscriptions
Dedan (al-'Ula). © author

Tomb of the Two Lions – Dedan (al-Khurayba, al-'Ula). © author

Plate XVI

Rawwafa Temple and Camels © author

Plate XVII

Dīsa © author

Maqnā (NW Saudi Arabia) © author

Plate XVIII

Midian (al-Bid', Maghayer Shu'ayb). © author

Midian (Qurayyah). © author

Plate XIX

Egra (Kurkumah). © author

Leuce Kome ('Aynūnah). © author

PLATE XX

OLD QUARTER AND OMAR MOSQUE FROM MĀRID CASTLE
© AUTHOR

MĀRID CASTLE, DUMAH (DUMAT-AL-JANDAL). © AUTHOR

Plate XXI

In Dumah alleys (al-Dir' quarter, Dumat al-Jandal)
© author

Dumah's Inscription 27 CE (Theeb 1994: ins 13, Starcky 1970: ins 16). © author

PLATE XXII

AL-ṢA'ĪDĪ CASTLE, AL KĀF, WĀDĪ AL-SIRḤĀN. © AUTHOR

MANṬAR BANI ATIYYAH, TAYMA. © AUTHOR

Plate XXIII

al-Khazne. © author

Plate XXIV

Middle of Sīq
© author

End of Sīq, Raqamū-Petra.
© author

PLATE XXV

TOMB OF 'UNAIS, QUEEN OF ŠAQĪLAH'S VEZIR. © AUTHOR

AL-ḪUBṮA MOUNTAIN, RAQAMŪ-PETRA. © AUTHOR

Plate XXVI

Theatre, Raqamū-Petra. © author

The 'Palace', Qaṣr Bint Far'un, al-Bayyarah, view from the south. © author

Plate XXVII

The way to the High-Place, Raqamū-Petra.

al-Baida, north of Raqamū-Petra.

PLATE XXVIII

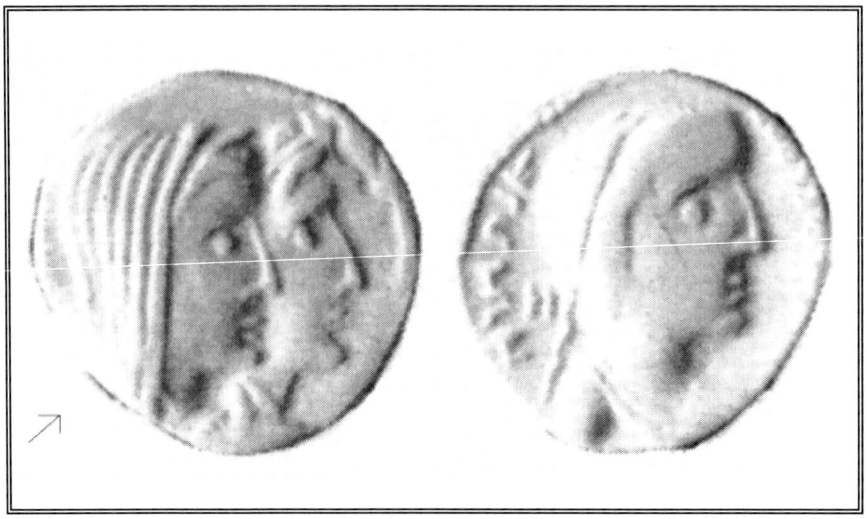

UNKNOWN (MOTHER) QUEEN IN THE FOREGROUND WITH KING ḤĀRIṮAH IV
(MESHORER 1975: NO. 47, 47A)

QUEEN CLEOPATRA THEA IN THE FOREGROUND WITH HER SON (SNG IV-III: NO. 359)

Plate XXIX

Queen Ḫuld and King Ḥāriṯah IV (9/8 BCE)
(Meshorer 1975: no. 49)

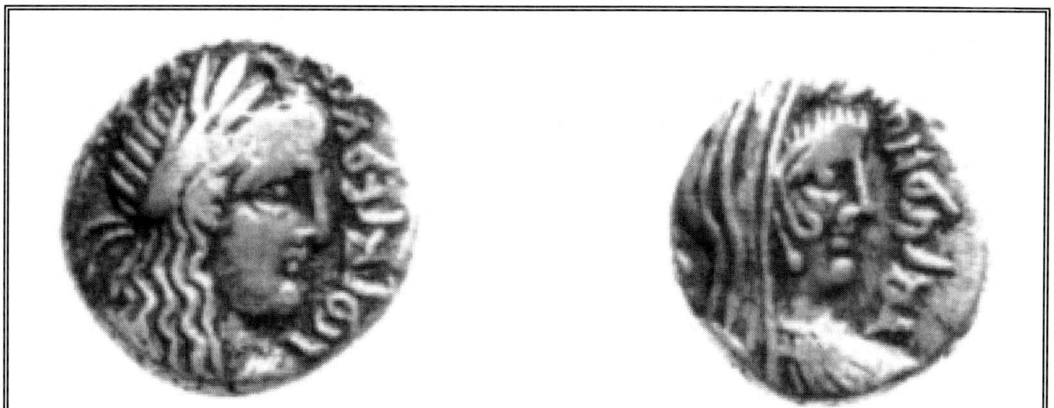

Minor Rab'el II — Šaqīlah II, the Mother Queen (71-76 CE)
(Meshorer 1975: no. 142-147)

Plate XXX

Umm al-Jimāl. © author

Sī', Ḥauran. © author

PLATE XXXI

BOṢRA, THE NABATAEAN TEMPLE. © AUTHOR

MAQAWIR (MACHAERUS), HEROD'S CASTLE. © AUTHOR

Plate XXXII

Allāt's Temple, Wādī Ramm, Jordan. © author

Allāt's Temple, Wādī Ramm, Jordan. © author

Plate XXXIII

Muhammad Radwan of al-'Ulayqat reads Nabataean inscriptions. © author

Wādī Mukattab, Sinai. © author

Plate XXXIV

Palmyrene women watching a procession (Bel Temple). © author

A lady from Palmyra (Palmyra Museum). © author

Plate XXXV

A Bride from Dura Europos (Cumont 1926: 64ff. Pl. xxxv)

Plate XXXVI

Two Nabataean female musicians with a man in the middle, in their local dress and veil. (Amman museum, Zayadine 1991: 55)

Nabataean female terracotta veiled. (Museum of Anthropology, Irbid). © author

Plate XXXVII

Head of a Nabataean King (?)
(Murray & Ellis 1940)

Cleopatra VII as Isis (Samson 1985)